Primate Models
of Human Neurogenic Disorders

Primate Models of Human Neurogenic Disorders

V. G. STARTSEV

TRANSLATED BY

MARIENNE SCHWEINLER
VADIM PAHN

EDITOR OF THE ENGLISH TRANSLATION

DOUGLAS M. BOWDEN
UNIVERSITY OF WASHINGTON

 LAWRENCE ERLBAUM ASSOCIATES, PUBLISHERS
1976   Hillsdale, New Jersey

DISTRIBUTED BY THE HALSTED PRESS DIVISION OF

JOHN WILEY & SONS

New York   Toronto   London   Sydney

Lawrence Erlbaum Associates, Inc., Publishers
62 Maria Drive
Hillsdale, New Jersey 07642

Distributed solely by Halsted Press Division
John Wiley & Sons, Inc., New York

Originally published in Russian as *Modelirovanie Nevrogennykh Zabolevanii
Cheloveka v Eksperimente na Obez'ianakh.* "Meditsina Press" by
recommendation of Editorial-Publication Council of the Academy of
Medical Sciences of the USSR, Moscow, 1971. Chapter VIII originally
appeared as a research article: Novaia model' nevrogennoi ishemicheskoi
bolezni serdtsa v eksperimente na obez'ianakh, by V. G. Startsev, Iu. M.
Repin, & S. K. Shestopalova, *Biull. Eksp. Biol. i Med.*, 1972, 73(1), 35–38.

Library of Congress Cataloging in Publication Data

Startsev, Valentin Georgievich.
    Primate models of human neurogenic disorders.

    Translation of Modelirovanie nevrogennykh
zabolevanii cheloveka v éksperimente na obez'ianakh.
    Bibliography: p.
    1. Nervous system—Diseases.   2. Psychosomatic
research.   3. Diseases—Animal models.   4. Primates
as laboratory animals.   I. Title.   [DNLM:
1. Disease models, animal.   2. Models, Neurologic.
3. Monkey diseases.   4. Neuroses. WM170 S796m]
RC347.S7313   616.8'0724   76-21626
ISBN 0-470-15193-5

Printed in the United States of America

Contents

Preface to Startsev's
Primate Models of Human Neurogenic Disorders

David T. Graham

In this book are described experiments that help us understand the reasons for illness. Most readers no doubt will consider as "psychosomatic" the illnesses under discussion. Why? A full-scale examination of possible definitions of "psychosomatic illness" would be out of place here, but perhaps it can be said that the two most important ingredients are (1) that the illness is a response to external sensory stimulation, and (2) that a state (of long or short duration) of the person that is described in psychological language is relevant to the illness. It is important to recognize that these two criteria are different and separable, though they are very often simultaneously satisfied. Much of the work in psychosomatic medicine in Western Europe and North America has been aimed at showing that various illnesses satisfy one or both of them.

The book does not deal directly with matters to which Criterion (2) applies. It does, however, concern itself with many findings directly related to Criterion (1), and the reported experiments are pertinent to the so-called specificity problem in psychosomatic medicine.

Startsev summarizes and formulates his conclusions as follows: "The repeated pairing of activation of a given organic system with intense nervous stress directs the pathological influence of the stressor primarily upon the system activated; subsequently the natural stimuli which would ordinarily activate the system in a normal manner sustain the pathological stressor's effect as a conditioned stimulus for the stressor effect."

The circumstance that produces the "intense nervous stress" in this research is immobilization. It is not clear that this is related to Criterion (1), since we do not know by what means the immobilization affects the animal. It could be that it is through his external sense organs, but it could also be through his proprioceptors, or through some direct effect on, for example, the velocity of blood flow. If the last were the case, we would probably not be inclined to consider the resulting changes in the animal as "psychosomatic." On the other hand, the natural activators of the system which was active at the time of immobilization are very often sensory stimuli (e.g., the sight of food.) This book tells of ways in which the animal's experience confers on such stimuli the power to produce diseases that we therefore call psychosomatic.

The author is clearly interested in the application of his work to human health and disease, and at one point says, "The causes of many human illnesses are rooted in the living environment of the patient, in the effects of everyday stimuli activating different functional systems of the organism." This is a remark that will draw hearty agreement from clinicians who pay close attention to the exact circumstances in which their patients improve or worsen, and who therefore can precisely identify the stimuli responsible for exacerbations or remissions of illness. There are, of course, major gaps to fill before one can see the connections leading from "naturally activating" stimuli such as food, to the kinds of sensory stimuli that produce disease in human patients.

These stimuli arise very commonly in the behavior of other persons. A husband's angry criticism, a superior's rebuke, a letter containing bad news, the demands of an aging parent are everyday stimuli that make people sick. It is not easy to see how these can be natural activators of the system in which the patient's disease lies. This observation is not a criticism of Startsev and his collaborators, who could not be expected to solve every problem in psychosomatic medicine; it is merely pointing out that the road from the laboratory to the clinical situation may be long. One might perhaps hope to bridge the gaps by finding a learned association, perhaps something that could be called "conditioning," between primitive stimuli, such as food, and other stimuli, like those just mentioned, whose effects are derived from the association. On the other hand, it is conceivable that, contrary to Startsev's formulation, the pathogenic stimuli of daily life are related, not to natural activators of a system, but rather to the original stressor.

It is worthwhile to look at the contribution this research makes to the specificity question, but it is necessary first to give some idea of what that question is. In a general way, it is whether there are predictable associations between a psychosomatic disease and something else. The "something else" can be the nature of the stimulus, some enduring characteristic of the patient that antedates the appearance of the disease, or some state of the patient that changes more or less simultaneously with the disease (e.g., an "emotion"). Usually, the effort in American psychosomatic research has been to find something about the patient that is described in psychological terms—for instance, personality traits, or unconscious conflicts, or emotions, or attitudes, that can be correlated with the presence of a particular disease. If the effort is successful, one can then say, "All patients with disease X have psychological state or characteristic Y."

The whole question is complicated, and only certain aspects of it need to be discussed here. It may first be repeated that Startsev's work leads to no conclusions about association of disease with particular psychological variables of the kinds just mentioned. Statements about such variables are usually derived from clinical interviewing or from psychological tests that require verbal responses, and neither procedure is suitable for baboons. Startsev's results put the specificity—the correlation of disease with "something else"—in the life experiences of the animal, and in the long-lasting effects of those experiences. He can say that an animal responds to feeding by developing gastric disease because activation of the stomach had previously occurred while the animal was immobilized. The explanation of the gastric disease is that the animal is now different—has a different nervous system—from animals that have not had its special experience. Its history explains both the disease it has (or at least explains why a particular organ is diseased), and its susceptibility to certain stimuli. It does not, of course, account for the occurrence of different diseases within the same organ system, though one might perhaps suppose that these differences could result from the use of different stressors during conditioning. Immersion in cold water, for instance, might lead to diseases different from those produced by immobilization.

Two approaches to the specificity problem that do not make use of psychological descriptions of the patient or his states have often been examined. One, stimulus—response specificity, stated here for simplicity in its extreme form, says that a particular stimulus gives rise to the same disease in every person; different diseases are responses to different stimuli, but specific stimulus—response connections are the same in all persons. The second approach, individual response stereotypy, is that each person has his own preferred disease, with which he responds to all stimuli, or at least to all "disturbing" stimuli. This, again an oversimplified statement, is one way of putting the "organ weakness" theory, which is that everybody has a weak organ (e.g., his heart), in which he has all his diseases.

As is obvious from clinical observation, neither of these views even approximates the complete truth. Stimuli that produce peptic ulcer in one person are not the same as those that produce it in another. There may well be similarities in the meaning of the stimuli to the two persons, but to consider meaning introduces an entirely new concept. Also, it is easy to see that no patient has only one disease, though one may predominate. Every person has an enormous repertory of responses; which response he actually makes depends on, among other things, the stimuli that are acting on him.

Startsev's animals do not fit into either the stimulus—response specificity or the individual response stereotypy model. They demonstrate, it is true, a kind of stimulus—response specificity, but only in the sense that animals with similar life histories, of which the essential features were imposed by the experimenters, show the same predictable relations between stimuli and diseases. One might also say that there was a certain degree of individual response stereotypy, in the organ weakness sense, in that an organ system was predisposed to illness by association of its activation with the immobilization stress. On the other hand, it is logical to infer that several organ systems in the same animal could be made vulnerable by activating each of them during immobilization. The stimuli to illness would be different for each system.

The experimental procedures described in this book therefore suggest ways in which several different psychosomatic diseases could occur in the same person, each of them as a response to a set of stimuli, the natural activators, different from the stimuli that elicit the others. Of course, in examining the relations between what Startsev and his collaborators have done and the general trend of clinical research and thinking elsewhere, one must exercise caution in assuming that what is true of apes is also true of man.

Editor's Introduction

Many a disease has defied understanding until an appropriate animal model has been established. The defeat of poliomyelitis awaited the discovery that polio virus would grow in monkey tissue culture. Successful treatment of renal hypertension awaited the Goldblatt kidney. Open heart surgery and kidney transplantation returned health to human patients only after hundreds of dogs had given their lives for the evaluation of the required surgical techniques. Because biomedical investigators recognize the extreme usefulness of such models, the push is now on to establish animal analogs of human leukemia, lung cancer, sudden infant death, and a variety of other major diseases.

Although the value of animal models has been recognized in medical and surgical research for decades, it has not been so widely appreciated in psychosomatic research. This is particularly true in the United States, where the major psychiatric and medical approach to psychosomatic disease has grown out of the Freudian and Alexandrian traditions. Primary emphasis has been placed on psychic mechanisms and verbally expressed attitudes as determinants or correlates of various psychosomatic disorders. Because introspection, attitudes, and language are functions generally attributed only to the human organism, the research efforts growing out of these traditions have been restricted largely to studies of human subjects. Animals respond to stress as well, however, and the research reported by Dr. Startsev explores some of the important similarities between man and other primate species in the way their bodies respond to psychological stress.

Our purpose in translating this work is to bring to the attention of western investigators new and, it is hoped, useful models of stress-induced disorders involving the gastrointestinal system, cardiovascular system, metabolism, and motor and sexual functions. It has been translated with two audiences in mind, viz., research investigators and readers with particular interest in the theory of

1

psychosomatic mechanisms. Research investigators will be primarily interested in the methods the author has used to produce specific disorders, the indices by which he has identified the disorders, and the strength of the evidence that the disorders have been produced by the factors the author claims. They can get this information by going directly to the various chapters that discuss diseases of interest. The psychosomatic theorist will find it useful to read the remainder of this preface, Chapter II, Chapter I, and then the chapters dealing with specific disorders.

Vast differences in theoretical perspective create unusual opportunities for misunderstanding between Soviet investigators and their western counterparts. This is particularly true in an area where interest is great and the base of scientific data is small. The Soviet reader rapidly becomes impatient with studies in the Freudian and Alexandrian traditions where the pathogenesis of gastric disorders, EKG changes, and hysterical paralyses is discussed in terms of such concepts as "dependency," "ego threat," "secondary gain," and the like. In the same way, many a western reader will undoubtedly bridle at the regularity with which the soviet author invokes such concepts as "clash of excitation and inhibition," "reciprocal induction," "pathological cerebral dominant," and the like in explaining the same kinds of phenomena.

There are two ways for the translator to deal with this problem. One is to provide the foreign reader with sufficient historical and theoretical background to allow him to appreciate the author's interpretations. The second is to translate as much of the terminology as possible into the kinds of words that the reader ordinarily uses when referring to the same phenomena. The difficulty with the first approach is that it would take several volumes the size of this to convey the full extent of the Pavlovian theory of higher nervous activity and the kind of data on which it is based. There is a danger in the second approach, however, in that in the interest of making things easily comprehensible to the foreign reader one may do a disservice to the author by obscuring the theoretical significance of the work he has performed; the concepts in his theory that have no real equivalents in the second language may sound more bizarre than ever to the untutored reader.

A little of each approach has been used here in an attempt to produce a translation that is comprehensible and still true to the author's intent. The remainder of this preface defines a few major modifications of terminology and, it is hoped, explains enough of the conceptual framework underlying the author's work to enable the western reader to understand his methods and interpretations as described in his own terms.

One of the strengths of the Pavlovian terminology lies in its adherence to physiological concepts in dealing with processes in which the brain is presumed to play a role. We have therefore avoided substituting such terms as "psychogenic" for the author's "neurogenic," "anxiety" for his "defensive excitation," "perseveration" for his "immobility of central neural processes," and the like. However, there are several important terms used in the Russian text that if translated directly into their English cognates can engender unnecessary confusion in the western reader. Such terms as "reflex" and "neurotic" have specific meanings in western psychosomatic theory that are, in some ways, quite different from the meanings ascribed to them in contemporary Soviet theory. These must be translated into different terms that more nearly convey the author's meaning. The following is a list of such freehand translations and the reasons for using them.

In most instances where the author has used the terms "uslovnyi refleks" and "refleks," they have been translated "conditional response" and "response mechanism," respectively. Translating the Russian "refleks" as "reflex" may be misleading to western psychologists who adhere to a terminology in which reflex conditioning refers only to classical Pavlovian, or respondent, conditioning. In this translation the English word "reflex" has only been used in contexts where the classical, respondent conditioning procedure has been clearly implied. In other contexts "response" is a better translation. However, "response" alone lacks an important connotation of the Soviet "refleks," namely the connotation of a series of anatomical structures via which some kind of input, e.g., the sound of a bell, evokes a behavioral output, e.g., approach to the feeder. Therefore, wherever the term "refleks" clearly has been used to denote such an anatomical construct it has been translated "response mechanism."

"Response system" has been substituted for the author's term "natural conditioned reflex." Again, the rationale was to retain the concept of a mechanism in the nervous system mediating a particular kind of behavior without using a sequence of words that, to the western ear, would evoke a conglomerate of self-contradictory images. The "natural conditioned sexual reflex" thus becomes the "sexual response system of the brain," "natural conditioned alimentary reflex" becomes the "alimentary response system," etc.

The term "system-specific disorder" has been substituted for the author's term "sistemnoe porazhenie." In this case the Russian word "sistemnoe" is used in a more narrow sense than the English "systemic." To western ears a systemic disorder relates to the whole organism; when the Soviet author uses the term, he means a disorder confined to one physiological system, e.g., the alimentary system or the motor system.

The term "nevroticheskii" has been translated with some flexibility. Where the Russian text clearly referred to disrupted performance on learning tasks or inappropriate, nonadaptive behavior it has been translated "neurotic." Where it was used to refer to a period of time following stress during which animals showed persistent behavioral and physiological disorders, it has been translated "poststressor," e.g., "postressor period" or "poststressor changes in gastric secretion" instead of "neurotic period" or "neurotic changes in gastric secretion."

With these exceptions, most of the author's terminology has been retained. Because most of it derives from investigations carried out in Pavlov's laboratories in the early part of this century, it is worth reviewing some of the major concepts that grew out of that work, particularly concepts relating to functional disorders of the brain.

The term *experimental neurosis* first came into use between 1912 and 1920. The basic design of experiments to study functional disorders was established at that time, and various aspects of it have been applied in hundreds of studies in the decades following 1920.

Most of the experiments consist of three phases: a prestressor phase, a stressor phase, and a poststressor phase. In the prestressor or baseline phase an animal is trained on a series of conditional reflexes or motor responses. Baseline data are collected regarding his performance on the conditional responses, his general behavior within and outside the test chamber, and normal patterns of fluctuation in physiological functions that are of interest to the investigator. The duration of the prestressor phase ranges from one to several months.

The stressor phase is usually very short. The stressors range from subtle changes in the schedule of presentation of stimuli in the conditioning sessions to grossly traumatic procedures, such as shocking the animal through the food bowl when it is taking food. Typically one or two stressor trails are embedded in otherwise unaltered test sessions for one to five daily sessions. The animal's performance, general behavior, and physiological functions are disrupted during the sessions in which the stressor is imposed. Such disruptions are referred to as *reactive* changes and are not regarded as pathological.

In the poststressor phase, the test sessions return to the prestressor pattern. This is the phase of the experiment in which the investigator looks for *neurotic* phenomena, i.e., inappropriate performance on the conditioning task and disturbances of general behavior and physiological functions that persist long after the stressor trials have been dropped from the experimental sessions. Observations may continue in this phase for several months to a year or more.

The first and now classic case of experimental neurosis was that of "Vampire," a dog that suffered a dramatic nervous breakdown when confronted with an impossibly difficult form discrimination (Shenger-Krestovnikova, 1921). The investigator trained the animal to salivate at the sight of a circle by giving it food whenever the circle was projected on a screen. Then she trained it not to salivate to oval forms by projecting ovals and not presenting food. The goal of the experiment was to determine the limits of Vampire's ability to discriminate between circles and ovals by presenting ovals closer and closer to the shape of the circle and observing at what point he salivated as though they were circles. The test sessions ran smoothly for several months. As each new oval was introduced, he salivated to it once or twice, but this response rapidly disappeared after the food failed to appear. Suddenly, as the fifth oval was introduced his behavior changed dramatically. Whereas before he had performed quietly and cooperatively, he became agitated, whined, tore at the loose restraints that held him in the test stand, ripped the saliva collector from his cheek, and began to salivate profusely to all stimuli, ovals and circles alike. When the "impossible" oval was removed from the series of test stimuli for a number of sessions his general behavior and performance of salivary responses slowly improved, but whenever it was reintroduced, his behavior and performance suddenly deteriorated and remained disrupted for days and weeks at a time. During these periods he barked and resisted entering the test chamber and, when there, salivated in response to oval forms that he had mastered months before.

This case is worth analyzing in some detail because it is a dramatic example of the kind of disorder that dominated the research interests of many Soviet investigators over the next 20 years. Furthermore, it provides a good basis for illustrating the terminology of experimental neurosis research. The experimental approach to psychological phenomena using patterns of salivation as an index of brain function was referred to as the *physiology of higher nervous activity*. Vampire's syndrome represented a breakdown in functioning of higher nervous activity remarkable for its abruptness, its link to a specific stressor of neural function (an impossible form discrimination), and its persistence long after the stressor was removed. The goal physiologists set themselves was to determine what was going on in the animal's brain that could result in such a sudden, massive, and prolonged disruption of normal behavior and performance.

The terms *experimental neurosis* and *pathology of higher nervous activity* were coined very early to refer to the field in general. It soon became apparent, however, that the disorders generated by various stressors were not limited to the spheres of general behavior and performance of conditional responses but included major vegetative disorders as well: weight loss, increased susceptibility to infection, diarrhea, and the like. Because these appeared to result from stress-induced disorders of the central neural mechanisms that regulate the function of peripheral organs, they came to be referred to as "corticovisceral pathology."

Most of the hundreds of studies that were carried out in the 1920s and 1930s were designed to analyze the disorders in terms of neurophysiological mechanisms which were known at that time. Sherrington had demonstrated spinal reflexes, i.e., sequences of neurons whereby electrical stimulation of sensory nerves from the leg reliably elicited a direct motor response. Sechenov had proposed that similar neural reflexes, involving links within the brain, mediated more complex physiological responses, and Pavlov had demonstrated reliable reflex control of gastric secretion in the dog. Indeed, in 1904, Pavlov received the Nobel prize for his studies demonstrating that the secretion of gastric juice which occurred when an animal saw food was mediated by nerves coming from the brain. It was presumed that such a reflex was mediated by a series of nerves linking the eyes, the brain, and the gastric glands and no less fixed than the series of nerves whereby a tap on the patellar ligament was translated into extension of the knee.

At about the same time Pavlov first reported studies of another kind of reflex, which he referred to as a *temporary connection* or *conditional reflex* (CR). The establishment of temporary connections in the brain was postulated to account for the process of conditioning, i.e., the fact that a signal (such as a circle) which ordinarily did not elicit a particular response (such as salivation) could be made to do so if it were presented a number of times in combination with a stimulus (such as food) which did elicit the response. The connection was "temporary" in the sense that it persisted only as long as the new stimulus was paired with food, the *natural* or *unconditional stimulus* (US); again, it was a "conditional" reflex in the sense that its continued existence was conditional on the signal's being paired with food. If the US was food, the CR was called an *alimentary CR;* if the US was shock, it was called a *defensive CR;* and so forth. If the signal were presented a number of times without the unconditional stimulus, it soon failed to elicit the response and the conditional reflex was said to have undergone *extinction.* A stimulus that, through conditioning, has acquired the capacity to elicit a response is referred to as a *conditioned stimulus* (CS).

In addition to the laws of conditioning, two other laws of normal higher nervous activity assumed great importance in the attempts of early investigators to analyze the brain mechanisms underlying experimental neurosis, viz., the "law of intensity" and "differentiation." Very simply, the *law of intensity* referred to the fact that if several different stimuli were conditioned to elicit a given response, the stronger the stimulus, the more intense the response it elicited; for example, a loud bell was found to elicit greater salivation than a weak tone.

The concept of a *differential reflex* (DR) was developed to account for the observation that whereas initially stimuli similar to a CS elicited salivation, if they were presented a number of times without the natural stimulus they soon ceased to do so. In fact, they appeared to become signals for inhibition of the CR. If they were presented very shortly before the CS, the salivation elicited by the CS was markedly reduced. A signal that acquired the capacity to inhibit a CR was referred to as an *inhibitory stimulus* or *differential stimulus* (DS). Sometimes CSs and DSs for the same response mechanism were referred to as *positive stimuli* and *negative stimuli,* respectively.

Describing the experiment with Vampire in these terms, a salivation CR was established to the circle and a DR was established to ovals. The circle elicited excitation of the salivation mechanism; the oval elicited inhibition of that mechanism. Pavlov's interpretation of Vampire's nervous breakdown was that the presentation of a signal which the visual system was incapable of resolving into a circle or an oval resulted in an intolerable clash of excitatory and inhibitory neural processes within the brain. Many subsequent experiments were carried out in attempts to discover where in the brain such a clash might occur and what kind of lasting damage it might produce.

In general, Pavlov postulated, breakdowns in central neural functions resulted from *excessive strain on excitatory or inhibitory processes or their mobility.* The excessive strain was generally believed to result in *overstress* and *exhaustion* of nerve cells somewhere in the brain. Indeed, in recent years a group of investigators in Leningrad has used the electron microscope to look for histological changes in the brains of dogs subjected to experimental neurosis (Manina, Khananashvili, & Lazuko, 1971). They report that dogs with nervous breakdowns induced by clashing visual stimuli show pathological changes in neurons of the visual cortex.

Within a few years after the pathology of higher nervous activity became a recognized field of physiological research, five commonly observed patterns of breakdown in the performance of conditional salivation reflexes had been identified. The subtlest changes were disturbances of the law of intensity. In the *equalization pattern*, the magnitude of response (volume of salivation) to weak CSs became no different from that to strong CSs. In the *paradoxical pattern*, the response to weak stimuli was greater than to strong stimuli. In the *ultraparadoxical pattern* salivation was greater to DSs than to CSs. In the *inhibitory pattern* all signals, CSs and DSs alike, ceased to elicit salivation. And in the *excitatory pattern*, all signals came to elicit salivation. The excitatory pattern was also described as *disinhibition of differentiation*, because DSs that had previously, and appropriately, inhibited salivation reverted to stimulating it. (Vampire's nervous breakdown fit the excitatory pattern.)

Many attempts were made to predict what pattern of breakdown particular dogs would show when subjected to nervous stress (Ivanov-Smolenskii, 1952; Iakovleva, 1967). These early approaches to the question of symptom specificity demonstrated that the nature of the stressor had little to do with the pattern of breakdown an animal developed. All dogs subjected to the same stressor did not develop the same pattern of breakdown, and a variety of different stressors were capable of producing the same pattern of breakdown in different dogs.

The second and most widely tested hypothesis regarding symptom specificity was that the pattern of breakdown could be predicted on the basis of previous knowledge about the animal's type of nervous system. Type of nervous system was assessed by a battery of tests requiring several months to administer. Most of the tests were designed to evaluate the strength, balance, and mobility of excitatory and inhibitory processes controlling the salivary response. An animal in which it was possible to establish reliable salivation CRs with large volume of saliva output was described as having a strong excitatory type of nervous system. If he also developed reliable DRs with total suppression of salivation when DSs were presented, his nervous system was said to be of the balanced type. If he maintained clearcut and appropriate responses when the CSs and DSs were presented in rapid succession, or if he readily reversed his responses when the CSs were made DSs and vice versa, he was said to possess nervous processes of high mobility.

To a certain extent, data of this kind proved fruitful in predicting the vulnerability of dogs to experimental neurosis. Those with weak nervous systems turned out to be more vulnerable to nervous breakdown than did dogs with strong, balanced nervous systems. However, determining the type of nervous system turned out to be of little use in predicting what pattern of disorder an animal would show when the breakdown occurred. Nevertheless, the tests for type of nervous system have remained a part of many investigators' procedures as they establish performance baselines in the prestressor phase of neurosis experiments.

It appears that no measure has been identified that reliably predicts the pattern of disruption in the law of intensity which different animals show when subjected to nervous stress. Soviet physiologists have had success, however, in establishing the determinants of other kinds of disorders, such as phobias and system-specific physiological disorders.

One of two approaches that have dealt more successfully with the question of symptom specificity grew out of the idea that the disorder an animal shows under stress may represent a relapse into dysfunction of a behavioral or physiological system which was traumatized at an earlier time. Evidence supporting this theory in the behavioral sphere was reported by M. K. Petrova (1945). She showed that when a dog was dropped from a great height it reacted with an appropriate, reactive fear of heights, which lasted a few days and then disappeared. If at a much later date the animal was subjected to nonspecific nervous stress, such as that induced by confrontation with an impossible task in the conditioning chamber, it developed an intense height phobia. When led up and down stairs it hugged the wall away from the bannister, refused to eat near the stairwell, and, in the conditioning chamber, huddled on the test stand as if afraid of falling off. An observer unaware of the animal's past experience might interpret this behavior as a bizarre and arbitrary response to stress, whereas the investigator was able to interpret it as the pathological reemergence of a fear response pattern established at an earlier date by a specific kind of nervous trauma.

Evidence for the same theory in the physiological sphere has been accumulated by I. T. Kurtsin and colleagues in the years since World War II (Kurtsin, 1968). They have reported, for instance, that dogs in which the gastric mucosa has been traumatized by nitric acid lavage and then allowed to recover develop gastric ulcers when subjected to nonspecific nervous stress (Kurtsin, 1965). Dogs subjected to hypertension by frequent injections of ephedrine for 2–3 weeks and then allowed to recover developed disturbances of blood pressure when subjected to nervous stress (Sergeeva, 1966).

The experiments described by Dr. Startsev in this book represent another of the more successful approaches to the question of symptom specificity that have emerged from experiments in the Pavlovian tradition. As has that of proponents of the theory of corticovisceral pathology, Dr. Startsev's major interest has been directed toward the physiological disorders produced by the procedures of experimental neurosis research. His hypothesis, as the reader will see, is that the physiological system likely to become chronically disturbed when an animal is subjected to nervous stress is one which has happened to be particularly active when the stress is imposed. For instance, animals repeatedly stressed shortly after eating develop gastrointestinal disorders, whereas animals stressed immediately after exercise are likely to develop cardiovascular disorders.

Dr. Startsev's investigations differ from much of the early experimental neurosis research in that (1) he works with primates rather than dogs, (2) the performance he records as an index of the functional state of the central nervous system involves motor responses rather than salivation, and (3) he uses an operant conditioning paradigm rather than a respondent paradigm; i.e., the animal must respond to the CS in order for the food to appear, whereas in earlier studies the food appeared whether the animal responded to the CS or not. The reader interested in relating the performance disorders reported in this work on primates to the earlier studies on dogs may want to consider the implications of these methodological differences in some detail. Clearly, the author finds no great difficulty in analyzing disruptions of operantly conditioned lever pressing behavior in terms of brain mechanisms originally postulated to account for disorders of classically conditioned salivation. His behavioral studies, as have most of those carried out at Sukhumi (see Chapter I), have contributed greatly to extending the concept of pathology of higher nervous activity to include responses mediated by the somatic nervous system as well as those of the autonomic nervous system. He believes that functional disorders of the motor system hold particular significance for psychosomatic disease in primates.

The interpretation of neurogenic disorders that Dr. Startsev proposes incorporates most of the Pavlovian concepts described above plus one other important concept of Soviet physiology which derived from another school of physiological research, the Vvedenskii–Ukhtomskii school. The term *cerebral dominant* was coined by Ukhtomskii (1949) to refer to the response system of the brain in control of the organism at any point in time. According to his theory, control of the entire organism shifts from one system to another, e.g., from the alimentary system, to the sexual system, to the defensive system, etc., depending on a variety of internal and external factors. This concept grew out of experiments in which he found that the effects of electrical brain stimulation depended on what system, if any, was active at the time the stimulation was applied. Stimulating a cortical area that ordinarily evoked limb flexion failed to do so if the animal was in the process of defecating. In this case, the stimulation accelerated the defecatory mechanism. Only after control of the organism had shifted away from the brain system mediating the complex act of defecation did stimulation of the cortical area elicit limb flexion again.

Initially, the concept of the dominant was developed to explain phenomena surrounding "subcortical functions," such as defecation, scratching, and vomiting. In time, however, Ukhtomskii extended the theory to include the animal's major behavior response systems as well. The *defensive dominant,* for example, was defined as the *constellation* of brain structures, cortical and subcortical, that is triggered into control of the rest of the nervous system by threatening or painful stimuli. When the defensive system is dominant, the thresholds for fighting, fleeing, and other defensive acts drop and stimuli that ordinarily evoke other responses, such as exploration or friendly approach, may trigger defensive behavior instead.

The dominant system inhibits and raises the activation threshold of competing systems and thus maintains a certain inertia of its own activated state. Its control persists until terminated by stimuli that deactivate it just as lawfully as the initiating stimuli activate it. The signal for deactivation of the defecation mechanism is presumably collapse of the colon and anal sphincter after a bolus has passed. A stimulus that can terminate the defensive dominant is removal of the stimulus that triggered it, i.e., escape.

Startsev and others (Miminoshvili, 1960; Magakian, 1968) have postulated that if the defensive dominant is repeatedly triggered but not allowed to terminate (as occurs with the immobilization stressor used in this work) a *pathological defensive dominant* may result. When, by classical conditioning procedures, such ubiquitous stimuli as food or exercise are conditioned to activate this pathological response system, the stage is set for the serious derangements of cortico-visceral functions described in the following chapters.

I wish to express my appreciation to Marienne Schweinler and Vadim Pahn, who performed the basic translation of this work, to Ida Smith, who typed the several revisions, and to Mary Morgan, who assisted in a number of ways. Every editor must feel some need to apologize to the author whose work he has presumed to translate and prepare for publication. In this case the urge is overwhelming. I thank Dr. Startsev for the honor of bringing this important work to the attention of his English-reading colleagues. At the same time, I sincerely apologize for any distortions it may have suffered in the process.

DOUGLAS M. BOWDEN

Author's Introduction

I. P. Pavlov's studies of experimental neuroses in dogs were the first to demonstrate convincingly the role of functional disorders of the brain in causing pathological states in animals. A wealth of experimental material accumulated by students of Pavlov, particularly by K. M. Bykov and his school, leaves no doubt that animal studies dealing with experimentally induced functional, or neurotic, disorders have legitimate significance and implications for clinical research on human somatic and nervous diseases.

For the medical practitioner, however, it is not sufficient simply to demonstrate that certain disorders in animals are neurogenic or psychological in nature. Unfortunately, up to the present time, the causal connection established between somatic or nervous diseases and chronic disturbances of brain function in animals has been conceptualized in terms too general to be of practical benefit to the practicing physician.

The theory of corticovisceral pathology, which grew out of Pavlov's concept of neurosis as a disorder of cortical excitatory and inhibitory processes or their mobility, states in a convincing, albeit general, way the dependence of visceral illnesses on chronic disturbances of brain function. This theory has been confirmed both experimentally and in clinical practice where drug therapy with neurotropic agents is employed to remove pathological nervous tension and ensure temporary "rest" for the central nervous system and internal organs.

The theory of experimental neurosis, stated in its most sophisticated form as the theory of corticovisceral pathology, has not as yet dealt satisfactorily, however, with one of the central problems of medical research, viz., the question of system specificity. As K. M. Bykov and I. T. Kurtsin wrote in 1952: "This question probably represents one of the most complex problems in medicine." A. L. Miasnikov (1958) wrote as follows regarding the scientific status of the problem of specificity of somatic illness during neurosis: "unfortunately, we are still poorly informed about the mechanisms relating cortical functions and vegetative reactions and, consequently, do not understand in concrete terms the manner in which the nervous system acts upon specific organs (i.e., effectors) to determine the specificity of a disease. In this regard, the visceral theory of physiology and pathology, as developed by K. M. Bykov and his associates, is incomplete in an aspect which is most readily apparent to the clinician."

In our attempts to develop experimental neurosis in monkeys using immobilization stress, we discovered certain conditions that had to be met if this neurogenic stress was to have a pathological effect on particular functional systems (Startsev, 1964a). The basic task of the research was to identify the mechanisms that determine the specific and nonspecific disturbances of the functional systems underlying higher nervous activity, motor behavior, sexual behavior, gastric secretion, carbohydrate metabolism, and cardiovascular activity seen in different cases of experimental neurosis in monkeys.

Completion of work at this stage has made it possible to formulate a general principle regarding the question of which system breaks down in monkeys subjected to immobilization neurosis. In essence, the conditioned and unconditioned stimuli, which normally stimulate a certain physiological system, are transformed into conditioned signals of a defensive or other pathological dominant. They lose, to a certain degree, their former physiological significance and become the chief pathogenetic factor in chronic disorders of the system they formerly activated more appropriately.

Selectivity of damage to a particular physiological system may be achieved by transforming any normal physiological stimulus, whether alimentary, sexual, somatomotor, interoceptive–chemical, or cardiovascular into a conditioned signal for the pathological dominant.

According to the laws of classical conditioning, the stimuli for this purpose must be repeatedly paired with the activation of defensive response mechanisms of the motor system, which, in our experiments, was evoked by physical restraint of the monkey's body and the extremities.

The principles that we have demonstrated emerged from experiments designed to produce chronic disorders, specifically of higher nervous activity (as reflected in the acquisition and performance of conditioned alimentary–motor responses), and neurogenic gastric disorders (gastric achylia with precancerous changes of the gastric mucosa) in monkeys. Working in terms of the principles established there, we were able to produce and analyze other neurogenic disorders: hysterical-like paralyses and hyperkineses in baboons, amenorrhea in female and impotence in male baboons, and a prediabetic condition in rhesus monkeys.

The experimental data on the modeling of these neurogenic diseases in monkeys were gathered between 1961 and 1967 at the Institute of Experimental Pathology and Therapy of the Academy of Medical Sciences of the USSR in Sukhumi.

I
Experimental Neuroses in Monkeys—A Review

In no other branch of medicine have there accumulated so many and varied preconceptions, misconceptions, and methodological errors as in the study of neuroses (Davidenkov, 1963). Nevertheless the practical demands of the clinic present an urgent need for theories that can clarify the nature and mechanism of these functional and reversible disorders of the central nervous system. The only strictly scientific theory of neuroses, that of I. P. Pavlov, is in a continual state of development. Its fundamental postulate, that the neuroses represent excessive strain of excitatory and inhibitory processes or of their mobility, has as yet received little direct study at a neurophysiological level (Iakovleva, 1967). Numerous observations have suggested that in addition to the functional breakdown of cortical cells, which is postulated to occur in chronic disturbances of higher nervous activity, the change in biological significance of stimuli present at the time of extreme stress is also of major importance. The role of pathological conditioned reflexes (including reflexes to the general environment in which stress has occurred) in neurosis has been considered in a number of monographs (Bykov & Kurtsin, 1952, 1960; Dolin, 1962; Iakovleva, 1967). In discussions of the mechanisms of pathology of higher nervous activity, however, major emphasis has been placed on the mechanism of general neurosis, i.e., excessive strain of the basic nervous processes and their mobility in the cerebral cortex.

In the Pavlovian laboratories, the concept of experimental neurosis originally grew out of attempts to explain chronic impairment in the acquisition and performance of conditioned salivary reflexes to exteroceptive stimuli. Later it was broadened to cover disorders of interoceptive conditioned reflexes and somatic disorders that developed in animals with behaviorally defined neurosis. The latter culminated in the theory of corticovisceral pathology (Bykov & Kurtsin, 1960).

The early work in this field was carried out primarily on dogs, cats, and rats. It is natural to expect that systematic research into the problem of experimental neurosis in nonhuman primates can contribute further to our understanding of the causes and mechanisms of neurosis in man.

The first attempt to produce experimental neurosis in monkeys was undertaken by S. D. Kaminskii (1935). An anubis baboon and two pigtail macaques with established conditioned alimentary motor responses were subjected to the kinds of stressors traditionally used to produce nervous breakdown in dogs (presentation of differential stimuli for up to 6–20 min; "clashes," i.e., rapid alternation of positive and negative conditioned stimuli; and reversal of the significance of positive and negative conditioned stimuli). Unlike dogs, the monkeys showed only short-lived neurotic disorders, which disappeared after a week's rest. Later, another series of studies on monkeys, two rhesus monkeys and an ovariectomized chacma baboon, confirmed the finding that classical methods of overstraining cerebral inhibitory mechanisms were relatively ineffective in producing neurosis in monkeys (Kaminskii, 1936, 1937a, b, 1939a, b, c; Bam, 1936, 1939; Bam & Kaminskii, 1942). Kaminskii attributed the instability of the pathological effects to a characteristic of the organization of neural mechanisms in monkeys allowing ready adaptation to changing significance of environmental stimuli.

The two studies showed that whereas chronic breakdowns in higher nervous activity were less likely to occur using the traditional stressors on monkeys, they still developed in certain cases. Neurosis did not develop in monkeys with unbalanced nervous processes but was comparatively easy to produce in monkeys with weak nervous systems. Two of the subjects (pigtail macaque and ovariectomized chacma baboon) with weakened nervous processes showed stable ultraparadoxical response patterns that did not respond to treatment by rest and bromides but that disappeared on repeated administration of caffeine and strychnine.

Disruption of conditioned response performance was further evidenced by intermittent perseveration and reduced intensity of motor responses, general motor agitation alternating with sluggishness, omission of responses (particularly to strong conditioned stimuli), weakening of response inhibition to differential stimuli, reduced responsivity, and fear of the feed box.

The pigtail macaque had been trained to leave a start box and approach a feeder for food in response to a metronome beating 120 times a minute (M 120+) and not to approach in response to its beating 60 times a minute (M 60–) (no food reinforcement). After exposure to the stressor (prolonged presentation of M 60), he no longer responded appropriately to either stimulus. He responded in an ultraparadoxical pattern in that he responded positively to M 60– and negatively to M 120+. The neurotic state generating this response pattern lasted for $1\frac{1}{2}$ years. Tests involving reduced food deprivation did not produce any result. Exclusion of M 120+ from the stimulus sequence resulted in reestablishment of the proper differential response to M 60− and the animal's behavior reverted to normal. Removal of M 60− and reintroduction of M 120+ into the stereotype did not restore the positive reaction toward M 120+, however. Two-months treatment with bromides followed by a 4-month rest did not remove the ultraparadoxical pattern. Negative reactions to M 120+ even intensified and responses to other conditioned stimuli also disappeared. Attempts to establish conditioned responses to new stimuli failed. However, after all of the old stimuli were excluded from the conditioning sessions conditioned responses to new stimuli were successfully established. Reintroduction of the old conditioned stimuli resulted in exacerbation of the neurotic disturbance.

We would explain the mechanism of the ultraparadoxical phase in terms of inertness of the inhibitory process and inductive factors.

In Voronin's (1953) opinion the nervous system of monkeys is quite stable in the face of frequent and abrupt changes in the external environment. Therefore, it is difficult to produce neuroses under the usual experimental conditions. However, by altering the significance of stimuli or imposing tasks involving difficult discriminations a number of disorders of higher nervous activity have been induced in certain species (baboon, capuchin, chimpanzee). These have tended either toward inhibition leading to a total disappearance of established responses or to excitatory breakdowns involving intense motor activity.

In the work of Miminoshvili (1953a, b) with rhesus monkeys and hamadryas baboons it was demonstrated that the method of multiple clashes of positive and inhibitory conditioned response mechanisms led to a brief disruption of higher nervous activity for a period of 1–2 weeks; later on, normal responses were quickly reestablished and further disruption by the clash method was not possible. Analogous data were obtained by Kriazhev (1955) in two baboons and two pigtail macaques. Overstrain of excitatory and inhibitory processes did not cause neuroses except in one monkey with a weak type of nervous system. It became apparent that during various forms of nervous strain monkeys, contrary to dogs, proved capable of switching to various types of motor activity (self-grooming, scratching, etc.) and thereby to preserve the state of vital activity.

L. N. Norkina (1957, 1958) carried out an extensive study exposing monkeys to the usual laboratory stresses used to produce neurosis in dogs. Working with four hamadryas baboons with a firmly established stereotype of conditioned motor alimentary responses she presented a differential stimulus for successively longer durations up to 3 min. She also repeatedly substituted positive signals for negative ones, and vice versa; carried out whole sessions with only one of the signals, rather than the stereotype; or disrupted the stereotype by altering intertrial intervals. Finally, she imposed stimuli of extreme intensity. All of these methods, which are sufficient for disruption of higher nervous activity in dogs (as judged by disruption of classically conditioned salivation reflexes), did not disturb conditioned motor responses in monkeys for more than a very brief time. Apparently these manipulations do not overtax the limits of functional mobility of the motor analyzer in monkeys.

Later experiments involving greater complexity in the stereotypes produced neurotic motor responses but even these performance disorders disappeared within 20 days. Neurotic states were obtained in two of four monkeys subjected to a difficult problem in response differentiation where the appropriate responses were to press a lever upward in response to one stimulus and downward in response to another. One of these monkeys developed an inhibitory neurosis, the other an excitatory neurosis.

Norkina concluded that, in principle, the classical methods of obtaining experimental neurosis in dogs are also applicable to monkeys, but that the stimulus manipulations necessary to disrupt learned motor responses in monkeys are more complex and more prolonged than those sufficient to disrupt conditioned salivation responses in the dog.

The work of Miminoshvili and his colleagues (Miminoshvili, 1953a, b, 1960, 1957; Miminoshvili, Magakian, & Kokaia, 1954, 1960; Magakian, Miminoshvili, & Kokaia, 1953) represented a new stage in the study of experimental neuroses in monkeys. These investigations were performed on five animals: two rhesus monkeys and three hamadryas baboons. Two of the animals were trained on a stereotype of food- and shock-reinforced motor responses in a restraint stand; the stressors consisted of lengthening the duration of the signal for impending electroshock up to 1–2 min, rapid alternation of signals for food and shock, etc. The neuroses produced by this method were characterized by general motor agitation, sustained lever presses, disinhibition of differential responses, paradoxical and ultraparadoxical responses, and partial or total elimination of the unconditioned alimentary responses.

In the other three animals neuroses were produced over the course of 4–6 months by imposing conflict situations that evoked clashes of various biological responses: alimentary, sexual, affiliative, and defensive. In Miminoshvili's opinion disruption can be obtained more readily by clashing the stimuli that naturally activate various response mechanisms than by artificial stimuli, such as lights and tones. This is attributed to the fact that the natural stimuli activate neural processes of greater intensity than do the artificial stimuli.

The basic theoretical conclusions that emerged from Miminoshvili's research were as follows.

1. It is difficult to establish a neurotic state in monkeys on the basis of alimentary response mechanisms; neurosis is more easily produced on the basis of defensive response mechanisms, in which it appears that neural activity proceeds with greater intensity in the monkey so that clashing or excessively straining these mechanisms can rapidly lead to a serious disruption of cortical function.

2. The method of creating conflicting excitatory inputs directed toward various subcortical and cortical areas leads to a clash of excitatory and inhibitory

processes in the cerebral cortex; the simultaneous appearance of competing foci of excitation in the cortical representation of a number of unconditioned reflexes leads to a disruption of higher nervous activity faster than conflicts between conditioned excitatory and inhibitory response mechanisms limited to the cerebral representation of the alimentary system.

3. The most appropriate methods for studying both normal and pathological higher nervous activity in monkeys involve the manipulation of defensive, sexual, and orienting–exploratory responses rather than alimentary responses. The methods worked out by Miminoshvili for establishing neuroses in monkeys by creating conflict situations on the basis of natural alimentary, sexual, social, and defensive response mechanism have been used successfully by other researchers in experiments on hamadryas baboons (Alekseeva, 1957a, b, 1959a, b; Markov, 1957, 1959). Sh. L. Dzhalagoniia (1960), using this method, obtained relatively mild and transient changes in the higher nervous activity of hamadryas baboons.

The research of G. M. Cherkovich (1956, 1957, 1960) has developed further the idea of clashing, and thus stressing, various natural response mechanisms to produce experimental neuroses in monkeys. She has used disruption of the daily living routine of hamadryas baboons as an effective stressor. This method is analogous to other clash techniques and makes it possible to obtain neurotic behavior in a short period of time (1.5–2 months). In one animal she produced an excitatory nervous breakdown manifested by excessively high rates of lever pressing, frequent pressing in the intervals between trials, and breakdown in discrimination on an operant paradigm; another animal developed an inhibitory breakdown, i.e., refusal to press the response lever.

Clashing alimentary (food elicited) and defensive (shock elicited) neural mechanisms to produce neurosis was first used on dogs by Kriazhev (1945), and later by Kurtsin (1951) in Bykov's laboratory. Successful application of this technique for producing neurosis in monkeys has been accomplished by a number of researchers (Miminoshvili, 1953b; Kriazhev, 1955; Gavlichek, 1962). Kriazhev attributes the disappearance of active motor responses (including positive responses) following the pairing of food and shock to the formation of a stable inhibitory focus in the motor cortex. It should be noted that this neurotic state has been established in monkeys with the very first clash of alimentary and defensive response mechanisms. Gavlichek (1962), experimenting on two rhesus monkeys, repeatedly coupled the sound of a siren with painful electrocutaneous stimulation according to the Bechterev–Protopopov method. After a number of trials the conditioned stimulus for the defensive response presented alone came to evoke the entire complex of disturbances typically elicited by the painful unconditioned stimulus. Considering the stability of the conditioned defensive response over many months time, the fact that it was established while the animals were responding to conditioned stimuli for alimentary behavior, and the fact that defensive behavior came to dominate the conditioned and unconditioned alimentary responses, the author concluded that neurosis in monkeys develops through the establishment of a defensive dominant in the central nervous system that inhibits other response mechanisms.

Masserman and Pechtel (1953) also produced neurosis in rhesus monkeys by clashing natural alimentary and defensive reflexes. Chronic disruption of conditioned alimentary responses developed immediately after a toy snake was placed in the box where food ordinarily appeared.

More recent experiments have substantiated earlier findings concerning the development of chronic disturbances of conditioned responses following collision of the neural mechanisms that mediate natural biological response patterns.

Dzhalagoniia (1962, 1967), working with hamadryas baboons, investigated the influence of chronic (2–3 months) taxing of natural biological responses (food-reinforced motor responses) on animals previously subjected to physical stress. In one study, the influence of this procedure was tested on normal animals and on animals which had been subjected to total body x irradiation (400 rads) 18 months previously. In the normal animals, only transient changes in higher nervous activity were noted with repeated clashes of sexual, affiliative, and alimentary response mechanisms. In the irradiated group, however, the same stimulus manipulations produced severe neurotic syndromes manifested behaviorally as motor agitation; food-reinforced motor responses were chronically inhibited in one animal and excessively excited in the other.

Two groups of hamadryas baboons, one intact and the other with lesions of the visual cortex inflicted in infancy, were trained on a series of food-reinforced motor responses to light and sound stimuli. Then they were subjected to 5 months of stress induced by random manipulations of the light—dark cycle. Experimental neurosis developed in both groups of monkeys but was considerably more severe in the group with cortical ablations. During the first 10–20 days, the changes in higher nervous activity were reactive in character. The conditioned responses became unstable, the normal relationship between stimulus intensity and response (lever press) intensity was lost, lever pressing was protracted, and cyclical excitatory and inhibitory disruptions of performance developed. At a later stage the conditioned behaviors became weaker (gradual decrease in the frequency and force of pressing) and responses completely disappeared toward the end of each day's experiment; finally an ultraparadoxical stage was reached in which the animals pressed more frequently to the unreinforced stimulus than to the reinforced stimulus. They came to respond negatively and even with revulsion to the unconditioned stimulus, food. A 40-day rest improved performance on the conditioning paradigm only in the unoperated monkeys.

After the rest, the disrupted light—dark cycles were imposed anew for 10 days with the addition of periodic electrocutaneous shock (40 V) with a noxious sound stimulus. After the latter stressor period ended the subjects showed signs of inhibition both in their free behavior and in performance on the conditioning paradigms: motor activity diminished and the animals frequently appeared drowsy. This was accompanied by ultraparadoxical performance in response to conditioned stimuli. There was little stability in the performance of conditioned responses. Administration of a number of neurotropic substances that would ordinarily potentiate performance of conditioned motor responses (amphetamine, ephedrine in combination with adrenalin) caused drowsiness and response inhibition instead.

The development in monkeys of neurotic conditions induced by various functional stressors of central nervous mechanisms involves an early stage of reactive disturbances of higher nervous activity. In some cases normalization ensues, but in other cases a neurosis coupled with secondary vegetative—somatic disorders develops. In analyzing the various methods that have been used to induce experimental neurosis, one must conclude that the determinants of the specific symptoms which emerge in neuroses in humans, monkeys, and dogs have not been sufficiently elucidated and require further study.

Sysoeva (1965) studied the establishment of new conditioned responses in four hamadryas baboons that previously had been subjected to severe functional stress. She found that their acquisition of such responses deviated considerably from the norm. Two of the subjects with defensive behavior patterns acquired conditioned responses as quickly as normal animals, but their performance deteriorated rapidly on the introduction of a differentiatial stimulus. The subjects in which passive defensive behavior patterns predominated showed a marked retardation in the rate of acquisition of conditioned responses. After more than a year of conditioning sessions, involving more than 1800 conditioning trials and 600 discrimination trials, appropriate responses to the conditioning stimuli fluctuated between 80 and 100%, whereas appropriate withholding of the response occurred only with 0–50% of presentations of the differential stimulus.

Panina (1965) studied four hamadryas baboons that appeared to have recovered from a previous experiment involving severe functional stress of the central nervous system and two control animals of the same species. She found that the acquisition of conditioned orienting—investigatory responses was retarded in the subjects previously subjected to stress.

In another study, the same investigator (Panina, 1967) produced neurosis in five hamadryas baboons in which had been established conditioned responses involving three different biological response systems: alimentary, defensive, and orienting—investigatory.

The defensive response mechanism was overstressed to produce neurosis in each of the animals. The stressor environment consisted of a special chamber in which a loud bell followed by electrocutaneous stimulation (80 V) was applied for 1 min every half hour around the clock. The baboons were subjected to this condition for 25 days. Some showed strengthening of the defensive conditioned responses with disruption of alimentary and orientating—investigatory responses.

Others suffered different disorders. The changes in higher nervous activity developed in the course of 3 weeks of the stressor condition. With the termination of the stressor condition and return of the baboons to their home cages, a general suppression of the conditioned responses ensued. This was seen in a rapid falling off or even disappearance of the conditioned orientation—exploratory responses for 4—6 months, with a lesser degree of suppression of the alimentary and defensive responses; if the alimentary responses predominated, then the defensive responses were suppressed to a greater degree and vice versa.

Inhibition of conditioned response mechanisms is presumably related to overstress and exhaustion of cortical cells in the neurotic mechanism. Typical symptoms of neurosis in the way the baboons performed conditioned responses were: chaotic responses (the responses elicited by conditioned stimuli were directed randomly at all of the response levers, not just the appropriate one), stimulus weakness (the response chain broke off at the first link, i.e., during approach to the lever, or the last link, approach to the feed box), and a tendency toward ultraparadoxical responding. Recovery from the latter symptom leveled off in 3—4 months after cessation of the stressor condition and remained incomplete thereafter.

Among the more recently reported findings regarding experimental neurosis in monkeys is the observation that monkeys gradually adapt to disruption of the daily light—dark cycle (Lagutina *et al.*, 1966). This implies the development of compensatory processes in the cerebral cortex. The limited nature of this compensation, however, can be demonstrated by imposing additional functional stressors.

Research on experimental neurosis in monkeys has generally failed to demonstrate homogeneous disruption of all cerebral functions. Instead the concepts of system-specific neuroses, i.e., functional disruption of specific organ systems, have come to the fore. The system disrupted depends on both the typological peculiarities of the nervous system of the animals and the type of stressor. In rhesus monkeys, especially during acclimatization, dyspepsia and dysentery predominate. In hamadryas baboons pathology of the cardiovascular system is most frequently observed. Under specific conditions of clash between alimentary and defensive response mechanisms, however, it is possible to produce serious gastric disease (neurogenic gastric achylia) even in baboons (Chapter III). Female baboons subjected to disruption of social relationships develop irregular sexual cycles and amenorrhea (Chapter VI). It is important to note that such somatic disorders frequently continue long after the renewal of appropriate conditioned response performance. The more primitive regulatory systems (functions of the so-called visceral brain) therefore possess less compensatory capacity than the higher neocortical systems.

Investigators who have induced experimental neuroses in monkeys by creating conflict situations, i.e., by clashing various natural conditioned biological reflexes (affiliative, sexual, defensive, and alimentary), have observed a number of profound autonomic and somatic disorders. Greatest attention has been directed at chronic increases and decreases in arterial blood pressure, coronary insufficiency, and myocardial infarction (Miminoshvili, 1953a, 1957; Miminoshvili *et al.* 1954, 1956, 1961; Magakian, 1953a, b, 1957, 1966, 1967; Magakian *et al.*, 1953; Cherkovich, 1957, 1959, 1960; Markov, 1957, 1959; Gavlichek, 1962).

The most extensive report of neurogenic hypertensive disease and coronary insufficiency appears in the work of Miminoshvili *et al.*, (1960). Five animals were studied—three hamadryas baboons and two rhesus monkeys. In three of the subjects neurosis was produced by laboratory methods. They were subjected to constant conflict between alimentary and defensive response mechanisms in one setting and tested intermittently for conditioned response performance in a different chamber. In the other two subjects neurosis was produced by clashing natural conditioned stimuli eliciting alimentary, sexual, defensive, and affiliative behavior.

The first three animals developed hypotension (78/45 mm Hg) within 4 months of the onset of neurotic behavior. This period coincided with the predominance of excitatory disruption of conditioned response performance. The authors interpreted the hypotension in terms of negative induction by the cortex on subcortical vasomotor centers. After a period of normalization the arterial pressure began to increase. This was accompanied by the onset of behavioral sluggishness and disappearance of all previously acquired conditioned responses and by refusal to eat in the test chamber. Eventually, arterial pressures reached 170/110 mm Hg and 180/120 mm Hg. This hypertensive phase was interpreted as a result of positive induction from an inhibited cortex to the subcortex, i.e., as a removal of inhibition of the subcortical vasomotor centers.

With the onset of neurosis the reactivity of the autonomic nervous system to such pharmacological agents as pilocarpine, atropine, and nitroglycerin changed. Whereas under normal conditions pilocarpine and nitroglycerin lowered arterial pressure, they increased it in neurosis; tachycardia ensued. Atropine under normal conditions raised the arterial pressure, whereas during neurosis it lowered blood pressure. The hypertensive reaction to the cold pressor test was more marked and prolonged in neurosis, lasting up to 18 min rather than the usual 2–3 min.

The other two monkeys, the neurotic condition of which was caused by clashes of various natural stimuli, showed a tendency toward increased arterial pressure within 3–6 months after the beginning of the stressor condition. The onset of hypertension coincided with the disappearance of conditioned responses and refusal to eat. No hypotensive phase was observed in these animals, and the hypertension continued for 20 months.

In some monkeys coronary insufficiency appeared after the onset of hypertension, and in others it emerged as an independent neurogenic disease in the absence of hypertension. In one monkey the electrocardiogram (EKG) remained normal, despite a clearcut hypertensive syndrome. For the animals developing coronary insufficiency, repeated electrocardiograms in the course of a year showed progressive cardiac pathology and disclosed transformation of the functional disturbance of coronary circulation into a chronic disorder comparable in stability to organic disease. Nitroglycerin restored the EKG to normal in all monkeys except one, suggesting that even though the coronary insufficiency is quite stable in such monkeys, it is functional in nature. Albeit for a short time (only a few minutes), nitroglycerin was capable of eliminating the coronary spasm. Presumably, in cases where nitroglycerin does not improve the EKG a local organic process or an especially stable spasm has been established (Miminoshvili *et al.*, 1960).

The investigators differentiated two types of functional coronary insufficiency in monkeys: a cortical type and a subcortical type. The cortical type appeared during waking hours and disappeared during medication-induced sleep; the second, on the contrary, was not seen during the waking hours but appeared during sleep or in the transitions between sleep and waking. The authors explained the cortical type of coronary insufficiency as follows. A chronic excitatory focus develops in an area of the cortex, which causes a stable spasm of the coronary vessels. The exclusion of cortical influences during sleep has a beneficial effect in that the coronarospasm is reduced and the ischemia is removed.

In the subcortical type, the normally active cortical influences maintain control of the functionally impaired subcortical vascular centers during waking. In this case, inhibition of the cortex during sleep results in the exclusion of this compensatory function and allows coronary insufficiency to emerge. Positive induction from the inhibited cortex facilitates the pathological processes at the subcortical level during sleep.

In two of the subjects the coronary insufficiency resulted in myocardial infarction, and one of these suffered two infarctions with probable development of a cardiac aneurysm.

The experiments cited suggest that sleep and the transitory hypnotic states of falling asleep and awakening may play an important initiating role in the angina and myocardial infarction sometimes observed in human patients. They have suggested new ways of using functional electrocardiography for the detection of hidden forms of coronary insufficiency in man. They also have provided a physiological basis for defining indications and contraindications for sleep therapy, for on some occasions this treatment has been associated with myocardial infarction in man.

Studies of experimental neurosis in monkeys have therefore demonstrated both coronary insufficiency and myocardial infarctions of a functional nature. These disorders can develop in the absence of atherosclerosis or other morphological pathology. Animal studies in this area have substantiated the view of Soviet clinicians that disorders of function in the central nervous system can constitute the leading factors in disturbances of arterial pressure and the coronary circulation (Lang, 1950).

Magakian (1966, 1967) studied changes in blood pressure and electrocardiograms in 20 hamadryas baboons that were subjected to chronic traumatization of the nervous system as a result of living in a special electrified cage. Even though no special investigations of higher nervous activity were conducted, one might presume that the monkeys suffered from chronic nervous disorders. Eight monkeys of the first three groups noted in Table 1 developed hypotension by the end of the fourth month of stress. The hypotensive phase lasted about 2 months and then was followed in 8–10 months by a steady rise of the maximal and minimal arterial pressures and symptoms of coronary insufficiency. Myocardial infarction developed in four monkeys, and in three of them it appeared 8–10 months after the discontinuation of the stressor condition while they were living in an open air cage. Eight of the monkeys were found by Startsev (1964a, b, c) to suffer from gastric achylia. Interestingly, Magakian (1967) found that chlorpromazine had a marked prophylactic effect in preventing the development of neurogenic pathology.

The most impressive pathological findings in this study included instances of paroxysmal ventricular tachycardia during infarction, x-ray cinematographic evidence of a left ventricular aneurism in one monkey, and several instances at autopsy of massive foci of myocardial necrosis. Given the young age of the monkeys involved, the author was able to demonstrate that all of the pathological findings had occurred with a complete absence of atherosclerosis in the coronary vessels.

Cherkovich (1957, 1959, 1960) produced similar disorders using a different kind of stressor, viz., repeated disruption of the diurnal light–dark and feeding

TABLE 1

Pathological Changes in Visceral Organs of Monkeys Subjected to Stressors after the Administration of Pharmacologic Agents (Magakian, 1967)

Experimental group	Total	With coronary insufficiency	With myocardial infarction	With hypertension	With gastric achylia[a]
		Number of monkeys with different disorders			
I No drug	5	5	2	2	3(4)
II Pituitrin	5	4	1	3	2(4)
III Vicasol[b]	5	5	1	3	2(4)
IV Chlorpromazine	5	–	–	–	1(5)

[a]Numbers in parentheses represent numbers of subjects examined for gastric achylia.

[b]Bisulfite derivative of 2-methyl-1,4-naphthoquinone (water-soluble analog of vitamin K_3).

schedules. Six to eight weeks after cessation of the stressor condition, two of her hamadryas baboons were found to suffer from coronary insufficiency that, in one case, terminated in myocardial infarction.

Markov (1957, 1959) produced neurotic disorders by a combination of excessive strain on basic biological response mechanisms (à la Miminoshvili) and disruption of diurnal schedules (à la Cherkovich) in four hamadryas (two normal and two sensitized by injections of horse serum). Neurotic disorders developed in the sensitized monkeys in 7—10 days after the onset of nervous stress, whereas in the control monkeys the onset did not occur for over 40 days. In addition to behavioral signs of neurosis, hypertension developed. The author, in accordance with the views of P. K. Anokhin, pointed out that the genesis of neurotic conditions in humans lies in an abrupt conflict between two or more systems of excitation competing to dislodge one another and associated with negative emotional saturation as the conflicting urges tend to cancel one another.

The literature dealing with experimental neurosis in monkeys is essentially limited to the studies cited above. Almost all of this work has been done in the last 30 years at the Sukhumi primate facility by investigators in the Laboratory of Physiology and Pathology of Higher Nervous Activity. Our own work on experimental neurosis in monkeys belongs in the same category (Startsev, 1961a, b, 1963, 1964b, c, 1965, 1966a, b, 1968a, b, 1972; Shestopalova & Startsev, 1968; Startsev & Kuraev, 1967).

Experimental neuroses in monkeys clearly represent a new and far from finished page in the text of experimental pathology. The difficulty in producing neurosis in monkeys and the relatively rapid reestablishment of normal higher nervous activity after disruption can be explained by the advanced development of the primate brain, especially of the motor system and the frontal lobes. The rich connections of the frontal cortex with other cortical areas and with subcortical structures in nonhuman primates provide enormous compensatory possibilities and therefore reduced vulnerability to neurogenic stress by accelerating the termination of neurotic processes. The importance of advanced central neural control mechanisms is also evidenced in studies on animals with less complex nervous systems. Chechulin (1963) showed that dogs with intact cerebral hemispheres recover from neurosis more quickly and easily than dogs with the cortical hemispheres removed. As some of the studies cited above have demonstrated, the compensatory function of higher areas of the brain can be reduced in monkeys by traumatic injury to the brain, radiation sickness, etc. Under such conditions, neurotic disorders are more profound and more persistent than in intact animals.

The fact that the various traditional methods of producing neurosis in dogs have proved ineffective in monkeys can probably be explained by the higher level of development of the frontal cortex in monkeys. They are similar to man in the major characteristic of their response to central nervous system stressors.

A second important characteristic of neuroses in monkeys is that they develop in conflict situations as a result of gross and chronic disruption of normal affiliative, sexual, and parental relationships, which establishes a defensive dominant. The use of distorted environmental situations to disrupt various natural conditioned and unconditioned reflexes is not only a new method more appropriate to the neural organization of primates but is also a method of producing neurosis more comparable to human neurosis than the methods traditionally used with other animals.

Finally, the development of serious cardiovascular pathology during the induction of behavioral neurosis in monkeys is extremely important. The experimental production of hypertension and, more particularly, of coronary insufficiency and myocardial infarction, which are primarily diseases of man, raises the significance of experimental neurosis research in monkeys to a level unattainable with other animals. It is probable that other pathological conditions peculiar to man may be successfully simulated in monkeys as well by procedures involving nervous stress.

As far as our knowledge of the mechanisms of experimental neurosis is concerned, the studies in monkeys have contributed little beyond what has been earlier established on the basis of work with dogs. The basic concepts regarding the mechanism of neurosis derive from Pavlov's ideas concerning overstrain of excitatory and inhibitory processes and their mobility in cortical and subcortical areas. It is possible that the same mechanism postulated to account for the general neurotic breakdowns in dogs stressed by the traditional experimental paradigms holds for the neuroses induced in monkeys by diverse stressors. These methods, although quite reliable in producing neurotic breakdowns, are so gross as to make it difficult to analyze the causes of pathological changes in particular functional systems. Methods involving multiple stressors directed at a variety of response mechanisms provide little opportunity for comprehending the mechanism whereby particular functional or organic systems undergo chronic pathological changes while other systems remain relatively unaffected. It is likely that the mechanism underlying functional disruption of specific systems consists in the hyperfunction of a given system evoked by its natural stimulus combined with the action of a nonspecific nervous stressor on the organism. The repeated pairing of activation of a given organic system with intense nervous stress directs the pathological influence of the stressor primarily to the system activated; subsequently the natural stimuli that ordinarily activate the system in a normal manner sustain the pathological stressor's effect on the system as a conditioned stimulus for the stressor effect. The following pages explain this hypothesis in greater detail. In general our investigations have been directed toward the detection and analysis of diseases of specific organ systems and their neural regulation during neurosis.

II
Immobilization Neurosis in Hamadryas Baboons

Up to the present time, the majority of studies of experimental neurosis and its somatic symptoms in monkeys has involved the manipulation of various social, sexual, and alimentary response mechanisms. This approach to neurogenic stress has proved to be very fruitful in monkeys, which have highly organized social relationships. It requires, however, a large expenditure of time—from a few months to a year—to produce chronic disorders of higher nervous activity and visceral disturbances by such methods. It was desirable to accelerate the production of experimental neurosis, while preserving the biological appropriateness of the stressors and their conformity with the peculiarities of higher nervous activity and behavior in primates. For this purpose we have worked out a different type of procedure, wherein the stressor consists of temporary immobilization of the animal.

The question arose, of course, as to the appropriateness of using immobilization as a stressor in attempts to simulate diseases of man. It is unlikely that forcible restraint or limitation of movement is the cause of every case of psychosomatic disease in humans. Nevertheless, there are a number of instances in a person's life when forcible immobilization or compulsory limitations of activity are accompanied by strong negative emotions capable of creating foci of pathological defensive dominance in the brain. From the cradle, literally, man is subjected to immobilization of arms and legs that may coincide in time with a strong feeling of hunger, the pain of a childhood disease, itching, etc.

The activation of defensive response mechanisms in an immobilized child, when caused by pain, can certainly give rise to pathological phenomena in the young organism. Are the etiologies of infantile gastric anacidity, dyspepsias, and dystrophies frequently seen in babies really so clear? And is it not true that chronic immobilization of children is related to a number of nervous and motor disorders of childhood, as well as to the lowering of resistance to a number of childhood infections?

These issues demand special investigation. One of the most common methods of punishing older children for actual or imaginary misdemeanors is to have them stand and face a corner for many hours. Another is to spank a child while he is squeezed between the knees! And is it not a fact that an individual may carry a psychic trauma for life following an experience of immobilization associated with being beaten or sexually molested? Intense fear of being restrained on an operating table or of being restricted to bed for months is by no means uncommon among people suffering temporary paralysis, recuperating from a heart attack, or bedridden after physical trauma.

It is safe to say that no consistent physiological approach to questions of this kind has been actively pursued, and, in fact, such has been proposed only in barest outline. W. B. Cannon (1929), a noted American physiologist, took the view that under conditions of forced immobilization an animal mobilizes all its strength and energy to struggle against the restraining object. Another aspect of the phenomenon is important as well, namely the futile ineffectiveness of the activated neural mechanisms that mediate the tremendous muscular effort expended by the animal. There arises not only a progressive overwhelming strain on central neural mechanisms, primarily of the motor system, but also a profound mismatch between the expected effect of motor reactions acquired throughout the life of the individual and the sudden impossibility of reaching a goal despite desperate muscular effort.

The defensive excitation of the motor system generated in this process bears a number of features characteristic of a "cerebral dominant" as defined by A. A. Ukhtomskii (1949): inertia, summation, and the capacity to inhibit various other response mechanisms.

Excitation of defensive response mechanisms became extremely intense in our experiments, where otherwise healthy monkeys, when immobilized, developed profound behavioral and visceral disorders. Some of the animals suddenly died, probably because of functional cardiac paralysis. We have interpreted the prolonged disorders of the functional state of the brain, particularly of the motor system, as manifestations of a pathological defensive dominant, the effect of which can be channeled into disease of a particular physiological system, e.g., the gastrointestinal system, the motor system, sexual system, or the system regulating carbohydrate metabolism (Startsev, 1964a, b, c). A particular system becomes affected when stimuli that ordinarily stimulate it to activity, e.g., food, exercise, or sexual stimuli, are transformed into conditioned signals eliciting the defensive dominant. This occurs when excitation of the specific system is repeatedly combined with the excitation of defensive response mechanisms caused by immobilization of the monkey's body and extremities in a restraint stand.

METHODS

The subjects for this investigation were nine adult male hamadryas baboons. They lived in groups in large home cages allowing observation of a wide range of activities: motor (walking, running, jumping, climbing), orienting–investigatory, alimentary, defensive, vocal, social, etc. They were fed at the same time every day and were not food deprived for the conditioning sessions. The large size of the home cage provided an opportunity to immobilize the monkeys of a group all at the same time on restraint stands set up in the home cage.

Before the animals were subjected to immobilization stress, they were all trained on a sequence of conditioned motor responses using food as reinforcement. The conditioning sessions were carried out in a separate, specially constructed cage 2.5 X 2.5 X 3.0 m in size, which was located at some distance from the home cage. During testing they could hear their cagemates and animals in nearby cages but not see them. They were tested individually in this setting. During conditioning sessions, food was delivered immediately to a feeder when the animal pulled a lever on one wall in response to various conditioning stimuli. The conditioning stimuli and differential stimuli were tones of different pitches and lights of different colors presented in a stereotyped sequence (Table 2). The stimulus duration was 10 sec with a constant intertrial interval of 2 min. Training was continued until the subject's performance had been stable and appropriate for many sessions.

TABLE 2
Fixed Sequence of Stimulus Presentation

Stimulus	Significance	Designation of the stimulus on strip chart records
Low tone	Positive	LT+
High tone	Differential	HT−
Low tone	Positive	LT+
High tone	Differential	HT−
White light	Positive	WL+
Red light	Differential	RL−
White light	Positive	WL+
Red light	Differential	RL−
Low tone	Positive	LT+
High tone	Differential	HT−
White light	Positive	WL+
Red light	Differential	RL−
Low tone	Positive	LT+
White light	Positive	WL+

The following response indices were recorded: (a) the number of appropriate responses to positive stimuli; (b) the number of disinhibited differentiations (lever press responses to differential stimuli); (c) the latency of conditioned responses to positive signals; (d) the total number of lever presses during the conditioning session.

In addition, the large size of the test cage made it possible to observe the motor activity of the animal under relatively natural circumstances. Particular attention was given to recording various aspects of the alimentary motor response mechanism as reflected in search for food, rate of lever pressing approach to the feeder, and style of eating.

The stressor conditions used to produce chronic disruptions of the conditioned motor responses consisted of five sessions in which the baboon was prefed and then fixed to a restraint stand or restraint chair in the home cage; the arms and legs were totally immobilized for 5 hr.

The response of the animals to the restraint stand was to struggle violently; they screeched, trembled, chewed the stand, and tore at the vests that held them in place (Figure 1). The negative emotional reaction as reflected in active and passive defensive behavior was especially striking. The animal was in a constant state of motor excitement, except for transient periods when he hung limp from exhaustion. His face became pale or flushed and was covered with perspiration.

FIG. 1 Hamadryas baboon immobilized in the restraint stand.

Urination and defecation were frequent. After release from the stand, the baboon sometimes lay in its cage for some time and did not eat. On several occasions, animals died in the restraint stand, evidently from acute cardiac failure, for autopsy failed to reveal organic lesions of any sort.

The experiments with feeding in the home cage followed by 5 hr of fixation in the restraint stand alternated with 1–2 days of rest, during which performance of the conditioned alimentary motor responses was tested. Such testing sessions were repeated for many months through various phases of the stressor and poststressor conditions. After three or four immobilization sessions the baboons developed a negative reaction toward food, and particularly to the kind of food that they had received just before being fixed in the restraint stand (Table 3). With repeated combinations of normal eating and subsequent immobilization in the home cage, the act of eating became a conditioned stimulus for the defensive dominant. Furthermore, the conditioned alimentary motor responses were disrupted simultaneously with the unconditioned responses to food.

Because the baboon received food before each experiment in the conditioning chamber, the testing of performance of responses to conditioned alimentary stimuli always occurred against a background of preliminary stimulation of the alimentary system. This constant aspect of the conditioning experiments acquired special and permanent significance through the repeated combinations of home cage feeding and immobilization in or near the test chamber.

It was found that anticipation of immobilization in the stand caused the animals to develop a fear of eating, manifested at first by a partial refusal to eat and, over a period of time, by weight loss. Later, however, food intake returned to normal, although the food did not stimulate the gastric glands; in fact, it sometimes produced vomiting and inhibition of gastric secretion. Insofar as conditioned and unconditioned alimentary response mechanisms comprise a single functional system, the disorder of the unconditioned alimentary responses (approach to food and eating) was inevitably reflected in a chronic disorder of conditioned alimentary motor responses (lever pressing) as well.

Special investigations were carried out to evaluate the significance of the act of eating as a stimulus to the defensive dominant and, therefore, the most probable cause of chronic disorders of conditioned alimentary motor responses. If the behavioral neurosis was based on transformation of the act of feeding into a signal activating the defensive dominant, then immobilization without preliminary feeding should not produce the same effect. Likewise, if the same experiments were performed under conditions that eliminated the defensive excitation, e.g., under the influence of psychotropic pharmacological agents, long-term functional disruptions should not arise. In either case the conditions necessary for transformation of the act of feeding into a stimulus to the defensive dominant would not be met.

Before the effectiveness of psychopharmacological agents in preventing the development of neurosis was investigated, it was necessary to test their influence

TABLE 3
Lowering of Alimentary Excitability in Two Baboons (Larn and Abo) as a Result
of Repeated Combinations of Normal Feeding in the Home Cage with Subsequent
5-hr Fixation in the Restraint Stand (similar results were obtained
with subjects Antil, Nochnitsa, and Kleshchevina)

Subject	Date	Experiment No.	Feeding in home cage just before immobilization	Feeding between immo-bilization sessions
Larn (1962)	Mar. 13	1	Consumed an egg, bread, fresh apples, and stewed fruit (20 min)	Ate peas off floor; did not touch food with hands; ingested own urine
	Mar. 15	2	Ate an egg, bread, 3 apples and some stewed fruit (25 min)	Ate poorly: apples, candy, and sunflower seeds; drank milk
	Mar. 20	3	Ate 3 apples, no eggs, and little bread or stewed fruit (45 min)	The following morning, ate poorly: an egg, stewed fruit, bread; did not touch peas and seeds; did not eat candy, nuts, or seeds during testing of conditioned responses
	Mar. 22	4	Ate no bread, a little apple; consumed all of stewed fruit (15 min)	Ate nothing after testing
	Mar. 26	5	Ate no bread; consumed all of stewed fruit (30 min)	Drank milk after testing; did not eat nuts or peas
Abo (1964)	May 18	1	Ate 3 eggs and drank 200 ml of milk	Ate poorly after testing
	May 21	2	Ate 2 eggs and drank 200 ml of milk	Ate little after testing
	May 25	3	Ate 1 egg and drank some milk	Ate little
	May 28	4	Ate 1 egg, spilled milk; consumed all of stewed fruit	Ate little
	June 1	5	Refused egg; consumed a little milk and stewed fruit	Ate little

on general motor activity and conditioned alimentary motor responses under normal conditions.

The last part of this chapter describes the short- and long-term effects of immobilization stress on conditioned alimentary motor responses (1) with and without prefeeding, and (2) with and without pretreatment with psychotropic agents.

NEUROTIC CHANGES IN
HIGHER NERVOUS ACTIVITY

In the study of the baboon Larn, five experiments involving home cage prefeeding followed by immobilization of the body and extremities for 5-hr periods precipitated a breakdown of higher nervous activity. Figures 2 and 3 illustrate the differences between conditioned alimentary motor responses under normal conditions (I) and during the development of experimental neurosis (II, III, IV, V). Conditioned responses were completely inhibited during the first month after the immobilization sessions. The total inhibition of responses to conditioned stimuli was frequently accompanied by ultraparadoxical responses, i.e., lever presses to the differential stimulus or more intense pressing to the differen-

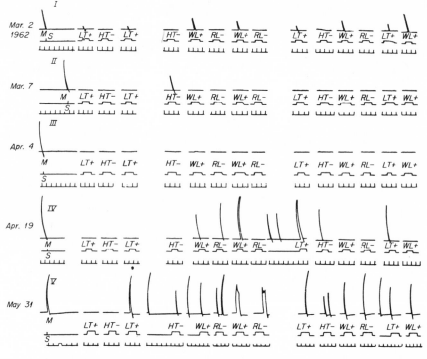

FIG. 2 Changes in conditioned alimentary motor responses in the hamadryas baboon Larn (I) under normal conditions; (II and III) during stressor sessions; (IV and V) during recovery from the disruption of nervous activity. From top to bottom: strip chart records of lever pressing, stimulus marker for conditioned signals, time marker (1-sec intervals). M, deflection representing maximal pressure on the lever; S, calibration representing synchrony of onset of a conditioned signal with lever press M; LT+, low tone conditioned stimulus (CS); WL+, white light CS; HT−, high tone differential stimulus (DS); RL−, red light DS. Date and number of experimental series appears to the left of each record.

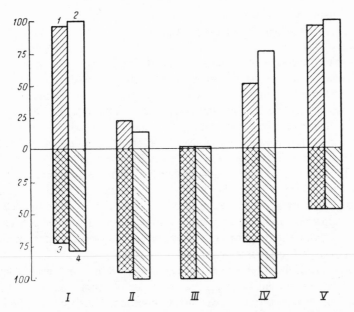

FIG. 3 Changes in conditioned alimentary motor responses in hamadryas baboon (Larn): (I) prestressor condition; (II) during sessions with prefeeding followed by fixation in stand; (III) during onset of disorder of higher nervous activity; (IV and V) during normalization of higher nervous activity. Abscissa: stages of change in conditioned response performance; ordinate: upper histograms represent percent correct responses to positive conditioned stimuli; lower histograms represent percent stability of differential responses; (1) low tone (CS); (2) white light (CS); (3) high tone (DS); (4) red light (DS). (I) mean of five experiments (Jan. 26 to Mar. 10, 1962); (II) Mean of four experiments (Mar. 17–24, 1962); (III) Mean of five experiments (Mar. 27 to April 11, 1962); IV. Mean of four experiments (April 14–23, 1962); (V) Mean of five experiments (May 31 to June 7, 1962). Experiments with 5-hr immobilization of subject in restraint stand after prefeeding in home cage conducted Mar. 13, 15, 20, and 26, 1962.

tial stimulus than to the conditioned stimuli. Later the disorders of higher nervous activity were intermittent; i.e., appropriate responses alternated with inappropriate responses to signal stimuli, either in the course of the same experiment or from experiment to experiment. Normal conditioned alimentary motor responses were reestablished gradually in the course of 4 months, subsequent to the immobilization sessions. In summary, the neurotic state during these 4 months was characterized by marked inhibition of conditioned motor responses and an intermittent ultraparadoxical pattern of responding.

By $2\frac{1}{2}$ months after the immobilization stress, the conditioned responses were almost completely restored, whereas differentiation was still only restored to 50% of normal stability. Even after appropriate conditioned responses had been reestablished, the character of lever pressing remained different from that seen in the prestressor period. The intensity of pressure on the lever was increased and individual presses were often of greater duration.

Judging by the state of the conditioned alimentary motor responses, therefore, Larn showed disruption of higher nervous activity during the very first week of stressor sessions, when the pathological connection between the act of eating and the defensive dominant was being conditioned. The disorder progressed through three phases: (1) inhibition (Figure 2, II and III), (2) predominance of excitation (Figure 2, IV and V), and (3) spontaneous reversion to normal.

As the animal developed the above disorders of conditioned behavior his general behavior changed as well, both within and outside the experimental setting. Defensive, aggressive responses that had been absent previously came to dominate his behavior. When the disorders of higher nervous activity were most severe the animal's appetite was reduced and major distortions of alimentary function appeared: vomiting after eating, urine ingestion, and weight loss. Five months from the beginning of the immobilization sessions Larn was found to be suffering from gastric adenomatosis.

Once chronic disorders of conditioned alimentary motor responses following a comparatively small number of pairings of the act of eating with immobilization stress had been demonstrated, two further questions presented themselves: (1) how would immobilization neurosis affect the acquisition and retention of conditioned food-oriented responses in an animal with no experience in the conditioning paradigm before or during the immobilization sessions and (2) what changes would take place in the higher nervous activity of monkeys subjected to repeated immobilization after complete restoration of previously disrupted conditioned response mechanisms? The second question had to do with the significance of a previously experienced nervous trauma in determining the susceptibility to remission and exacerbation of the defensive dominant with rest and repetition of the same kind of stress. Experiments to answer the first question were conducted with the baboon, Zlak; experiments relating to the second were carried out on two baboons, Antil and Abo.

Zlak was subjected to five experiments in which feeding apples in the home cage was followed by 5-hr fixation in the restraint stand. This procedure resulted in his developing gastric achylia. Experiments dealing with gastric secretion were discontinued and 6 months later conditioning sessions were begun to establish motor conditioned responses with food as reinforcement. The system of responses was simplified for this animal. The stimuli and sequence of presentation were: low tone (CS), high tone (DS), low tone (CS), high tone (DS), low tone (CS), high tone (DS), low tone (CS).

The establishment of conditioned reflexes progressed with difficulty. On being placed in the conditioning chamber, Zlak showed extreme motor excitation; he tried to open the cage door, climbed to the top of the cage, and shrieked constantly; defecation of liquid feces was frequent, although there had been no sign of intestinal dysfunction in the home cage. Once appropriate conditioned responses appeared, they were unstable and repeatedly inhibited; at the same time motor responses sometimes occurred to the differential stimuli (ultraparadoxical response pattern).

Multiple, prolonged lever presses were recorded between stimulus presentations. Explosive bursts of excited motor activity alternated with weak responsivity and wide fluctuations in the character of higher nervous activity. The latency of motor responses was frequently prolonged. Typical records from two experiments are presented in Figure 4, I and II. After 6 months of conditioning experiments (a year after the prefeeding–immobilization experiments) the monkey was subjected to a new series of investigations of gastric secretion. He underwent a second surgery for the implantation of a gastric fistula because the original fistula had evulsed 6 months earlier as a result of adenomatous proliferation of the gastric mucosa. Eleven days after the operation, gastric secretion was measured in the same setting where the immobilization neurosis associated with gastric achylia had been produced. In this and subsequent experiments over the course of a number of years the gastric achylia was found to persist. In addition, resumption of the tests of gastric secretion led to total and permanent inhibition of conditioned alimentary motor responses (Figure 4, III, and Figure 5).

The experiments with Zlak showed that a previously acquired immobilization neurosis, based on the conditioning of the act of eating as a signal for the defensive dominant, hampers the subsequent acquisition of alimentary motor conditioned responses. The conditioning mechanisms of higher nervous activity were dominated by inhibitory processes and ultraparadoxical response mechanisms. Furthermore, the defensive dominant was not completely extinguished even a year after the immobilization stress was imposed.

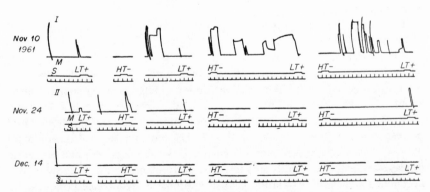

FIG. 4 Character of conditioned alimentary motor responses acquired after prefeeding–immobilization sessions that had induced neurogenic gastric achylia: (I and II) under normal conditions when gastric samples were not being taken; (III) total inhibition of conditioned responses after resumption of gastric juice sampling in the setting where 6 months previously the stressor sessions had been carried out. Designations same as in Fig. 2 except that the light stimuli were omitted.

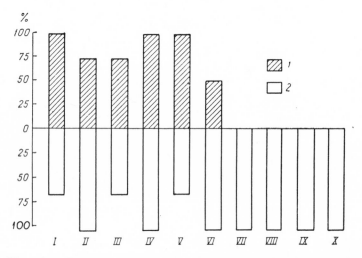

FIG. 5 Disruption of acquisition of food-reinforced motor responses in the hamadryas baboon Zlak after feeding established as conditioned stimulus for pathological defensive dominant. Abscissa, time; ordinate, percent correct responses to conditioned stimuli (upper histograms) and percent stability of differentiations (lower histograms). (1) Low tone (CS); (2) high tone (DS); Roman numerals I–X represent experiments Nov. 10, 14, 21, 23, 25, Dec. 12, 14, 16, 18, and Jan. 26, 1961–1962, respectively. Resumption of sampling gastric secretion after a 6 months interruption occurred Dec. 11, the day before date VI (see text for further explanation).

The resumption of gastric sampling, a prominent element of the stimulus setting in which immobilization neurosis had been produced, restored the defensive dominant as evidenced by the complete suppression of conditioned alimentary motor responses.

The investigation of higher nervous activity with repeated periods of immobilization stress was conducted with the hamadryas baboons Antil and Abo. Figure 6 shows the results obtained from Antil. The first series of stressor experiments, which involved the combination of prefeeding with apples and 5-hr fixation in the restraint stand produced marked disruption of higher nervous activity lasting about 3 weeks. This disruption was reflected in performance as a failure to respond to one to three of the eight CS presentations per session, disinhibition of responses to one to three of the six DS presentations (ultraparadoxical pattern), and increase in response latencies. This baboon, which had previously displayed very stable conditioned response performance, came to show signs of heightened alimentary excitation evidenced primarily by increased frequency of lever pressing between stimuli. During the period of most acute behavioral change, he showed reduced unconditioned alimentary reponsivity (food refusal), vomiting either on an empty stomach or after taking food, and hair loss.

Performance on the conditioning paradigm returned to normal within about 6 weeks and remained stable for 6 months, at which time another series of five

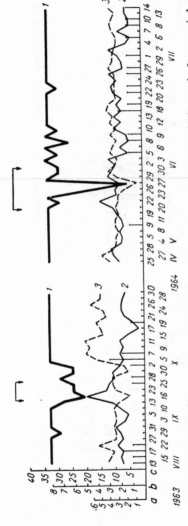

FIG. 6 Changes in conditioned alimentary motor responses in the hamadryas baboon Antil before, during, and after a period of immobilization stress. Arrows: onset and offset of stressor period. Abscissa: dates of experiments. Ordinate: (a) number of inappropriate responses to DSs per experiment and average response latency (sec); (b) number of correct responses to positive conditioned stimuli; (c) number of lever presses per experiment; (1) number of correct responses to light and sound CSs; (2) responses latencies (sec); (3) total lever presses per experiment; columns, number of inappropriate responses to DSs.

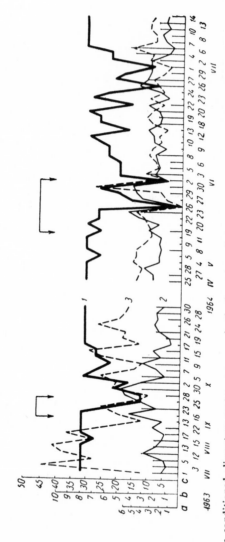

FIG. 7 Changes in conditioned alimentary motor responses in the hamadryas baboon Abo before, during, and after immobilization stress. Designations same as in Fig. 6.

40

prefeeding–immobilization sessions was carried out. The disruption of higher nervous activity produced by this series was more pronounced and more prolonged than that seen with the first series. The ultraparadoxical pattern of responding with disruption of differential responses was especially long lasting. Later Antil died, displaying hysterical-like motor disorders and, at autopsy, he was found to have multiple adenomatous gastric polyps.

Even more profound and persistent disorders of conditioned food-oriented motor responses were obtained as a result of experimental immobilization stress in Abo (Figure 7). The major effects of the first series of stressor experiments lasted more than a month. These changes were manifested in a sharp decrease in the total number of lever pressings per session, which persisted for almost 2 months. At the same time, the number of appropriate responses to CSs dropped from eight to between three and seven per session; responses to the DSs were disinhibited to a greater degree than in the prestressor phase of the study; and response latencies were increased. Typical records reflecting these alimentary motor responses are presented in Figure 8. Responses to CSs and DSs followed an ultraparadoxical pattern along with explosiveness of motor excitation in the form of numerous lever presses of unusually great intensity and long duration.

Repetition of the neurogenic stress 6 months later (5 months after the recovery of normal higher nervous activity) brought on more severe and

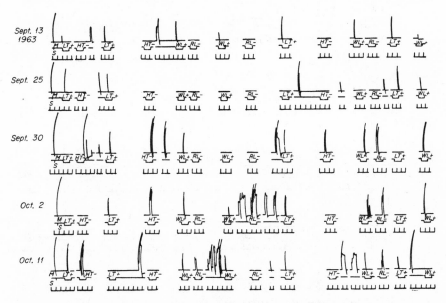

FIG. 8 Conditioned response performance in Abo in the prestressor period (Sept. 13, 1963), immediately after the immobilization sessions (Sept. 25 and 30), and in the subsequent 2 weeks (Oct. 2 and 11, 1963). Performance after the first series of sessions involved prefeeding and immobilization in the home cage. Legend same as in Fig. 2.

prolonged disruption of conditioned alimentary motor responses (Figures 7, 8, and 9).

Inhibition and ultraparadoxical response patterns dominated the animal's performance on the conditioning paradigm. The force of lever pressing gradually diminished (Figure 9). The animal sometimes vomited and for a time after the stressor sessions he showed reduced unconditioned alimentary responsivity in the form of refusal or hesitation to take the food reinforcement.

Comparison of the disruptions of conditioned alimentary motor responses in Antil and Abo with their patterns of gastric secretion before the second stressor period (May 14, 1964), at the height of disruption (June 4, 1964), and several weeks or months after the stressor period (August 11 and October 6, 1974), shows that these indices can either parallel one another, as in Abo, or run independent courses, as in Antil. Whereas gastric achylia was observed in Abo during inhibition of the conditioned alimentary motor responses and disappeared with the reestablishment of appropriate performance in the conditioning chamber, Antil's gastric achylia persisted even after the restoration of normal higher nervous activity (Table 4).

The inhibition and distortion of conditioned responses to food-reinforced stimuli during the immobilization neurosis suggests a disruption of neurally

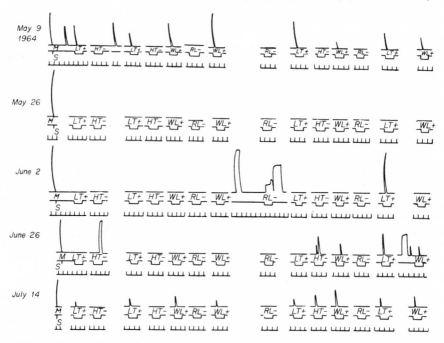

FIG. 9 Intensification of inhibition of conditioned alimentary motor responses in Abo following the second series of immobilization sessions; May 9, 1964: prestressor record; subsequent dates represent poststressor period. Legend same as in Fig. 2.

TABLE 4

Changes in Gastric Secretion in Hamadryas Baboons during Experimental Neurosis[a] (see Figures 6 and 7)

Subject	Date (1964)	Weight (kg)	Volume of secretions (ml)	pH	Free HCl[b]	Total acid[b]	Digestive strength (Mett units)	
							Without added HCl	Control (1 ml secretion + 1 ml 0.36% HCl)
Abo	May 14	26.3	2.5	2.5	10	40	0.5	12.0
	Jun. 4	25.4	4.0	7.0	0	10	0.0	7.0
	Aug. 11	24.4	6.0	1.0	45	82	7.0	13.0
	Oct. 6	24.6	9.0	1.5	36	70	7.0	16.0
Antil	May 14	19.6	4.0	4.0	0	50	0.0	2.5
	Jun. 4	18.6	3.0	4.5	0	8	0.0	6.0
	Aug. 11	19.5	6.0	7.0	0	20	0.0	12.0
	Oct. 6	19.0	3.0	5.0	0	30	0.0	6.0

[a]Gastric juice was obtained by gastric probe.
[b]In titration units.

mediated alimentary mechanisms. The development of gastric achylia, fasting and postprandial vomiting, and temporarily diminished appetite, primarily for the kind of food offered before immobilization, all point to the same conclusion.

There were several indices of excitability of alimentary mechanisms, including the force and latency of lever press responses to the conditioned stimuli. Figure 10 shows changes in these indices for Abo. An initial increase in the force of lever pressing (II) was followed by a gradual and steady decrease (IV, V, VI, VII). Only after a 6-month pause in the experiments was the original force of lever pressing reestablished (VIII). The latency of responses increased greatly during the most profound disruptions of higher nervous activity (II, IV). It should be noted, however, that the changes in force of pressing and in response latencies did not always parallel one another. During some phases long latencies were associated with lever presses of great force (II), whereas in others very short response latencies were associated with reduced force of pressing (V, VI, VII).

Judging from the fact that some months after the second stressor phase appropriate responses to the CSs returned to 100%, one might conclude that the conditioned alimentary motor response mechanism was restored. A persistent reduction in the force of pressing, however, indicated that the animal's higher nervous activity had not completely returned to normal.

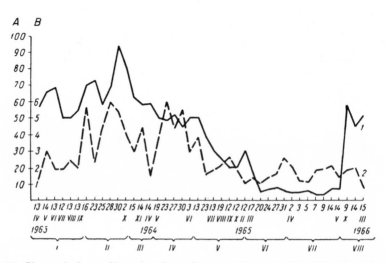

FIG. 10   Changes in force of lever pressing and response latency in Abo. Abscissa: dates and sequential phases of the study; ordinate: (A) force of conditioned lever press response (in mm excursion of recording pen), (B) latency (in sec); (1) force of lever presses; (2) latency of responses; (I) prestressor phase; (II and III) first stressor and poststressor phases; (IV and V) second stressor and poststressor phases; (VI and VII) third stressor phase with suppression of defensive excitation by chlorpromazine; (VIII) after prolonged pause between experiments.

The neural organization of the conditioned alimentary motor response mechanism is complex, but basically it consists of two components: a conditioned alimentary perceptual link (or perception of a conditioned alimentary signal by the alimentary center) and a motor response link. In the case where one observes short latency, 100% appropriate responses to alimentary CSs with marked decrease in the strength of these responses, one must presume that there is a certain dissonance between these two components of the response mechanism. Apparently in this animal the motor link was affected more severely and for a longer period of time by immobilization stress than the input link. This may be related to the fact that recurrent immobilizations of the body and extremities create an inert focus of activity, a defensive dominant in the motor analyzer. In the present experiments the dominant in the motor analyzer was closely associated with conditioned and unconditioned alimentary stimulation. In the first weeks and months after the prefeeding–immobilization experiments were carried out, activation of the defensive dominant evidently was tied in considerable degree to the act of eating or to conditioned alimentary stimuli. This would explain the apparent lowering of interest in food, particularly in food of the kind provided just before the animal was immobilized. For the same reason, the conditioned alimentary stimuli did not fail to elicit a response, but the response consisted in inhibition of the motor link of the conditioned alimentary response mechanism. This phenomenon was demonstrated by the inhibitory phase and negativism as manifested in the ultraparadoxical pattern of responding to CSs and DSs, prolonged response latencies, and reduced force of lever pressing. In other words, the reception of conditioned alimentary signals was preserved but their effect was reversed or distorted.

The hypothesis that a transformation of the act of feeding and conditioned alimentary stimuli into signals for the defensive dominant constituted the basic etiological and pathogenetic mechanism in immobilization neurosis demanded further control experiments. In particular it was necessary to study animals that were subjected to immobilization in the restraint stand without prefeeding. Such experiments were carried out on four baboons with previously established conditioned alimentary motor responses (Abo, Lolium, Pianch, and Zlak). As can be seen from Figures 11 and 12 (I), five repeated immobilizations of the animals for 5 hr at a time in the same conditioning chamber did not noticeably affect the performance of conditioned alimentary motor responses in any of the animals. This is especially clear in Figure 11, which presents the complete data from five conditioning sessions carried out the first day after immobilization sessions in which the baboons were not prefed. Comparable conditioning sessions on the day following immobilization of animals prefed in the home cage showed much more profound disruptions of conditioned alimentary motor

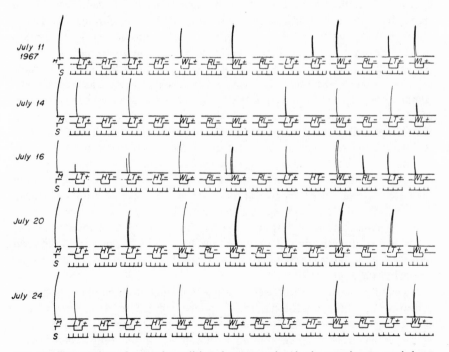

FIG. 11 Preservation of normal conditioned responses in Abo in experiments carried out the day following a 5-hr immobilization without prefeeding. Legend same as in Fig. 2.

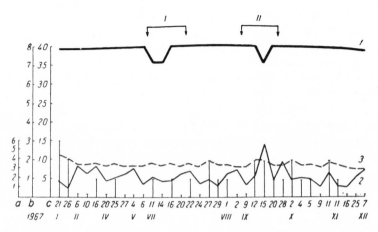

FIG. 12 Changes in conditioned alimentary motor responses in Abo; arrows I, before, during, and after immobilization sessions without prefeeding; arrows II, before, during, and after immobilization with prefeeding and administration of haloperidol to suppress defensive excitation; otherwise legend same as in Fig. 6.

performance. Because the activation of defensive response mechanisms elicited by fixation in the restraint stand has been presumably the same whether an animal has been prefed or not, one must conclude that the chronic disorders of higher nervous activity seen in the prefed animals was related to alimentary signals (the act of eating and its conditioned components) becoming signals for the defensive dominant. The features of these experiments that made it possible to think in terms of a temporary connection between feeding, as a conditional stimulus, and the defensive response mechanisms were as follows: (1) activation of the defense mechanism was consistently preceded by feeding; (2) combination of prefeeding and fixation of the body and the extremities was performed repeatedly; (3) the animal could not avoid the immobilization; and (4) the reinforcement factor: the defensive excitation caused by immobilization is a stronger stimulus for the monkey than the preceding food reinforcement. All of the necessary conditions for formation of a conditioned connection were therefore fulfilled. An important aspect of this connection lay in the fact that feeding is not a simple indifferent stimulus of the kind usually used in conditioning experiments but activation of a response mechanism itself, a mechanism of great biological importance, regular activation of which is essential in the day to day survival of the animal.

A second type of control was to subject animals to immobilization after activation of alimentary mechanisms by prefeeding, but to block the mobilization of defensive response mechanisms by administering such psychotropic agents as haloperidol, chlorpromazine, morphine, or the central cholinolytic substances benactyzine and metamizil (2-diethylaminopropylbenzylate hydrochloride). It was hypothesized that suppression of the defensive excitation

TABLE 5

Effects of Neurotropic Agents on Free Behavior and Conditioned Alimentary Motor Responses of Adult Male Hamadryas Baboons in the Conditioning Chamber

Drug	Dosage (mg/kg), subcutaneous or intramuscular injections	Decrease in general motor activity	Decrease in defensive activity	Duration of inhibition of conditioned responses (hr)	Number of subjects tested	Total number of sessions
Chlorpromazine	2.5	+	+	4–24	2	6
Haloperidol	0.1–0.2	+	+	1–4	2	10
Dicarbine	2.5	±	–	weak	2	6
Reserpine	0.03	–	–	weak	1	5
Benactyzine	1.0–5.0	–	–	0.5–4.0	7	22
Metamizil[a]	2.0–4.0	–	–	0.5–1.0	2	10
Atropine	0.2	–	–	0.5 (in first 2 experiments)	1	5
Adiphenine	20.0	±	–	weak	2	2
Phenobarbital	20.0	±	–	weak	2	6
Morphine	2.5–5.0	+	+	4+	5	21

[a]2-Diethylaminopropylbenzylate hydrochloride.

ordinarily evoked by 5-hr fixation in the restraint stand would preclude formation of the conditioned connection by eliminating an essential element, viz., the defensive reinforcement.

Before the animals were subjected to prefeeding–immobilization under these conditions, it was necessary to clarify whether the neurotropic agents themselves would influence conditioned response performance and, if so, the duration of such action. General findings regarding the direct influence of the drugs on free behavior (level of motor activity and defensive reactions) and on conditioned alimentary motor responses in the conditioning chamber are presented in Table 5.

Evaluation of ten drugs showed that chlorpromazine, haloperidol, and morphine were most effective for suppression of defensive excitation and for prolonged inhibition of alimentary conditioned response mechanisms. Chlorpromazine (2.5 mg/kg, intramuscular) produced drowsiness in 15–30 min and inhibition of conditioned alimentary motor responses for almost 24 hr (Figure 13). Similar results were recorded for haloperidol (0.1–0.2 mg/kg, intramuscular; Figure 14), and morphine (2.5–5.0 mg/kg, subcutaneous). It was interesting to note that morphine, although decreasing motor activity and defensive reactions and inhibiting conditioned responses, did not produce the drowsiness seen with the first two drugs.

Haloperidol, administered to Abo and Lolium immediately after they had fed on apples in the home cage and 10 min prior to fixation in the stand, removed defensive reactions before and during the 5-hr fixation. As Figure 15 shows,

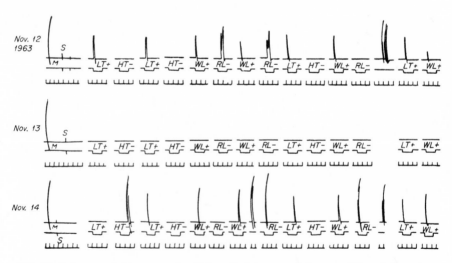

FIG. 13 Influence of chlorpromazine (2.5 mg/kg intramuscular) on conditioned alimentary motor responses 1 hr after injection; Nov. 11, 1963, without drug; Nov. 13, 1963, with drug; Nov. 14, 1963, 24 hr after drug. Legend same as in Fig. 2.

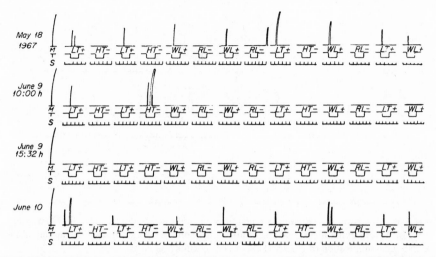

FIG. 14 Influence of haloperidol (0.1 mg/kg; intramuscular) on conditioned alimentary motor responses: May 18, 1967, without drug; June 9, 1967, 1 hr and 6.5 hr after administration of haloperidol; June 10, 1967, 24 hr after administration. Legend same as in Fig. 2.

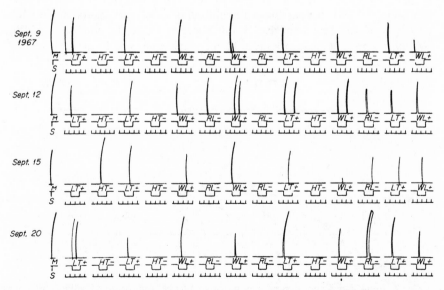

FIG. 15 Preservation of appropriate conditioned responses in Abo 1 day after combination of prefeeding and immobilization with suppression of defensive excitation by haloperidol. Legend same as in Fig. 2.

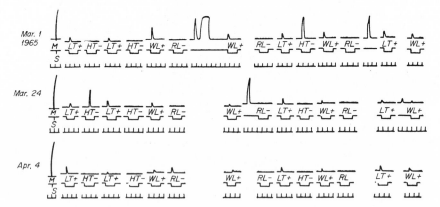

FIG. 16 Preservation of appropriate conditioned responses (although of diminished intensity) in Abo in experiments one day following the combination of prefeeding and immobilization with suppression of defensive excitation by chlorpromazine.

there was no disruption of conditioned alimentary motor responses the next day. The general changes in higher nervous activity during haloperidol prophylaxis are illustrated in Figure 12 (II). The development of immobilization neurosis was prevented in Abo and Antil by prophylaxis with chlorpromazine (Figures 16 and 17). Morphine produced a good result in one animal, Zlak (Figure 18). In the remaining three, the preventive effect of morphine was less pronounced. These animals showed inhibition of alimentary motor conditioned responses on the days immediately following prefeeding–immobilization. Still, this was observed only for the 10–15 days over which the prefeeding–

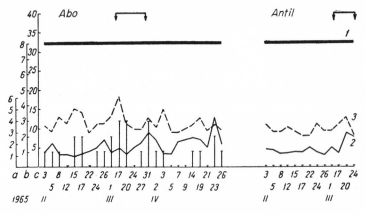

FIG. 17 Conditioned motor responses of baboons Abo and Antil reflecting protective effect of chlorpromazine when administered before immobilization stress. Double arrows indicate period during which sessions with prefeeding–immobilization under the influence of chlorpromazine were carried out.

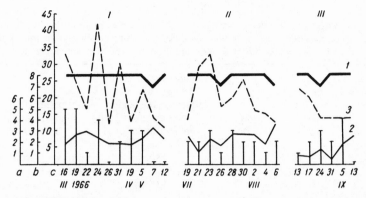

FIG. 18 Prevention of immobilization neurosis by morphine (5 mg/kg; subcutaneous) in the baboon Zlak. Indices of conditioned response performance (I) under normal conditions; (II) during stressor period involving repeated prefeeding–immobilization sessions under the influence of morphine; (III) in the poststressor period. Otherwise, legend same as in Fig. 6.

immobilization experiments were distributed. Once the stressor sessions were discontinued, performance in the conditioning chamber promptly returned to normal.

By removing the defensive excitation of a monkey fixed in the restraint stand, therefore, one can prevent the development of the immobilization neurosis. This again tends to support the view that the immobilization neurosis is based on transformation of feeding and conditioned stimuli for feeding into signals for the defensive dominant.

The central cholinolytic agents, benactyzine and metamizil, were not effective. Under nonstressful conditions they suppressed conditioned alimentary motor responses for .5–4 hr, but had little influence on the animal's defensive reactions. Neither agent suppressed defensive excitation during fixation in the restraint stand. On the contrary, they potentiated it and, as a result, four monkeys died in their very first prefeeding–immobilization sessions. After 2–3 hr of increasingly intense motor excitation they developed paralysis of the extremeties and expired.

In the experiments in which psychotropic agents prevented the development of immobilization neurosis, the animals' reactions to the food that had been fed to them just before immobilization were not altered (Table 6). The fact that the animals did not develop a negative reaction to the food, which repeatedly preceded their immobilization in the restraint stand, suggests indirectly that under conditions of immobilization neurosis unconditioned and conditioned alimentary stimuli become inhibitory signals.

We first proposed the term "immobilization neurosis" to designate new forms of chronic experimentally induced disorders of higher nervous activity in monkeys (Startsev, 1967). An important aspect of the concept is that it does not

TABLE 6
Preservation of Alimentary Excitability in Hamadryas Baboons during Repeated
Combinations of Prefeeding in the Home Cage with 5-hr Fixation in the Restraint
Stand When Chlorpromazine was Administered Just before Immobilization

Subject	Date (1965)	Experiment number	Amount consumed of 150 g of apples offered in the home cage prior to immobilization (g)	Feeding after immobilization sessions
Abo	Mar. 15	1	150	Ate food after the experiment
	Mar. 18	2	150	Ate poorly after the experiment; ate well the following day
	Mar. 22	3	150	Ate and drank after the experiment
	Mar. 25	4	150	Ate and drank after the experiment
	Mar. 27	5	150	Ate and drank after the experiment
Antil	Mar. 15	1	150	Ate well after the experiment
	Mar. 18	2	150	Ate candy, porridge, drank water
	Mar. 22	3	150	Drank water, ate candy

refer to the complex of reactions which the organism generates during the period of immobilization itself but to signs and symptoms which persist after the immobilization stressor is discontinued.

From the viewpoint of pathogenesis the immobilization neurosis in hamadryas baboons is a system-specific disorder, because the major factor in its establishment is transformation of conditioned and unconditioned aspects of eating, i.e., functions of the alimentary system, into signals for the defensive dominant; one of the chief manifestations of the neurosis is the disruption (inhibition and distortion) of conditioned alimentary motor responses to normally conditioned alimentary stimuli.

Immobilization unassociated with activation of the neural mechanisms that mediate alimentary behavior did not result in the breakdown of conditioned responses established by food reinforcement. Furthermore, the conditioned alimentary stimuli retained their normal effectiveness and the animals' attitude toward unconditioned alimentary stimulation, food, was not affected. One of the essential conditions for rapid, profound, and prolonged disruption of higher nervous activity in monkeys was the ecologically appropriate choice of the act of feeding as a signal for the defensive dominant. Conditioned and unconditioned alimentary stimuli ordinarily activate alimentary mechanisms of monkeys almost continuously, throughout the day. In immobilization neurosis, they act as continuous signals for the defensive dominant. In short, the immobilization neurosis is a chronic disorder of conditioned alimentary motor response mechanisms.

III

An Experimental Model of Neurogenic Gastric Achylia in the Hamadryas Baboon

The chronic gastric achylia that occurs in hamadryas baboons subjected to immobilization neurosis generally develops as a functional disease (Startsev, 1963, 1964b, c, 1965, 1966a, b, 1972; Startsev & Kuraev, 1967). At some stage of this neurogenic disorder, however, dystrophic changes have invariably appeared in the mucosa, usually as adenomatous foci and sometimes as multiple polyps and ulcers; anacidosis has been a constant finding. In other words, the neurogenic gastric achylia in baboons has ordinarily progressed to a true model of the precancerous state in the stomach.

This chapter describes our method of establishing an experimental model of neurogenic gastric achylia, the clinical and physiological characteristics of the syndrome, and an analysis of its neural mechanism. First, however, we offer a brief review of the literature on functional achylia in man and information that we have collected regarding so-called "spontaneous gastric achylia" in various species of monkey.

FUNCTIONAL GASTRIC ACHYLIA IN MAN

Einhorn, in 1892, introduced the term "achylia gastrica" for those conditions in which there is no indication that the stomach is producing gastric juice. The case histories he described were similar clinically to syndromes involving atrophy of the gastric mucous membrane but they did not represent serious, incurable disease. In his opinion the disease was very prolonged in nature, and although the subjective symptoms might improve, gastric secretion was seldom reestablished.

Einhorn succeeded in eliciting gastric secretion in patients with achylia by direct electrical stimulation of the gastric mucosa. Therefore, he concluded, the reduction in gastric secretion was functional and should be ascribed to a disturbance in the nervous system. In a number of cases he observed a transition from achylia to normal secretion and even, in a few cases, to hyperchlorhydria with subsequent reversion to achylia and then to a normal state. Such fluctuations were inconsistent with the previously held view that the cessation of gastric secretion was a permanent disorder resulting from atrophy of the mucosa.

In 1911, the Russian investigator M. P. Konchalovskii suggested a relationship between gastric achylia and neurasthenia. He worked out the following clinical classification:

Classification of Achylia Gastrica
(Konchalovskii, 1911)

The achylias
I. Organic
    1. Primary   a. Gastritis
                         b. General progressive
                            atrophy of the
                            gastrointestinal
                            tract
    2. Secondary   a. Cancerous achylia
                            (secondary to
                            gastric carcinoma)
                         b. Achylia secondary
                            to pernicious
                            anemia
                         c. Achylia secondary
                            to cancer of other
                            organs, cachexia,
                            or old age
II. Functional
    1. Simple functional achylia or
       heterochylia

At the present time there is little uniformity of opinion regarding the etiology and pathogenesis of the functional disease. Many clinicians attribute gastric achylia exclusively to atrophy of the mucous membrane of the stomach (Miasnikov, 1956; Beier, 1963). At the same time, a number of physicians' handbooks discuss a functional form of gastric achylia in addition to the organic forms (Brugsh & Schittengel'm, 1921; Osler, 1928; Luriia, 1935; Vasilenko, 1951; Tareev, 1952; Gukasian, 1958). These refer to psychophysiological stress as the major factor in the pathogenesis of functional achylia in man. A psychosomatic form of achylia has been recognized by many Soviet clinicians (Rakhman, 1929; Chireikin, 1931; Reizel'man & Govorchuk, 1935; Funt, 1947; and others).

R. A. Luriia (1935) discussed achylia in a chapter on functional diseases of the stomach. He cited a case, earlier reported by Brugsh, of a prisoner in whom gastric analysis yielded no free HCl for a number of years but who resumed secretion of normal gastric juice after his release from the penitentiary.

One sign of a functional gastric achylia is considered to be that the pepsin content of the gastric juice is reduced but not eliminated (Einhorn, 1892; Konchalovskii, 1911; Zimnitskii, 1926; Afanas'ev, 1934; Gordon, Motrenko, & Peredel'skii, 1935; Luriia, 1935; Shul'tsev & Bondar', 1941; Rasmussen & Brunschwig, 1941; Funt, 1947; Tareev, 1952; Rakov, Shemiakina & Ol'shanetskii, 1954; Gukasian, 1958; and others). In functional gastric achylia not only are the chief cells morphologically intact (Vasilenko, 1951) but they can secrete pepsin. Still, functional achylia with anacidity of the gastric juice may be associated with total apepsia (Einhorn, 1892; Afanas'ev, 1934; Luriia, 1935; Funt, 1947; Vasilenko, 1951; Gukasian, 1958). Clinical detection of achlorhydria and apepsia makes the diagnosis of organic achylia quite probable but does not entirely rule out functional achylia.

It should be pointed out that in most clinical research the primary question or, indeed, the only question raised has had to do with whether or not there is a disturbance in the ability of the glands to secrete hydrochloric acid and pepsin in response to histamine. The histamine test used to differentiate "true" achylia from "false" achylia, i.e., organic from functional (Babkin, 1960) is based entirely on the capacity of histamine to elicit the activity of the gastric glands if they are not morphologically damaged. It should be borne in mind when making a diagnosis of functional achylia, however, that in so far as pathogenesis is concerned, the primary consideration is not the glands themselves and their secretory ability but the conditions that brought about their inactive state. The restoration of secretory activity in functional achylia can be accomplished either by the application of effective stimulants to the gastric glands or by the removal of certain suppressive influences.

Secretion of gastric juice has been restored in patients suffering from achylia by (1) replacing a weak food stimulant with a stronger one (Trusevich & Shapiro, 1930; Martsinskovskii, 1931; Gordon et al., 1935); (2) by direct electrical stimulation of the gastric mucosa (Einhorn, 1892); (3) by administration of epinephrine (Zimnitskii, 1926); (4) by the elimination of negative emotional influences (Luriia, 1935; Gukasian, 1958); and (5) by histamine injection (Afanas'ev, 1934; Luriia, 1935; Gordon, et al., 1935; Kuznetsov, 1937; Shul'tsev & Bondar', 1941; Funt, 1947; Tareev, 1952; Miasnikov, 1956; Gukasian, 1958; Babkin, 1960).

Contrary to the opinion of some authoritative investigators (Tareev, 1952; Miasnikov, 1956; Gukasian, 1958; Babkin, 1960) detection of histamine-negative gastric achylia does not necessarily signify atrophy of the gastric glands. Histamine does not stimulate secretion of HCl in ascorbic acid deficiency or nicatinamide deficiency syndromes, yet after replacement therapy the achylia disappears and histamine produces the normal reaction (Zhodzishskii, 1938; Shul'tsev & Bondar', 1941). Levenson and Agol (1936) demonstrated that in some patients suffering from achylia histamine began to stimulate gastric secretion after treatment with protein hydrolyzates. On the basis of their experiments they concluded that the value of the histamine test in the differential diagnosis between organic and functional achylia must be considered doubtful. On the basis of other investigations, I. M. Funt (1947) reached the same conclusion and expressed the opinion that the irreversability of true achlorhydria remained to be proved, and atrophy of the gastric mucosa was especially questionable when the only evidence has a negative reaction of the gastric glands to histamine. Schnedorf and Ivy (1937a, b), working with rhesus macaques, were able to change a stable syndrome of gastric anacidity and histamine-negative reactivity into a normal condition after a long course of treatment with methacholine. A positive reaction to histamine was reestablished by this therapy. Various neural and humoral influences may therefore determine the reaction of the gastric glands to direct stimulation by histamine.

The functional gastric achylias are of great interest to both clinicians and physiologists. Although they usually respond to treatment more readily than the organic forms, they in all probability represent the initial stages of organic disease. From this perspective, it is important to analyze the functional achylias in terms of the primary causes of the disease in its initial stages, to which such secondary features as morphological changes in the mucosa, pancreatic and intestinal disorders, and compensatory responses of the pancreas and intestine accrue later on. The initial disorder of gastric secretion in functional achylia may be identified as having a neural mechanism by a number of physiological and pharmacological tests. In the stage of advanced morphological changes, when atrophy of the gastric mucosa has developed, the neural mechanism is difficult to detect by physiological and pharmacological techniques, and that is precisely the stage of development at which a patient usually goes to see a physician with complaints of chronic stomach trouble.

The suspected role of a neural mechanism and, more specifically, of a central neural mechanism in the initial stages of gastric achylia in man merits experimental test in animals. The assertion by V. V. Kudrevetskii (1904), one of Pavlov's students, remains true to this day: the supposition of a neural origin of gastric achylia remains just that, a supposition.

Some experimental attempts to produce achlorhydria in man and dogs were unsuccessful (Atkinson & Ivy, 1938). In experiments performed on dogs in Pavlov's laboratories (Soborov, 1899; Zavriev, 1900; Kazanskii, 1901), scalding or traumatizing the gastric mucosa with hot water or chemical substances produced relatively short-lived suppression of HCl and pepsin secretion. Clearly, the gastric achylia that in human patients lasts many months or years is quite different from such temporary disorders of gastric digestion in dogs. The production of simple achylia in an isolated stomach preparation in the dog by sectioning the vagus nerve (Orbeli, 1905) is open to similar criticism. Neurogenic disorders of gastric digestion in dogs and cats produced in the laboratory of K. M. Bykov (Bykov & Kurtsin, 1952, 1960) led as a rule to hypersecretion and hyperacidity of gastric juice accompanied by the appearance of gastric ulcers but not to gastric achylia. Either dogs and cats are unsuitable species for the experimental production of gastric achylia or the methods used on them to date have been inappropriate for producing chronic suppression of gastric secretion.

SPONTANEOUS GASTRIC ACHYLIA IN MONKEYS

In human cases the etiology of gastric achylia is generally unknown; either the signs are detected accidentally during routine gastric analysis or the patient develops complaints long after he has forgotten all possible causes of the disease. Therefore, gastric achylia in man is usually seen as a "spontaneous" illness.

The detection of spontaneous gastric achylia in monkeys is of special interest, because the investigation of such cases can throw light on a number of the questions regarding etiology and treatment that have arisen from clinical studies of the disease in man.

Spontaneous anacidity of the gastric juice in nonhuman primates was first described by Schnedorf and Ivy (1937). They discovered histamine-resistant anacidity in several otherwise healthy rhesus monkeys. After treatment with methacholine, however, the anacidity disappeared and a positive response to histamine developed. The authors referred to the etiology of the anacidic state in these monkeys as "inexplicable." Other investigators have reported similar puzzling observations in which alcohol, nonfood substances, or such natural foods as cabbage failed to activate secretion of HCl in intact animals or in rhesus monkeys and green marmosets with gastric fistulas (Ferguson, 1932; Ferguson, McGavran, & Smith, 1934; Ferguson & Smith, 1935; Bosheniatova, 1938; Bosheniatova & Voronin, 1943; Voronin, 1949; Startsev, 1961a, b).

To illustrate this phenomenon, which incidentally we did not encounter in our experiments on dogs, we can cite data from an experiment on a rhesus monkey named Kan.

Subject: Kan (rhesus; 6.6 kg)
Experiment: 21
Date: Jan. 28, 1960

At 9:20 am the animal was placed unfed in a restraint stand; he showed mild motor agitation. At 9:25 am the gastric fistula was opened and a balloon to register gastric contractions was inserted into the stomach; a cup was positioned below the fistula to collect the gastric juice. The juice produced was alkaline (pH = 8).

Time	Volume of juice (ml)	pH	Digestive activity (Mett units)	Remarks
9:45	6.0	8	0	Secretions thick,
10:00	5.5	8	0	color of sunflower
10:15	3.6	8	0	oil with mucus;
10:30	5.3	8	0	monkey restless
Total	20.1			
10:45	4.7	8	0	Secretions thick,
11:00	4.3	8	0	color of sunflower
11:15	5.0	8	0	oil; monkey restless
11:30	5.0	8	0	
Total	19.0			

At 11:30, drinking milk with gastric fistula open; 70 ml consumed in 20 min.

Time	Volume of juice (ml)	pH	Digestive activity (Mett units)	Remarks
11:45	5.2	7	0	Milk, mucus,
12:00	3.0	7	0	pinkish juice;
12:15	12.5	7	0	monkey restless
12:30	4.0	7	0	
Total	24.7			
12:45	5.5	7	0	Light pink juice
13:00	3.8	7	0	with mucus; monkey
13:15	4.6	7	0	restless
13:30	3.0	7	0	
Total	16.9			
13:45	5.5	7	0	Yellowish juice
14:00	3.0	7	0	with mucus;
14:15	2.0	7	0	monkey restless
14:30	5.0	7	0	
Total	15.0			

The failure of rhesus monkeys and green marmosets to secrete acidic gastric juice in the fasting state did not surprise investigators, for by analogy with dogs, it was to be expected (Ferguson and colleagues, 1932–1935; Voronin, 1949; Kipiani & Miminoshvili, 1956a, b; Porter, Brady, Conrad, & Mason, 1957; Porter, Brady, Conrad, Mason, Galambos, & MacRioch, 1958; Polish et al., 1962; De Los Santos, Bucaille, Delgado, & Spiro, 1962).

A thorough discussion of the inaccuracy of the analogy between monkeys and dogs is beyond the scope of the present investigation and is to be found in several of our research reports. Briefly, however, a new method that we developed in 1960 for investigating gastric secretion in hamadryas baboons living in groups in open compounds revealed that, under fasting conditions, anacidity is not the rule in monkeys. Acidic gastric juice rich in pepsin is secreted continuously throughout the day. Such findings, originally obtained from baboons, were later confirmed by numerous investigators to be true of spider monkeys (Smith,

Brooks, Davis, & Rothman, 1960; Brooks, Ridley, Attinger, & Neff, 1963; Brooks, Ridley, Attinger, Bjovedt, & Neff, 1963), squirrel monkeys (De Los Santos *et al.,* 1962; Brodie & Marshall, 1963), tatarin baboons, capuchins, squirrel monkeys and chimpanzees (Brodie & Marshall, 1963a, b) and hamadryas baboons and pigtail macaques (Nguen Tkhyong, 1967). The secretion of gastric juice in the fasting state is therefore typical for a variety of species of monkeys.

In this respect, nonhuman primates show a definite similarity to man. Samples of gastric secretions obtained by nasogastric tubes and fistulas in healthy human beings have established that there is a continuous secretion of gastric juice in the fasting state. Contrary to earlier opinions commonly held in physiology and medicine, therefore, the continuous secretion of acidic gastric juice is a normal phenomenon in healthy people and monkeys. Anacidity during fasting, especially after the administration of one of the agents known to stimulate the gastric glandular apparatus, is definite evidence for some factor inhibiting secretion. Specifically, such procedures as catching a baboon in a squeeze cage for clinical or experimental purposes, insertion of a gastric tube, and immobilization of the body and extremities in a restraint stand effectively inhibit gastric secretion (Startsev, 1961a, b, 1963, 1964a, b, c). The inhibitory effect of such procedures explains in part the "spontaneous" anacidity or gastric achylia that have sometimes been reported for rhesus monkeys and green marmosets, because the investigations in which these features of gastric secretion were noted invariably involved catching the monkey, immobilizing it, and probing the stomach by nasogastric or orogastric tube.

There are a number of observations, nevertheless, which suggest that the problem of spontaneous anacidity is more complex. For instance, it some cases anacidic gastric juice has been found for months, and even years in the so-called "zero samples," i.e., the first fasting specimens of gastric juice obtained in the morning (either by fistula or by tube). Such specimens represent the gastric juice secreted and accumulated overnight outside of the experimental setting (Figures 19 and 20). This phenomenon has been noted in rhesus macaques and green marmosets. One might ascribe it to species characteristics of the gastric secretory apparatus in these monkeys or to long-term inhibitory effects of repeated fixations in the restraint stand. Still, functional deficiency of the gastric glands has been demonstrated in two rhesus macaques with gastric fistulas that have never been fixed in an experimental stand (Table 7). These monkeys had been subjected for a prolonged period of time to hematological investigations that involved the taking of blood samples and bone marrow biopsies before they entered our experiment. Whatever the reason for the cessation of gastric juice secretion in these monkeys, it was clear that their state was very stable. The physiological significance of their chronic gastric anacidity merited analysis. For this purpose the digestive activity of the stomach was tested by introducing a protein stick through the fistula and leaving it for 24 hr (Mett's method; Table 8). Similar experiments on hamadryas baboons showed considerable digestion of protein (Startsev, 1964).

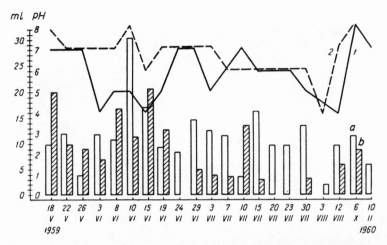

FIG. 19   Fluctuations in gastric juice as reflected in zero samples from rhesus monkeys with gastric fistulas. Abscissa, dates of experiments; ordinates, pH and volume of juice (ml); (a) volume of juice from the monkey Kan; (b) volume of juice from the monkey Ifag; (1) pH of secretions from Kan; (2) pH of secretions from Ifag.

The absence of digestive activity in gastric juice from these monkeys living under normal Primate Center conditions indicated pathology of gastric digestion; it certainly did not suggest a species peculiarity of the rhesus macaque or green marmoset. In addition to the pathological signs already mentioned (lack of free HCl and inability of the gastric juice to digest protein) these monkeys also failed to respond to histamine, the direct stimulus of gastric gland secretion, or to such

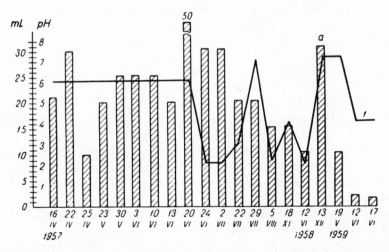

FIG. 20   Chronic spontaneous anacidity of gastric juice as demonstrated by zero samples obtained by gastric fistula from the green marmoset Beglets. Abscissa, dates of experiments; ordinates, pH and volume of gastric juice (in ml); (a) volume of juice; (1) pH.

TABLE 7

Chronic Functional Deficiency of the Gastric Glands Induced in Adult
Sukhumi-Bred Rhesus Macaques by the Unfavorable Conditions of Living in
Captivity for Prolonged Periods of Time[a]

| Subject | Date (1961) | Volume of juice (ml) | pH | Free HCl | Total acid | Digestive strength (Mett units) | |
						Without added HCl	Control (1 ml of juice plus 1 ml 0.36% HCl)
Galantus	Aug. 28	4.0	7.0	0	21	0	14.5
	Aug. 30	2.5	7.0	0	38	0	12.0
	Sep. 4	0.5	5.5	0	42	–	–
	Sep. 8	3.0	7.0	0	25	0	–
	Sep. 11	1.5	7.5	0	33	0	9.0
	Means	2.3 ± 0.6	6.8 ± 0.3	0	32 ± 4	0	11.3
Darzeb	Aug. 28	9.0	7.5	0	30	0	0.5
	Aug. 30	3.0	7.0	0	47	0	10.0
	Sep. 4	5.0	4.5	0	72	2	11.0
	Sep. 8	8.0	8.0	0	19	0	4.0
	Sep. 29	55.0	4.5	0	74	0	2.0
	Means	16.0 ± 10.0	6.3 ± 0.8	0	48 ± 11	0.4 ± 0.4	5.5 ± 1.8

[a]These data are based on zero samples obtained by gastric fistula.

chemical and reflex stimulants of gastric secretion as cabbage juice, alcohol, fruits and vegetables, or milk (either by mouth or directly into the stomach by fistula). We also noted spontaneous anacidity of the gastric juice, increased friability and vulnerability to trauma of the gastric mucosa, vomiting, and dyspeptic symptoms (e.g., watery stools).

The results of a comparative study of gastric secretions in various species of monkeys at the Sukhumi Primate Center are presented in Table 9. The data are based on a single fasting sample obtained by gastric tube from each subject. Intact hamadryas baboons of various ages and sexes from the breeding colony yielded appropriately acidic secretions rich in pepsin. No signs of gastric achylia were detected in any of the 28 such baboons tested. However, achylia did occur in half of 24 hamadryas baboons that had been systematically subjected to nervous stress; hypoacidity and hypopepsia were characteristic of all the animals in this group.

In contrast to the baboons living in the breeding colony, almost all of the green marmosets and rhesus monkeys from breeding compounds proved to be suffering from spontaneous gastric achylia. The only exceptions were two adult males and one female who were the dominant members of their groups. This suggested that the difference in gastric acidity of rhesus monkeys and baboons

TABLE 8

Acidity and Digestive Strength of Gastric Juice in Kan, an Adult Rhesus
Macaque with a Gastric Fistula Implanted March 25, 1959

Date (February 1960)	pH of gastric juice at the moment of removal of Mett stick from the stomach after 24 hr incubation	Digestive strength (Mett units) after 24 hr incubation of the protein in the stomach
1	7	0
2	7	0
3	7	0
4	7	0
9	7	0
11	7	0
12	3	0
17	8	0
18	5	0

might be a species difference. An analysis of gastric secretions from rhesus macaques imported from Vietnam, however, completely refuted this supposition. From Table 9 it is evident that for all eight rhesus macaques received from North Vietnam on January 7, 1962, the first examination a week after arrival yielded acidic gastric juice. By following the changes in gastric secretion of these monkeys over 7 months time, it was repeatedly demonstrated that the gastric juice was acid and possessed considerable digestive strength (Figure 21). For their first 4–6 weeks at the Primate Center the fasting gastric secretions of most of these monkeys were acidic, but later they became anacidic. The gastric achylia was of functional in nature, for histamine had a strong stimulatory effect. In the course of the next 2 years, a portion of the surviving animals from this group developed chronic functional achylia.

Gastric achylia developed much earlier in other rhesus monkeys that arrived from Vietnam in the same shipment (January 7, 1962). Their gastric secretions were first assayed 1 month after arrival at Sukhumi and gastric achylia was revealed in nine of them. A second investigation a week later showed it in 14; and a third investigation a week after that showed it in 13. These monkeys, up to the time of the first testing of gastric juice, had been subjected to numerous experimental procedures, including daily venipuncture to obtain blood samples.

Therefore, the more intense the nervous stress imposed on imported monkeys, the faster they developed gastric achylia. In contrast to these two groups, 20 other members of the same shipment and 25 received on July 17, 1963 yielded acidic fasting gastric samples when first tested 20–60 days after arrival (Table 9). These monkeys were not subjected to systematic examinations and/or experimental procedures, i.e., they were stressed to a lesser degree than the monkeys of the previous groups.

TABLE 9

Comparative Characteristics of Gastric Juice in Various Monkey Species under Various Living Conditions[a]

Species	Living conditions	Amount of juice (ml)	pH	Free HCl	Total acid	Digestive strength (Mett units)		Number of monkeys		
						Without added HCl	Control: 1 ml of juice + 0.36% HCl	Total	Normal	Gastric achylia
Hamadryas Baboon	Breeding colony	3–20	1.2 ± 0.07	42 ± 3	83 ± 6	8.4 ± 0.7	12.6 ± 0.4	28	28	–
Hamadryas baboon	Systematically subjected to experimental and clinical procedures	5.2 ± 0.7	2.7 ± 0.4	17 ± 4	51 ± 4	3.8 ± 0.9	8.5 ± 0.5	24	12	12
Green marmoset	Breeding colony	3.0 ± 0.5	4.0 ± 0.3	2 ± 2	47 ± 17	0	8.8 ± 1.0	25	3	22
Rhesus macaque	Breeding colony	0.7 ± 0.4	5.8 ± 1.7	0	27 ± 3	–	5.5 ± 0.4	14	–	14
Rhesus macaque	Imported from Vietnam; first examination 7 days after arrival	6.7 ± 2.3	1.7 ± 0.4	24 ± 7	75 ± 9	3.5 ± 0.7	9.5 ± 0.7	8	7	1

Rhesus macaque	The same shipment; first investigation one month after arrival, during which daily blood samples were drawn by venipuncture	1.1 ± 0.1	3.5 ± 0.6	9 ± 2	42 ± 6	—	—	14	5	9
Rhesus macaque	The same shipment; not subjected to clinical procedures; first investigation 2 mo after arrival	2.1 ± 0.3	2.2 ± 0.3	20 ± 4	78 ± 16	4.9 ± 0.2	10.6 ± 0.5	20	12	8
Rhesus macaque	New shipment from Vietnam; not subjected to clinical or experimental procedures; first examination 22 days after arrival	2.0 ± 0.3	2.0 ± 0.2	33 ± 6	76 ± 4	6.6 ± 0.8	7.9 ± 0.7	25	18	7

[a] Averaged data from multiple subjects each providing one fasting zero sample of gastric juice obtained by gastric tube.

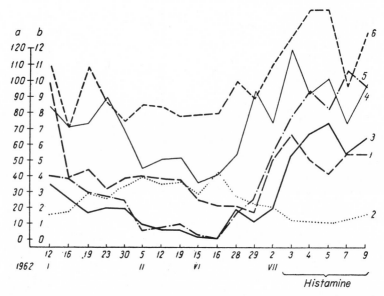

FIG. 21   Changes in quantitative and qualitative indices of gastric secretion in rhesus monkeys imported from Vietnam (Jan. 7, 1962) during acclimation at the Primate Center in Sukhumi (average data from experiments on eight monkeys). Ordinates: (a) acidity (titration units); (b) digestive strength (Mett units), pH, and volume of juice (ml). (1) volume of juice; (2) pH; (3) free HC1; (4) total acidity; (5) digestive strength; (6) control (digestive strength with addition of 1 ml 0.36% HC1 to 1 ml juice). The gastric juice was obtained from monkeys in the fasting state by means of a thin gastric tube; samples were taken for 7 months after arrival; at the end of the investigation five experiments were conducted involving administration of histamine (1 mg subcutaneously), after which the monkeys were returned to their home cage and then taken out in 45–60 min for gastric sampling.

In summary, it was evident that the secretory activity of the stomach of imported rhesus monkeys indicated normal secretory activity of the chief and parietal cells of the gastric mucosa during the first few months after transfer from the natural habitat. This was evidenced by the production of acidic fasting secretions containing high peptic activity. There was no difference in secretory function of the stomach between hamadryas baboons from the breeding colony and the imported rhesus monkeys. In captivity the imported monkeys gradually developed a functional form of gastric achylia, and the rate at which the disorder developed varied from individual to individual, depending on the intensity of nervous stress to which they were subjected, particularly on the frequency of clinical and experimental procedures. In this respect as well, the rhesus monkeys did not differ from the baboons, because various experimental and clinical procedures have induced functional gastric achylia in baboons. Apparently fasting gastric anacidity is not a species characteristic of rhesus monkeys but an acquired pathological symptom, most likely mediated by the central nervous system.

A mystery deserving experimental investigation is the question of why this functional disorder of gastric regulation should persist into the fourth to sixth generations of animals born and raised at the Primate Center. Perhaps the acquired characteristic of gastric achylia is inherited by subsequent generations. There is a description in the literature of gastric achylia in man as an inborn developmental defect of the stomach predisposing to breakdown in gastric functioning under stress (Martius, 1897). It concerns a 26-year-old patient suffering from gastric achylia who reported that his mother had suffered from a similar disorder for 15 years, his older brother for 2 years, and even his 15-year-old sister for a time. These patients experienced vomiting episodes that were triggered chiefly by eating meat.

The spontaneous gastric achylia that develops in imported monkeys may be one of the factors accounting for the high rates of morbidity and mortality from dysentery (20–70%) seen in such animals. A number of investigators at the Sukhumi Primate Center have written of the dysentery that so commonly develops in monkeys when they are transferred from the natural habitat to captivity (Lapin & Iakovleva, 1963; Dzhikidze, Gvazava, Stasilevich, Kavtaradze, Pekerman, Gasparian, Ivanov, & Bondar', 1963). Many clinical investigators have commented on the appearance of pathogenic microflora in the intestinal tract and the onset of gastrogenic diarrhea in human patients with gastric achylia (Orlik, 1950; Sazontov & Dobrolet, 1957). There may be a certain parallel between the consequences of spontaneous gastric achylia in man and in monkeys, therefore. Of course, most of the mortality from dysentery seen in imported monkeys results from still unexplained mechanisms of the disease and from the difficulties of maintaining and feeding such animals.

Studies showing that recently imported rhesus monkeys show signs of disrupted behavior and higher nervous activity support the view that nervous stress may play a role in the development and persistence of spontaneous gastric achylia in these animals (Lagutina, 1963). An experiment carried out in the early 1950s by Miminoshvili and Dzhikidze (1955) showed clearly that nervous stress influenced the susceptibility of healthy monkeys to dysentery when pathogenic bacteria were administered in known quantity by mouth. If, indeed, the high rate of dysentery in imported monkeys is related to gastric achylia of neurogenic origin, the problem of spontaneous gastric achylia has great practical significance both for the maintenance of monkeys in research centers and as an experimental model of similar diseases in man.

EXPERIMENTAL NEUROGENIC GASTRIC ACHYLIA IN HAMADRYAS BABOONS

Along with the chronic disruption of conditioned alimentary motor responses, gastric achylia is one of the most constant physiological findings in hamadryas baboons subjected to repeated immobilization stress. Whereas this disorder was readily reproducible by repeated immobilization of prefed animals in the

TABLE 10

Fasting Gastric Secretion of Hamadryas Baboon Florak during Unrestricted
Daytime Activity in the Home Cage and during Sham Feeding (Apples)

Condition	Hour from beginn- ing of exper- iment	Volume of secretion (ml)	pH	Free HCl[a]	Total acid[a]	Digestive strength (Mett units)	
						Without added HCl	Control (1 ml secretion + 1 ml 0.36% HCl
Fasting	0	8.0 ± 1.4	1.0 ± 0.0	52 ± 5	92 ± 6	8.6 ± 0.5	12.8 ± 0.4
	1	9.1 ± 1.4	1.0 ± 0.0	59 ± 5	96 ± 4	9.4 ± 0.4	12.6 ± 0.2
	2	6.8 ± 0.9	1.0 ± 0.0	54 ± 8	100 ± 8	8.4 ± 0.7	13.4 ± 0.9
	3	10.4 ± 2.5	1.0 ± 0.0	53 ± 5	92 ± 5	8.4 ± 0.7	11.8 ± 0.6
	4	6.0 ± 1.1	1.0 ± 0.0	45 ± 5	86 ± 5	8.8 ± 0.8	12.6 ± 0.8
	5	5.7 ± 0.8	1.0 ± 0.0	49 ± 4	86 ± 4	8.8 ± 0.2	14.4 ± 1.0
Sham feeding	0	8.1 ± 1.5	1.7 ± 0.3	29 ± 9	79 ± 10	6.6 ± 1.4	11.2 ± 1.2
	1x[b]	5.5 ± 0.7	1.5 ± 0.3	35 ± 6	64 ± 6	8.6 ± 1.1	11.4 ± 0.6
	2	6.5 ± 1.3	1.0 ± 0.0	51 ± 2	76 ± 6	9.5 ± 0.6	12.7 ± 1.0
	3	5.7 ± 1.4	1.0 ± 0.0	44 ± 4	66 ± 5	8.2 ± 0.6	11.8 ± 1.0
	4	5.2 ± 0.6	1.0 ± 0.0	46 ± 4	70 ± 6	9.2 ± 1.1	12.8 ± 0.4
	5	6.1 ± 1.1	1.0 ± 0.0	42 ± 4	65 ± 6	9.2 ± 0.5	11.8 ± 0.6

[a]In titration units.
[b]Note: The time of feeding and removal of chyme through the fistula is marked by (x). Each figure
represents mean of five sessions.

restraint stand, special experiments were required to demonstrate that the
mechanism consisted in the transformation of conditioned and unconditioned
alimentary stimuli into signals for the defensive dominant.

The experiments to produce neurogenic gastric achylia in hamadryas baboons
were preceded and accompanied by other investigations to evaluate normal
fasting gastric secretion and to test the effects of various physiological stimulants
of the gastric glands, e.g., the act of ingestion, insulin, cabbage juice, or
histamine. These preliminary experiments of many months duration demonstrated that baboons in the fasting state have a continuous gastric secretion of an
acidic, pepsin-containing juice during the daytime with inhibition of gastric
secretions at night. Apparently, the continuous gastric secretion in healthy
hamadryas baboons is maintained by a variety of natural conditioned alimentary
stimuli (Startsev, 1964c). Various kinds of stimulants were shown to increase
the acidity and digestive power of gastric secretions, and their stimulatory
effects were found to depend on the degree of activity of the gastric glands at
the time they were presented; the lower the baseline secretion, the stronger the
secretory response.

The effect of the act of ingestion and of insulin administration as central
stimulants of the gastric glands was to increase acidity and digestive activity to

levels not infrequently observed in the fasting state (Tables 10 and 11). Similar results were obtained using cabbage juice and histamine as gastric stimulants (Figure 22).

The continuity of rich secretion with a high content of free hydrochloric acid and intense digestive strength, the monophasic diurnal pattern of secretion, and the nature of secretions in hamadryas baboons proved to be quite similar to those of the healthy human; by the same token, they were quite different from those of the dog.

Altogether 21 hamadryas baboons were studied in experiments designed to establish neurogenic achylia, to analyze its mechanisms by physiological and pharmacological techniques, and to reverse it by various therapeutic techniques. Of this number, 14 had gastric fistulas, five had isolated gastric pouches of the types developed by Pavlov and Heidenhain (three of these also had fistulas), and two were intact. The research was conducted under standard conditions of the Sukhumi Primate Center; i.e., between collections of gastric secretions the

TABLE 11

Relationship between Secretory Activity of the Gastric Glands and Peripheral Blood Sugar Concentration in Fasting Hamadryas Baboons under Conditions of Free Behavior in the Home Cage Following Administration of Insulin (1 mg/kg; subcutaneous) (Experiments performed March 13, 1964)

Subject	Hour from beginning of experiment	Volume of gastric secretion (ml)	pH	Free acid[a]	Total acid[a]	Digestive strength (Mett units)		Blood sugar (mg%)
						Without added HCL	Control (1 ml secretion + 1ml 0.36% HCl)	
Azov	0	3.0	1	35	48	5.0	10.0	76
	1[b]	15.0	1	38	52	5.0	10.0	53
	2	3.0	1	60	75	7.0	9.0	55
	3	8.0	1	55	68	7.0	10.0	54
	4	3.0	1	50	60	8.0	11.0	57
	5	5.0	1	50	58	7.0	9.0	53
Takla	0	5.0	1	43	57	4.0	8.0	92
	1[b]	13.0	1	45	60	5.0	9.0	67
	2	10.0	1	30	45	3.0	8.0	72
	3	7.0	1	32	47	3.0	8.0	61
	4	5.0	1	34	50	4.0	9.0	64
	5	4.0	1	35	51	4.0	10.0	56

[a]In titration units.
[b]Time of administration of insulin.

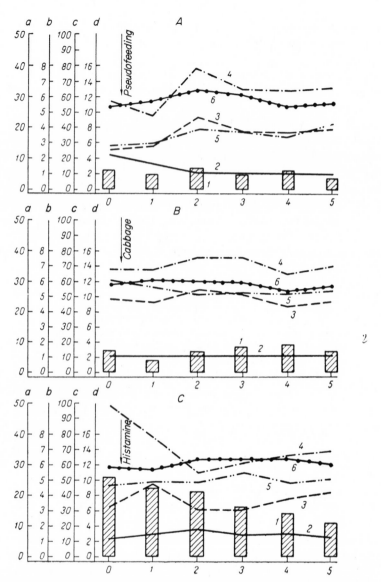

FIG. 22 Influence of various stimulants of gastric secretion on production of HC1 and pepsin in healthy hamadryas baboons with gastric fistulas. Abscissa: hour of experiment. Ordinates: (a) volume of secretion (ml), (b) pH, (c) acidity (titration units), (d) digestive strength (Mett units). Arrows indicate onset of stimulant presentation; (A) Sham feeding (125 g of apples removed through fistula after ingestion); (B) introduction of cabbage juice (50 ml) into the stomach through fistula for 1 hr; (C) injection of histamine (1 mg, subcutaneous); (1) volume of secretion; (2) pH; (3) free HCl; (4) total acid; (5) digestive strength; (6) digestive strength in control sample (addition of 1 ml of 0.36% HCl to 1 ml of secretion).

animals were unrestrained and remained free to interact with other members of their living group in the home cage. Every hour for 5–6 hr gastric juice was collected through a fistula in the stomach. A fasting zero sample was collected before the start of every experiment. From a physiological point of view this test was the best indicator of the long-term functional state of the gastric glands during various phases of prolonged studies. When disorders of secretion developed, the effects of various normal stimulants of gastric function were retested to evaluate the responsivity of the gastric glands under these conditions.

The chief question that had to be answered in establishing this animal model of neurogenic gastric achylia concerned the role of one major physiological stimulant of the gastric glands, viz., the act of ingestion in determining the onset and the chronic persistence of the gastric achylia. Answering this question would presumably establish the cause not only of experimental gastric achylia but also of spontaneous gastric achylia in baboons and man. Because the act of eating appeared to be a normal stimulant of gastric secretion, its implication as a factor in the development and maintenance of gastric pathology would further support the concept that neurogenic gastrointestinal disorders may derive from system-specific disturbances of conditioned and unconditioned alimentary response mechanisms in immobilization neurosis.

To begin with, it was demonstrated that immobilization following prefeeding gave rise to a more profound inhibition of secretory cell activity, particularly the acid-secreting parietal cells of the gastric mucosa, than did immobilization under fasting conditions (Table 12). Furthermore, the severity and duration of the inhibitory effects were considerably greater in the poststressor period if immobilization had been preceded by food than if it had been imposed on the animal in a fasting state (Table 13).

Of ten baboons, each subjected to five immobilization sessions under fasting conditions, none showed more than a transient hypoacidity in the poststressor period (Figures 23 and 24C). Of nine baboons subjected to the same number of stressor sessions immediately after eating in the home cage, every one developed an achylic condition that persisted after the stressor sessions were discontinued (Figure 25). A detailed account of their disorders is presented below.

These experiments, in many of which the food ingested just before immobilization was removed via the fistula before it could be digested (sham feeding), clearly implicated the act of eating as an important factor determining the emergence of chronic achylia in the poststressor period.

Why should preliminary eating cause the immobilization stress to have a stronger acute effect and a more prolonged and profound chronic inhibitory effect on the parietal cells and chief cells of the gastric glands than immobilization alone? It appears that the organ or functional system in the most intense state of activation at the time of stress is susceptible to the inhibitory influence of the defensive dominant of the motor system. Moreover, it is possible that the act of ingestion, by activating the alimentary system and gastric glands, opens

TABLE 12

Inhibition of Gastric Secretion in Hamadryas Baboon Zefir during Experiments Involving Fixation in the Stand in the Fasting State and with Sham Feeding in the Home Cage Followed by Fixation in the Stand

Experimental condition	Hour from beginning of experiment	Volume of secretion (ml)	pH	Free acid[a]	Total acid[a]	Digestive strength (Mett units) Without added acid	Control (1 ml secretion + 1 ml 0.36% HCl)
Fasting	0	14.6 ± 3.1	1.0 ± 0.0	42 ± 3	68 ± 4	10.6 ± 1.0	7.1 ± 2.9
	1	14.4 ± 2.9	4.2 ± 0.6	1 ± 1	27 ± 6	2.4 ± 1.5	5.1 ± 1.9
	2	9.2 ± 2.5	6.4 ± 0.4	0	21 ± 3	0.5 ± 0.5	6.6 ± 1.7
	3	7.4 ± 2.6	6.6 ± 0.4	0	28 ± 3	0	8.3 ± 2.6
	4	8.1 ± 2.4	6.4 ± 0.2	0	25 ± 4	0	9.2 ± 1.6
	5	9.1 ± 2.7	5.4 ± 0.9	4 ± 4	35 ± 5	1.0 ± 1.0	7.4 ± 1.9
Sham feeding of apples with subsequent fixation in the stand	0	22.4 ± 3.1	2.6 ± 1.4	17 ± 9	60 ± 13	6.8 ± 2.0	8.6 ± 1.5
	1[b]	23.2 ± 3.2	5.7 ± 0.9	0	28 ± 4	0	8.6 ± 1.3
	2	17.0 ± 3.0	6.4 ± 0.5	0	27 ± 3	0	7.1 ± 1.6
	3	12.8 ± 2.1	7.1 ± 0.5	0	21 ± 1	0	7.8 ± 1.9
	4	14.2 ± 3.0	7.2 ± 0.6	0	22 ± 1	0.8 ± 0.8	9.4 ± 1.3

[a]In titration units.
[b]Time at which chyme removed from stomach via fistula; averaged data from 5 sessions.

TABLE 13
Degree of Conditioned Reflex Inhibition of Gastric Secretion in the Hamadryas Baboon Zefir during Unrestricted Activities Following Repeated Experiments with Immobilization Alone or in Combination with Preliminary Sham Feeding[a]

Experimental condition	Hour from beginning of experiment	Volume of secretion (ml)	pH	Free acid[b]	Total acid[b]	Digestive strength (Mett units)	
						Without added acid	Control (1 ml secretion + 1 ml 0.36% HCl)
Fasting	0	29.8 ± 11.8	1.7 ± 0.4	24 ± 10	65 ± 7	8.6 ± 2.7	10.8 ± 0.5
	1	14.0 ± 3.0	1.9 ± 0.4	23 ± 4	56 ± 3	8.0 ± 3.6	11.2 ± 0.6
	2	17.6 ± 3.4	4.7 ± 1.3	13 ± 8	47 ± 8	3.8 ± 1.8	7.4 ± 2.0
	3	26.6 ± 5.6	3.7 ± 1.3	12 ± 7	41 ± 8	8.6 ± 2.0	8.6 ± 1.5
	4	16.4 ± 3.0	1.6 ± 0.2	32 ± 3	65 ± 3	11.2 ± 2.1	12.5 ± 0.7
	5	18.0 ± 5.7	2.5 ± 0.9	25 ± 7	51 ± 7	8.1 ± 1.5	11.4 ± 0.9
Sham feeding with subsequent fixation in the stand	0	11.4 ± 1.9	2.8 ± 1.1	18 ± 9	55 ± 9	5.0 ± 1.6	11.2 ± 1.2
	1[c]	22.0 ± 3.4	4.6 ± 0.8	3 ± 2	34 ± 2	0.6 ± 0.6	8.4 ± 0.7
	2	19.6 ± 5.7	4.6 ± 1.2	4 ± 2	36 ± 4	2.4 ± 1.0	8.8 ± 0.5
	3	16.0 ± 2.7	5.2 ± 0.7	2 ± 1	32 ± 2	2.2 ± 1.1	7.7 ± 1.7
	4	21.4 ± 2.4	6.2 ± 0.8	0	31 ± 2	0	9.0 ± 0.5
	5	22.4 ± 3.6	4.6 ± 0.5	2 ± 2	38 ± 4	0.4 ± 0.4	9.4 ± 1.1

[a]Experiments carried out with animal in fasting state; averaged data from five sessions.
[b]In titration units.
[c]Time of ingestion of fruit and its removal via gastric fistula.

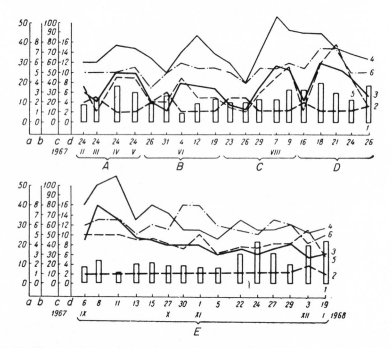

FIG. 23 Chronic changes in gastric secretions as reflected in zero samples from the hamadryas baboon Kuzbass; (A) normal fasting condition with free behavior in the home cage; (B) during immobilization experiments in fasting condition; (C) with free behavior under fasting conditions; (D) during immobilization experiments with prefeeding and administration of haloperidol to suppress defensive response mechanism; (E) with free behavior in the home cage in the following months. Otherwise legend same as in Fig. 22.

the way for pathological influences on the gastric glands, for the neural pathways that convey the inhibitory influence from the cerebral focus of the defensive dominant are the same pathways that conduct impulses to the stomach from the cerebral components of the alimentary system. Claude Bernard reported enhanced sensitivity of the vagal pathway conducting impulses from the alimentary center to the gastric glands with extreme painful stimulation of dogs who had been fed as opposed to little effect in fasting subjects.

Before the second part of the question was considered, i.e., that of the mechanism responsible for maintenance of chronic achylia, it was necessary to elucidate the role of defensive excitation in determining the development of gastric achylia. Neither the act of eating nor immobilization alone induces an achylic condition but the combination of the two does. To test the hypothesis that the intense activation of defensive response mechanisms mediated this effect, it was necessary to devise methods of eliminating the defensive excitation while leaving alimentary functions intact. With this aim, haloperidol (0.2 mg/kg) was administered to two baboons and metamizil (2 mg/kg) to two others between prefeeding and immobilization in the stressor experiments. (It had been

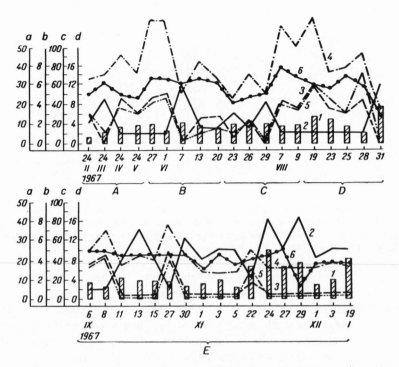

FIG. 24 Ineffectiveness of central cholinolytic substance metamizil (2 mg/kg; subcutaneously) in the prevention of neurogenic gastric achylia in the hamadryas baboon Vedun.
Graphs represent changes in zero samples of gastric secretions (A) under normal conditions;
(B) during immobilization stressor experiments under fasting conditions; (C) during poststressor period; (D) during immobilization stressor sessions with prefeeding (apples) and
administration of metamizil; (E) during second post stressor period characterized by
gradually developing gastric achylia. Otherwise legend same as in Fig. 22.

shown in previous experiments that the drugs in these dosages suppressed gastric
secretion in fasting, unrestrained baboons.)

The results of experiments in which the neurotropic agents were administered
are presented in Figure 26. The upper graph presents averaged data of five
sessions with haloperidol. Haloperidol, a major tranquilizer, suppressed the
defensive excitation during the entire experiment. The baboon was in a somno-
lent state until the last hours of the experiment, when he began to show some
weak defensive behavior. Inhibition of gastric secretion was not observed in the
first hour. Furthermore, the normal increases in total acidity, free hydrochloric
acid content, and digestive capacity normally induced by eating were observed.
These indices of gastric secretion began to subside in the third hour of immobilization. Pepsin activity remained high during the whole experiment (Figure 26A).

The administration of metamizil not only failed to suppress the defensive
excitation induced by fixation of the baboons in the restraint stand but markedly intensified their defensive behavior. Gastric secretion, in contrast, followed

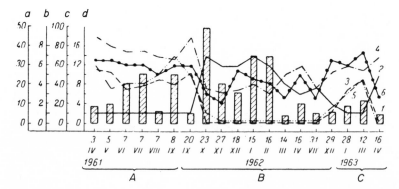

FIG. 25 Changes in zero samples of gastric secretions from Zefir (A) under normal conditions of fasting and free behavior in the home cage; (B) during neurogenic gastric achylia; (C) after transfer to new home cage and change in experimental setting. Symbols same as in Fig. 22.

the same course as was seen with haloperidol. The only difference was a somewhat earlier onset of the reversion of acidity and digestive strength to lower levels (Figure 26B, second hour of immobilization). Thus, the behavioral effects of the two agents were altogether different, but their effects on the functional status of the gastric glands were almost identical. It was interesting to note that when haloperidol and metamizil were administered in the context of immobilization stress, they did not produce the suppression of gastric secretion that was characteristic in the first hour after injection in the unrestrained animal.

The most important finding from this series of experiments was that when defensive excitation was blocked by haloperidol, gastric achylia did not develop (Figure 23, D and E). Testing 8 months after the sessions involving neurogenic stress revealed no signs of disturbed gastric secretory function. By contrast, the administration of metamizil had no protective effect against the development of gastric achylia (Figure 24, D and E). One of the baboons with achylia was autopsied $2\frac{1}{2}$ months later and found to have gastric adenomatosis. Changes in the secretion of gastric juice in the other animal are plotted in Figure 24. Achylia was recorded even 8 months after the stressor period.

Therefore, gastric achylia does not develop if the defensive activation ordinarily evoked by physical restraint is attenuated or eliminated by a psychotropic agent. By contrast, it does develop if defensive activation is not reduced or is potentiated by drugs following the act of eating. These results corroborated our findings regarding the prophylactic effectiveness of haloperidol, chlorpromazine, and morphine in protecting conditioned alimentary motor responses in similar prefeeding immobilization experiments on other baboons. Moreover, they give further support to the hypothesis that through repeated combinations of eating and immobilization the act of ingestion is converted into a signal for the defensive dominant.

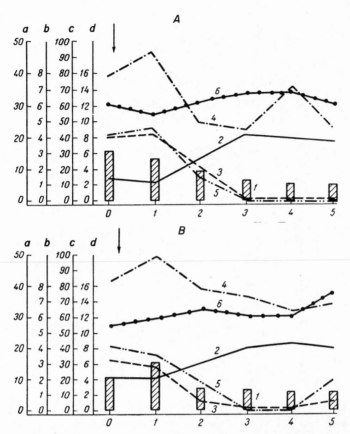

FIG. 26 Temporary preventive effects of (A) haloperidol (0.2 mg/kg) and (B) metamizil (2 mg/kg) on gastric secretion in hamadryas baboons subjected to 5-hr immobilization sessions with prefeeding in the home cage. Arrows indicate times of sham feeding apples, administering psychotropic agents, and immobilizing the subjects. Otherwise legend same as in Fig. 22.

The next step in the experimental analysis was to demonstrate conclusively that the act of eating continued to have an inhibitory effect on gastric secretion in the unrestrained animal under conditions of free behavior in the poststressor period, i.e., after cessation of the prefeeding–immobilization sessions. Figure 27 shows that for several months after the stressor sessions eating apples did not activate gastric secretion in hamadryas baboons in their home cage. On the contrary, decreases in total acid, free acid, and digestive strength and increased pH were recorded after eating. Peptic activity, with the addition of hydrochloric acid to optimize pH, either increased to abnormally high levels with progressive hypoacidity (Figure 27A) or decreased still further (Figure 27B). In either case the normal pattern of response of the parietal and chief cells to the act of eating was disrupted.

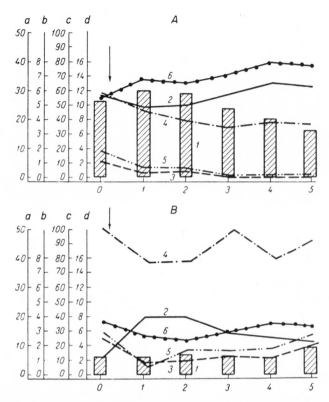

FIG. 27 Different patterns of inhibition of gastric secretion seen during sham feeding of hamadryas baboons with experimental neurogenic gastric achylia. Experiments conducted under conditions of free behavior in home cage. Arrows indicate time of sham feeding. Legend same as in Fig. 22.

Inhibition of gastric secretory responses under conditions of free behavior in baboons suffering experimental neurogenic gastric achylia was elicited by foods other than the kind of food that had been used for prefeeding in the immobilization sessions (Table 14). In fact, other factors besides eating were found to suppress the secretory response. The same effect was induced by other normal stimulants of gastric secretion, such as mechanical stimulation (Table 15), insulin, and histamine (Figure 28). In addition to the inhibitory influence of eating on gastric secretory responses, there was a sharp increase in the frequency of vomiting episodes following ingestion of food (Figure 29).

Other stressors besides repeated immobilization can convert the act of eating into a signal for the defensive dominant when they are preceded by eating. We observed the accidental conversion of ingestion into a signal for the defensive dominant in a baboon that was inadvertently set free from the cage for 20 min. His activity elicited intense aggressive reactions from the other baboons in adjacent open air compounds. The resulting defensive excitation inhibited gastric

TABLE 14

Chronic Neurogenic Deficit in Gastric Secretory Function in Hamadryas
Baboons: Influence of sham feeding (125 g of tangerines) on Gastric Secretion of Baboons under
Conditions of Free Behavior in the Home Cage (average data of five sessions)

Subject	Hour from beginning of experiment	Volume of secretion (ml)	pH	Free HCl^a	Total $acid^a$	Digestive strength (Mett units)	
						Without added HCl	Control (1 ml secretion + 1 ml 0.36% HCl)
Zlak	0	14.8 ± 2.0	1.6 ± 0.4	20 ± 5	60 ± 4	7.2 ± 2.7	11.0 ± 0.2
	1^b	15.9 ± 1.5	2.4 ± 0.4	9 ± 6	47 ± 5	2.8 ± 1.9	10.6 ± 1.1
	2	15.4 ± 1.4	4.2 ± 1.2	4 ± 3	36 ± 7	1.6 ± 1.0	10.2 ± 1.8
	3	13.7 ± 1.2	3.0 ± 0.7	9 ± 6	36 ± 8	3.6 ± 2.6	12.0 ± 1.0
	4	14.4 ± 1.5	4.2 ± 1.3	9 ± 9	32 ± 6	1.6 ± 1.6	12.4 ± 1.3
Pianch	0	24.4 ± 3.3	3.8 ± 0.8	6 ± 2	57 ± 10	5.8 ± 2.7	12.2 ± 0.6
	1^b	21.0 ± 3.7	3.4 ± 0.6	8 ± 5	64 ± 12	3.8 ± 2.4	16.0 ± 1.0
	2	25.0 ± 3.6	4.4 ± 0.2	0	53 ± 10	0	16.0 ± 1.0
	3	16.4 ± 1.6	5.3 ± 0.6	0	39 ± 5	0	15.2 ± 0.8
	4	13.6 ± 2.3	5.0 ± 0.3	0	36 ± 2	0	14.8 ± 1.0
	5	17.0 ± 0.9	4.8 ± 0.6	0	37 ± 2	0	14.0 ± 0.8

^{a}In titration units.
^{b}Time of ingestion of fruit and its removal via gastric fistula.

secretion throughout the remaining hours of the experiment (Figure 30A). This
experience turned out to be the initiating event for a suppression of gastric
secretion that was still evident a month later in a series of five sessions in which
the effects of feeding (apples) was tested under conditions of free behavior in
the home cage (Figure 30B). The animal gradually developed an achylic condition (Figure 31) and after his death, autopsy revealed an adenomatous polyp in
the stomach. This case of neurogenic gastric achylia is in no way inconsistent
with the syndrome of experimental gastric achylia produced by immobilization
stress. At the same time, it probably had a mode of onset more typical of that in
most baboons living in captivity where eating is not infrequently associated with
agressive attacks by stronger baboons or with seizure by laboratory personnel for
various clinical and experimental procedures. This case demonstrates graphically
the possible causes of so-called spontaneous gastric achylia in different monkey
species in captivity.

Conversion of the act of eating into a signal for activation of defensive
response mechanisms and the consequent inhibitory influences on gastric
response mechanisms is undoubtedly a widespread phenomenon in men as well.
How often one sees cases of appetite loss or even aversion to food in children in
their home surroundings where they are absolutely forced to finish the food

TABLE 15

Experimental Neurogenic Gastric Achylia in Hamadryas Baboons:
Inhibitory Influence of Continuous Mechanical Stimulation of the Stomach
(balloon inflated with 150 ml of water) on Gastric Secretion under
Conditions of Free Behavior in the Home Cage

Subject	Hour from beginning of experiment	Volume of secretion (ml)	pH	Free HCl[a]	Total acid[a]	Digestive strength (Mett units)	
						Without added HCl	Control (1 ml secretion + 1 ml 0.36% HCl)
Bakhmach	0	20.0	1.0	25	60	6.0	12.0
	1[b]	25.0	7.0	0	35	0	5.0
	2	15.0	7.0	0	25	0	7.0
	3	20.0	2.5	18	44	5.0	9.0
	4	25.0	4.0	11	29	4.0	8.0
	5	20.0	2.0	36	67	5.0	6.0
Zefir	0	100.0	4.0	0	92	0	17.0
	1[b]	15.0	6.0	0	33	0	6.0
	2	35.0	8.0	0	22	0	8.0
	3	18.0	7.0	0	35	4.0	9.0
	4	20.0	7.0	0	30	0	7.0
	5	10.0	7.0	0	30	0	9.0
Zlak	0	15.0	4.5	0	35	0	15.0
	1[b]	3.0	6.0	0	28	0	9.0
	2	5.0	5.0	0	33	0	9.0
	3	5.0	6.0	0	25	0	7.0
	4	3.5	5.0	0	28	0	9.0
	5	6.0	5.5	0	40	0	8.0
Pianch	0	35.0	4.0	0	50	0	19.0
	1[b]	10.0	4.0	0	40	0	11.0
	2	15.0	6.0	0	32	0	8.0
	3	12.0	6.0	0	30	0	6.0
	4	10.0	5.0	0	35	0	9.0
	5	35.0	5.0	0	23	0	10.0

[a]In titration units.
[b]Balloon inflated.

placed before them! The same children in other surroundings may possess a beautiful appetite for quite similar food. Haste in eating before going to kindergarten, school, or work may do especially great harm to gastric digestion in children and adults. Here probably lies the hidden cause of many disturbances of digestive function, among them the spontaneous gastric achylia of humans.

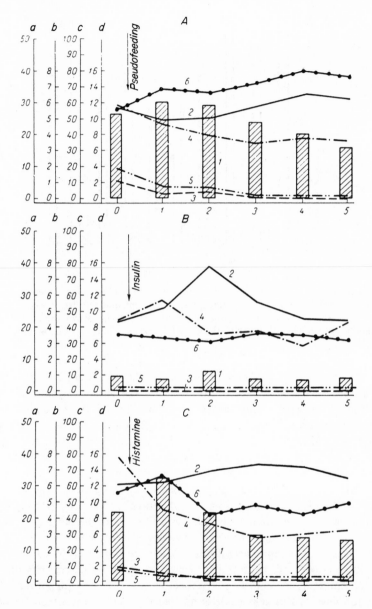

FIG. 28 Inhibitory influences of gastric stimulants when administered to hamadryas baboons with neurogenic gastric achylia. Arrows indicate time of presentation of stimulant: (A) sham feeding (125 g of apples); (B) insulin (0.5 units/kg, subcutaneous); (C) histamine (1 mg, subcutaneous). Otherwise legend same as in Fig. 22.

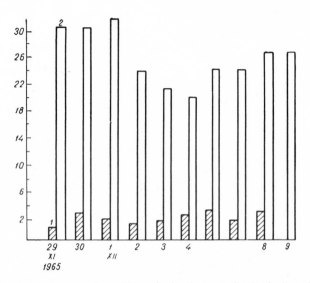

FIG. 29 Increased frequency of vomiting episodes during eating in the hamadryas baboon Zefir in the home cage 4 years after the onset of experimental neurogenic gastric achylia. Abscissa, dates of experiments; ordinate, number of attacks of vomiting in 1 hr of observation; (1) number of vomiting attacks in 1 hr before eating; (2) number of vomiting attacks in 1 hr after eating.

The neurogenic nature of chronic gastric achylia in baboons is evidenced not only by the fact that it is accompanied by behavioral neurosis and by the effectiveness of psychotropic agents in preventing it. If one compares the secretory activity of the gastric glands in the intact stomach and in the isolated Heindenhain pouch of a baboon with achylia, one finds the signs of achylia only in the stomach. In the pouch with its neural connections severed we found a continuous secretion of acidic gastric juice rich in pepsin (Table 16). Protein left in a Pavlovian pouch for 24 hr was inadequately digested, whereas in the denervated Heidenhain pouch digestion of protein proceeded normally (Table 17). The development of chronic achylia in this model therefore requires that neural connections between the gastric glands and the brain be intact.

An increase in the peptic activity of gastric juice from Pianch and Zlak under the influence of such neurotropic agents as atropine, chlorpromazine, and hexamethonium provide further evidence for a neurogenic inhibition of the pepsin-forming cells in achylia. It is noteworthy that in these baboons peptic activity increased almost to normal levels at night during sleep (Figure 32). These data not only establish the central neural, functional character of experimental gastric achylia but also have important implications for therapeutic intervention in the disease in humans.

The following are the most striking symptoms of the neurogenic gastric achylia established experimentally in baboons: vomiting in the fasting state or after

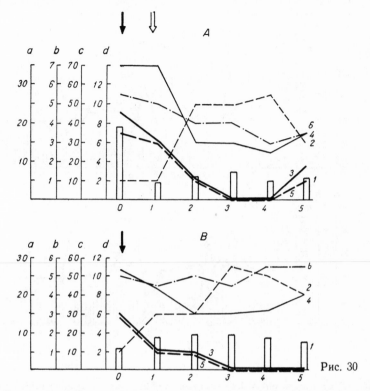

FIG. 30 Conversion of the act of eating into a signal for the defensive dominant by a stressor other than immobilization. (A) development of inhibition of gastric secretion in the hamadryas baboon Kholm after eating apples (indicated by black arrow) as a result of nervous stress (indicated by open arrow); (B) inhibitory influence of eating apples in the same baboon under conditions of free behavior in the home cage a month after the accidental combination of eating and defensive excitation. Abscissa, hours after eating. Otherwise legend same as in Fig. 22.

eating; residual undigested food in morning samples of gastric juice (although more often food is not retained overnight in the stomachs of baboons with achylia); lesions of the gastric mucous membrane such that traces of blood can almost always be detected in the gastric contents under fasting conditions; gastric juice with an intensely unpleasant odor; liquid stools reverting to normal with repeated administration of hydrochloric acid directly into the stomach; and ravenous eating despite the serious disruption of gastric digestion. The findings presented in Table 18 illustrate the decrease in proteolytic activity of gastric secretions in animals with gastric achylia. Comparative data from healthy hamadryas baboons are presented showing normal levels of proteolytic activity.

In a few animals with neurogenic achylia the volume of gastric secretion decreased sharply to 2–3 ml of mucous secretion per hourly sample. In the

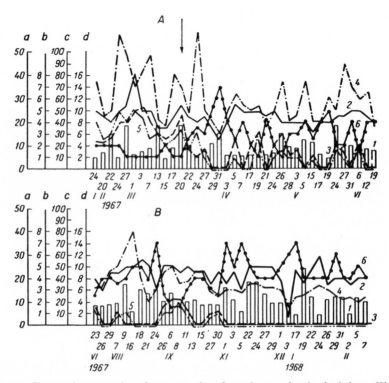

FIG. 31 Changes in properties of zero samples of gastric secretion in the baboon Kholm during the development of neurogenic gastric achylia. Arrow indicates time of accidental combination of eating and defensive excitation. Legend same as in Fig. 22.

majority of cases, however, the volume did not decrease and sometimes even increased. Total acid decreased to 20–40 titration units, free hydrochloric acid completely disappeared, and digestive strength diminished to zero but was restored to 4–8 Mett units with the addition of hydrochloric acid. In some cases apepsia occurred. In a number of others, in contrast, markedly increased peptic activity was recorded in the control sample (HCl added). It is characteristic of gastric achylia in baboons that many months of complete anacidity suddenly give way to a condition in which small quantities of free hydrochloric acid appear. Peptic activity fluctuates within and across days throughout the course of the disease.

Tables 19 and 20 compare gastric secretion in baboons suffering from experimental neurogenic gastric achylia with that of human patients who have suffered from gastric achylia for several years; the similarities are clear.

We have cited data demonstrating the inhibitory influence of the act of eating,

TABLE 16

Comparison of Secretory Activity of Gastric Glands of the Whole Stomach
and Heidenhain Denervated Pouch in Hamadryas Baboon Vik Suffering from
Spontaneous Gastric Achylia[a]

Time	Volume of secretion (ml)	pH	Free HCl	Total acid	Digestive strength (Mett units)	
					Without added HCl	Control (1 ml secretion + 1 ml 0.36% HCl)
			Stomach			
9:00	3.9 ± 0.4	5.3 ± 0.4	0	83 ± 8	0	0.9 ± 0.6
12:00	3.0 ± 0.7	5.8 ± 0.3	0	74 ± 8	0.1 ± 0.1	1.8 ± 0.6
15:00	3.1 ± 0.8	5.6 ± 0.5	0	54 ± 8	0.5 ± 0.5	1.6 ± 0.4
			Denervated Heidenhain pouch			
9:00	38.4 ± 2.9	1.0 ± 0.0	75 ± 3	108 ± 1	10.9 ± 0.5	12.0 ± 0.3
12:00	18.6 ± 3.2	1.0 ± 0.0	60 ± 5	88 ± 6	11.2 ± 0.5	12.4 ± 0.7
15:00	6.3 ± 0.9	1.0 ± 0.0	40 ± 4	70 ± 3	10.2 ± 0.9	12.2 ± 0.9

[a]Fasting samples taken under conditions of free behavior in the home cage (average data from 10 sessions).

of insulin, of mechanical stimuli, and of histamine on the secretion of acid and pepsin in baboons with gastric achylia.

Experiments with insulin and with sham feeding indicate that the first phase of excitation of gastric secretion completely disappears. These data are in accord with the view stated by M. P. Konchalovskii (1911) that the first phase of gastric secretion is disrupted in humans with the functional form of gastric achylia. In the human disease mechanical stimulation of the stomach also fails to elicit acid and pepsin secretion (Kurtsin & Slutsskii, 1935).

Because the depression of hydrochloric acid secretion in the hamadryas baboons tested was stable for many months, it appeared possible that the gastric glands had atrophied. Therefore it was necessary to test their ability to respond to the direct stimulant, histamine.

Two baboons administered histamine (1 mg, subcutaneously) failed to show any sign of free hydrochloric acid in the gastric juice. In fact, following the injection of histamine there was an increase in pH level and a noticeable decrease in the total acidity of gastric secretions. The absence of hydrochloric acid secretion in response to histamine in these cases indicates a true gastric achylia. In these baboons the second phase of gastric secretion was clearly disturbed (Figure 33A).

TABLE 17

Comparison of Gastric Secretions in Hamadryas Baboons
with Intact Gastric Innervation and Denervated Gastric Pouch under
Conditions of Free Behavior and Ingestion of Familiar Food Subsequent
to Immobilization Sessions with Prefeeding

Date	Baboon And, isolated pouch with central innervation intact		Baboon Kovboi, denervated, isolated pouch	
	pH of gastric juice at the moment Mett protein stick withdrawn from stomach	Digestive strength after 24 hr with Mett protein stick in the stomach (Mett units)	pH of gastric secretions at the moment Mett protein stick withdrawn from the pouch	Digestive strength as determined by Mett stick in gastric pouch for 24 hr (Mett units)
1960				
Jan. 29	7	1	2	10
30	7	0	2	4
Feb. 1	7	0	2	8
2	7	0	—	—
3	7	0	2	10
4	7	1	—	—
5	7	6	2	3
9	7	0	6	6
10	7	0	2	10
11	—	—	2	10
12	6	2	2	8
15	7	0	2	8
17	7	0	2	8
18	2	0	2	0
Mean:	6.5 ± 0.4	0.8 ± 0.5	2.3 ± 0.3	7.1 ± 0.9

In two other baboons histamine induced a positive reaction, i.e., secretion of hydrochloric acid in the first hour after injection (Figure 33B). Along with the increase in volume of free and total acid a noticeable increase in peptic activity was recorded. (The same increase in peptic activity had been noted in the first two subjects as well.)

In the second and following hours of the experiments all four animals showed profound depression of both chief cell and parietal cell functions. Taken together, these observations indicated that in reality histamine resistance of secretory elements of the stomach did not occur in a single one of the baboons. The glands responded to histamine but in a distorted way and sometimes in a pattern opposite to that seen in the normal, nonstressed animal. The first two subjects from the very first and the second two, beginning 2 hr after injection of

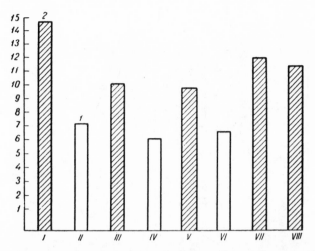

FIG. 32 Peptic activity of gastric secretions in the hamadryas baboon Pianch, suffering from neurogenic gastric achylia; stimulating effects of neurotropic agents and normal nocturnal sleep. Abscissa, number of experimental series; ordinate, digestive strength (Mett units) with addition of 1 ml 0.36% HCl to 1 ml of secretion. (1) Peptic activity of gastric secretions during gastric achylia (II, IV, VI); (2) digestive strength normally (I); under the influence of atropine (III), chlorpromazine, (V), hexamethonium, (VII), and during sleep (VIII). Columns represent means of five sessions, each carried out between Nov. 9, 1960 and May 27, 1961.

histamine, showed an intensification of functional inhibition of the chief and parietal cells. Therefore, the gastric secretory apparatus of baboons with neurogenic gastric achylia remains sensitive to the direct humoral stimulant histamine but its reaction is markedly distorted.

We have encountered similar distortions of the glandular response to histamine in experiments on healthy hamadryas baboons. Administration of histamine during a 10-min collection of gastric juice by esophageal tube, a procedure that induced an acute negative emotional reaction in baboons, not only did not stimulate secretion of hydrochloric acid and pepsin but abruptly intensified the inhibition of gastric secretion that was induced by the tubing procedure itself. It is probably possible, therefore, to identify reactions of the gastric glands to humoral stimulation by their potentiating effect on the central neural inhibition.

Because in the clinical literature negative reaction of the gastric glands to histamine is taken as an indication of atrophy of the gastric glands (Babkin, 1960), it was of interest to test the effect of the ganglionic blocking agent hexamethonium on histamine-resistant achylia in baboons. Hexamethonium blocks the transmission of central neural impulses through the sympathetic and parasympathetic ganglia (Denisenko, 1959), and to the extent that the achylia is a result of inhibitory neural influences it can be expected to remove the inhibition.

TABLE 18

Comparison of Gastric Digestion in Hamadryas Baboons Normally and with Neurogenic Gastric Achylia (average data from five sessions)[a]

| Subject | Volume of secretions (ml) | pH | Free acid | Total acid | Digestive strength (Mett units) | | Magnitude of digestion of protein stick in the stomach for 24 hr under customary living conditions and feeding outside experimental setting |
					Without added HCl	Control (1 ml secretion + 1 ml 0.36% HCl)	
				Normal			
Azov	39 ± 0.3	1.2 ± 0.2	34 ± 6	62 ± 7	8.0 ± 1.7	10.6 ± 1.7	7.4 ± 0.9
Zaimka	4.7 ± 0.5	1.0 ± 0.0	51 ± 6	93 ± 10	8.6 ± 0.8	12.2 ± 0.4	5.2 ± 0.4
Takla	5.4 ± 0.7	1.0 ± 0.0	32 ± 4	81 ± 7	7.0 ± 0.4	11.0 ± 0.1	5.8 ± 1.6
Florak	5.7 ± 0.5	1.0 ± 0.0	45 ± 7	82 ± 7	10.0 ± 0.2	12.6 ± 0.8	7.0 ± 1.4
				With neurogenic achylia			
Zefir	10.0 ± 2.7	3.9 ± 0.7	1 ± 1	46 ± 10	0.4 ± 0.4	7.2 ± 1.2	0
Zlak	2.5 ± 0.2	4.2 ± 0.4	0	33 ± 4	0	9.0 ± 0.4	0
Pianch	45.8 ± 5.9	1.7 ± 0.3	13 ± 4	57 ± 6	1.8 ± 0.5	7.4 ± 1.4	0.6 ± 0.4

[a]Zero sample of gastric secretion obtained before introduction of Mett protein stick into stomach.

TABLE 19

Characteristics of Zero Samples of Gastric Secretion in Baboons Suffering from Experimental Neurogenic Gastric Achylia Induced by Repeated Combination of Prefeeding with Immobilization in a Restraint Stand

Subject	Date	Duration of illness (months)	pH	Volume of secretion (ml)	Free HCl[a]	Total acid[a]	Digestive strength (Mett units)	
							Without added HCl	Control (1 ml of secretion + 1 ml 0.36% HCl)
Antil	Apr. 5, 1965	19	5	1.5	0	39	0	5
Bakhmach	Jan. 3, 1962	4	6	35.0	0	35	0	6
Vedun	Dec. 3, 1967	4	5	8.5	0	35	0	7
Zefir	Dec. 15, 1966	63	6	9.5	0	25	0	8
Zlak	Oct. 3, 1964	46	7	11.0	0	33	0	11
Kleshchevina	Oct. 16, 1965	12	5	50.0	0	165	0	6
Pianch	Mar. 14, 1962	6	3	25.0	0	53	0	6
Pianch	Aug. 10, 1964	37	6	5.0	0	30	0	9
Kholm	Mar. 20, 1967	10	6	9.5	0	15	0	1

[a]In titration units.

TABLE 20

Characteristics of Gastric Secretion in Patients with Gastric Achylia of Many Years Duration[a]

Patient	Age	Date	Duration of illness (years)	Volume of secretion (ml)	pH	Free HCl[b]	Total acid[b]	Digestive strength (Mett units)	
								Without added HCl	Control (1 ml secretion + 1 ml 0.36% HCl)
S.G.G.	52 yrs.	Sep. 13, 1965	13	48	7	0	8	0	5
V.I.K.	50 yrs.	Nov. 24, 1964	10	30	8	0	13	0	2
I.K.K.	55 yrs.	Aug. 15, 1964	Several	16	4	0	56	0	16
I.K.K.	55 yrs.	Aug. 17, 1964	Several	100	3	0	65	0	5
N.G.F.	56 yrs.	Mar. 27, 1967	20	13	7	0	18	0	5
R.G.Ch.	47 yrs.	Oct. 13, 1964	Several	60	7	0	27	0	5
V.I.Sh.	25 yrs.	Jun. 18, 1962	Several	50	7	0	20	0	6

[a]Fasting gastric secretions were obtained in the morning by a thin gastric tube.
[b]In titration units.

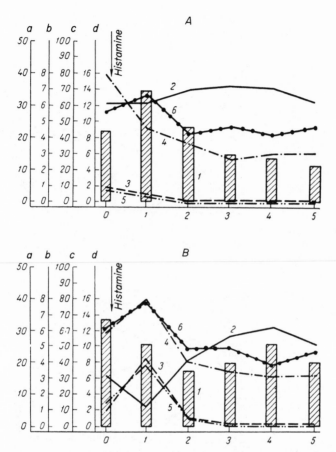

FIG. 33 Histamine-negative and short-term histamine-positive responses of acid-secreting gastric cells in hamadryas baboons with neurogenic gastric achylia (averaged data from five sessions). (A) Baboon Zefir; (B) baboon Pianch. Otherwise legend same as in Fig. 22.

In experiments on three baboons with gastric achylia, hexamethonium (1 mg/kg, subcutaneously) exerted a normalizing effect on the secretory activity of the stomach (Figure 34), again demonstrating the central neural mechanism and functional character of experimental gastric achylia in baboons. The fact that histamine failed to stimulate the secretion of hydrochloric acid in two of the baboons while hexamethonium stimulated it is evidence against atrophy of the parietal cells. Furthermore, this observation indicates that the apparent histamine resistance resulted from a central inhibitory influence on the activity of the gastric glands that was alleviated by blocking the autonomic ganglia. It is possible that blockade of the central inhibition at the ganglia creates more favorable conditions for the gastrin mechanism to excite gastric secretion. Therefore, it may well be more rational to test the effects not only of histamine

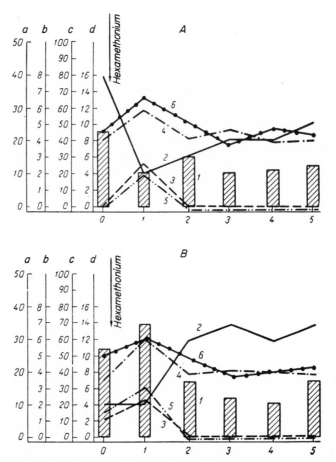

FIG. 34 Normalizing influence of the ganglionic blocking agent hexamethonium on gastric secretion in hamadryas baboons with neurogenic gastric achylia. (1) Hexamethonium administered (1 mg/kg, subcutaneous). Experiment Jan. 5, 1962. (A) Baboon Zefir; (B) baboon Pianch. Otherwise legend same as in Fig. 22.

in patients with histamine-resistant gastric achylia, but of hexamethonium as well, if one is to reach a valid differential diagnosis regarding functional versus organic forms of achylia.

Baboons with experimental gastric achylia were also retarded in growth and development. The onset of maturity, as judged by general appearance and hair length and distribution, occurred later than in normal hamadryas baboons. There was a significant deceleration of growth as measured by body weight (Figure 35). A number of trophic disturbances were recorded: hair loss, bleeding sores on the tail, ulcerative stomatitis, bleeding gastric ulcers, and gastric polyposis. Hematological investigations failed to demonstrate any deviation from normal in

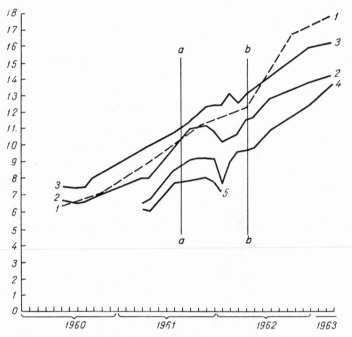

FIG. 35 Changes in weight of male hamadryas baboons: normally and with neurogenic gastric achylia. (1) Mean weight of healthy baboons; weights of Zlak (2), Pianch (3), Zefir (4), and Bakhmach (5). Abscissa, date; ordinate, weight (kg); (a) end of experiments with prefeeding and immobilization; (b) transfer of baboons to new living quarters.

red cell count, white cell count, hemoglobin concentration, or erythrocyte sedimentation rate (Table 21, data from M. I. Kuksova, 1956). It is interesting to note the absence of long-term disturbances in composition of the blood in the four baboons tested during gastric achylia, for they all showed marked leukocytosis (white cell count = 25,000–30,000) at the time they were caught and immobilized in the restraint stand early in the experiment (Kuksova, 1956). Despite this neurogenic rise in white cell count during the stressor phase of the experiment, during the long poststressor phase, when the animals showed symptoms of neurogenic gastric achylia, the white cell count fluctuated between 6000–7000 and 10,000–15,000, physiologically normal ranges for this species. Kuksova demonstrated that the leukocytosis seen during the initial immobilization of the baboons was not maintained but underwent extinction. This was contrary to the pattern seen with gastric secretory response, where initial inhibition of secretion under the direct influence of nervous stress persisted and even intensified in the poststressor period. Presumably the repeated combination of immobilization with prefeeding attached a system specificity to secretory function of the stomach that did not apply to the leukocytic reaction.

TABLE 21

Hematological Changes in Hamadryas Baboon Zlak during Neurogenic Gastric Achylia[a]

| Date | Erythrocytes | | Leucocytes | | | | Neutrophils | | | | Hemo-globin (%) | Erythrocyte sedimentation rate |
	Count (×10⁶)	Reticu-locytes (%)	Total (×10³)	Baso-phils	Eosino-phils	Immature forms	Nonseg-mented	Seg-mented	Lympho-cytes	Mono-cytes		
Before onset of achylia												
Aug. 25, 1958	5.35	—	6.650	—	3	—	8	51	34	4	74	2
Dec. 29, 1958	5.79	—	14.400	—	1	—	6	58	34	1	70	1
May 25, 1960	5.63	0.7	11.550	—	5	—	2	33	56	6	92	1
During achylia												
Sep. 30, 1961	6.16	0.5	10.500	—	5	—	1	32	59	3	92	2
Oct. 7, 1961	6.50	0.7	12.100	1	5	—	6	31	51	6	95	2
Oct. 14, 1961	6.30	0.6	7.800	1	1	—	6	36	51	6	90	2
Oct. 28, 1961	5.02	0.3	14.500	1	4	—	2	40	49	4	91	2

Nov. 4, 1961	6.09	0.5	8.200	—	1	3	45	48	3	95	2
Nov. 11, 1961	6.33	0.3	8.100	—	1	3	35	55	7	94	3
Nov. 25, 1961	5.49	—	9.000	—	2	7	47	31	10	98	2
Dec. 9, 1961	5.92	—	13.150	—	4	4	66	21	5	92	5
Dec. 23, 1961	5.28	—	9.250	—	—	—	—	—	—	90	2
Jan. 6, 1962	5.98	—	8.800	—	2	3	57	31	7	94	3
Jan. 20, 1962	6.30	—	12.000	—	—	—	—	—	—	84	3
Feb. 3, 1962	6.51	—	8.300	—	6	5	53	25	11	88	3
Feb. 17, 1962	5.28	—	10.700	—	3	7	45	40	5	78	3
Mar. 3, 1962	5.55	—	8.600	—	4	13	34	42	7	80	3
Mar. 17, 1962	5.90	—	12.600	—	3	6	49	38	4	87	2
Mar. 31, 1962	6.30	—	9.300	—	2	5	56	30	7	89	2
Apr. 14, 1962	6.10	—	11.800	—	—	—	—	—	—	92	5
May 5, 1962	4.86	—	14.600	—	—	—	—	—	—	80	3

[a]Blood samples obtained by ear incision under fasting conditions at the same hour daily. Animal born Dec. 21, 1957; fistula implanted May 5, 1960; onset of achylia Dec., 1960.

The absence of any change in erythrocyte count indicates that neurogenic gastric achylia in baboons, just as in man (Konchalovskii, 1911), does not always signify pernicious anemia. Bussabarger and Ivy (1936) demonstrated that complete removal of the stomach in the rhesus monkey did not induce severe anemia. Our data on baboons with gastric achylia corroborate the etiological independence of this disorder from pernicious anemia.

Investigations of fasting sugar concentration in blood taken by ear incision demonstrated hypoglycemia in all four baboons tested. Blood sugar varied from a clearly hypoglycemic level (50–70 mg %) up to the lower limit of normal (90 mg %). Although the levels fluctuated greatly from experiment to experiment and in the course of the same experiment in a particular subject, the decrease was unmistakable (Figure 36). Although its mechanism is totally unclear and remains a topic for special investigation, the observation is quite in accord with reports in the literature concerning hypoglycemia in humans suffering from gastric achylia (Pospelov & Maslennikov, 1936; Gordon & Zlatopol'skii, 1937).

The chronic hypoglycemia seen in baboons with experimental gastric achylia is also probably nonspecific with regard to the stressor conditions that induced the disorder in function of the gastric secretory apparatus. We found in the prefeeding–immobilization sessions that the blood sugar level increased to as much as 190 mg %. Therefore, the change in blood sugar specific to the stressor condition and emergence of hypoglycemia is evidence for nonspecific symptomatology

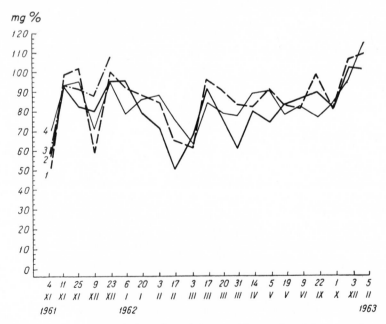

FIG. 36   Blood sugar changes in hamadryas baboons with experimental neurogenic gastric achylia. (1) Pianch; (2) Zlak; (3) Bakhmach; (4) Zefir. Abscissa, date of experiments; ordinate, blood sugar (mg %).

independent of the repeated combinations of eating with activation of defensive mechanisms.

Four therapeutic approaches have been explored with the syndrome of experimental neurogenic gastric achylia in baboons: (1) prevention of the disorder by the administration of various psychotropic agents during the time when the stressor was imposed; (2) administration of neurotropic agents with central and/or peripheral effects in the poststressor period; (3) administration of hydrochloric acid; and (4) removal of the subject from the surroundings in which immobilization neurosis was induced to a new environment.

Earlier in this chapter we presented experimental data showing that elimination of the excitation of defensive neural response mechanisms by the administration of psychotropic agents, such as haloperidol and chlorpromazine, prevented the development of neurogenic gastric achylia. This not only demonstrated a preventive technique for such chronic gastric illness but also showed the significance of the act of eating as a conditioned signal for the defensive dominant.

Neurogenic gastric achylia developed in hamadryas baboons in the first weeks after repeated sessions involving immobilization after prefeeding. With systematic

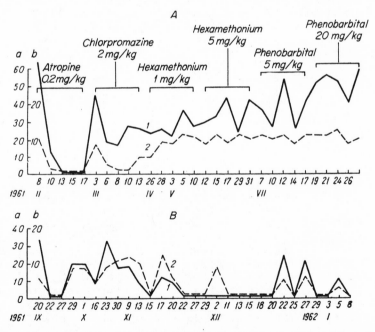

FIG. 37 Changes in zero samples of gastric secretion in Pianch after identical stressor sessions with pretreatment by different neurotropic agents. (A) With administration of different drugs; (B) with no drugs; abscissa, date of experiment; ordinates: (a) free HCl (titration units), (b) digestive strength of gastric juice without HCl supplementation (Mett units); (1) free HCl; (2) digestive strength.

administration of neurotropic agents (atropine, chlorpromazine, hexamethonium, phenobarbital), gastric secretions returned to normal within 6 months (Figure 37A). Repeated stress imposed on the same baboon without subsequent administration of such neurotropic agents led to a syndrome of gastric achylia that did not improve (Figure 37B).

We have had a certain amount of success in treating baboons that had suffered from neurogenic gastric achylia for several months by systematically introducing hydrochloric acid directly into the stomach after eating (Table 22) and by transferring them to new living environments (Table 23). For the present, the results of such treatment can only be taken as an indication of how important a role pathological conditioned interoceptive and exteroceptive reflexes play in the chronic inhibition of gastric secretion in achylia.

TABLE 22
Neurogenic Gastric Achylia in Hamadryas Baboons[a]

Subject	Hour from beginning of session	Volume of secretion (ml)	pH	Free HCl[b]	Total acid[b]	Digestive strength (Mett units)	
						Without added HCl	Control (1 ml secretion + 1 ml 0.36% HCl)
Zefir	0	27.5	4.5	0	29	0	9.0
	1	27.5	5.3	0	28	0	8.0
	2	15.0	6.0	0	30	0	8.5
	3	13.0	6.0	0	32	0	9.5
	4	20.0	7.5	0	30	0	8.5
	5	11.0	7.0	0	31	0	7.0
Zlak	0	5.8 ± 1.0	3.5 ± 0.5	3 ± 3	46 ± 6	1.6 ± 1.0	11.0 ± 2.1
	1	5.0 ± 0.6	4.4 ± 0.9	2 ± 2	29 ± 4	0.6 ± 0.6	6.4 ± 1.2
	2	4.9 ± 0.9	4.9 ± 0.6	2 ± 2	34 ± 3	0.4 ± 0.4	8.4 ± 1.6
	3	3.9 ± 0.3	4.6 ± 0.5	0	31 ± 3	0	7.6 ± 1.1
	4	3.7 ± 0.3	5.4 ± 0.9	2 ± 2	36 ± 4	0.8 ± 0.8	7.8 ± 1.6
	5	3.6 ± 0.6	4.8 ± 0.7	2 ± 2	34 ± 3	1.0 ± 1.0	7.4 ± 1.4
Pianch	0	34.0 ± 5.6	1.0 ± 0.0	31 ± 2	60 ± 7	5.8 ± 1.2	9.7 ± 1.0
	1	19.0 ± 4.9	2.0 ± 0.4	15 ± 6	50 ± 4	2.8 ± 1.3	8.8 ± 1.0
	2	15.0 ± 2.7	2.9 ± 0.9	10 ± 5	42 ± 5	2.2 ± 1.3	7.8 ± 1.0
	3	24.0 ± 6.9	5.3 ± 1.2	1 ± 1	40 ± 3	0.4 ± 0.4	9.8 ± 0.6
	4	25.2 ± 10.2	4.6 ± 1.1	2 ± 2	38 ± 0	0.8 ± 0.8	8.3 ± 1.5
	5	21.8 ± 3.5	4.0 ± 1.0	5 ± 4	38 ± 3	1.2 ± 1.2	7.8 ± 1.1

[a]Gastric secretory function after administration of HCl; under conditions of fasting and free behavior in the home cage.
[b]In titration units.

TABLE 23

Partial Restoration of Gastric Secretions in Hamadryas Baboons with
Neurogenic Gastric Achylia with Transfer to New Living Quarters and
Change of Experimental Surroundings

Subject	Hour from beginning of experiment	Volume of secretion (ml)	pH	Free HCl[a]	Total acid[a]	Digestive strength (Mett units)	
						Without added HCl	Control (1 ml secretion + 1 ml 0.36% HCl)
Zefir	0	5.4 ± 1.0	3.4 ± 0.2	0	50 ± 9	0	9.0 ± 0.5
	1	4.7 ± 0.8	2.8 ± 0.7	10 ± 4	41 ± 4	2.6 ± 1.1	8.4 ± 0.7
	2	4.8 ± 1.8	3.2 ± 0.8	7 ± 4	42 ± 13	2.0 ± 1.3	9.6 ± 0.8
	3	3.6 ± 1.0	2.1 ± 0.6	10 ± 4	35 ± 2	3.5 ± 1.4	9.7 ± 0.2
	4	5.4 ± 1.2	3.2 ± 1.1	9 ± 5	39 ± 8	1.7 ± 1.0	9.5 ± 0.6
	5	3.6 ± 1.1	3.2 ± 1.3	12 ± 9	39 ± 11	2.2 ± 1.6	10.5 ± 0.6
Zlak	0	4.0 ± 0.5	4.7 ± 1.1	6 ± 6	50 ± 6	1.0 ± 1.0	10.4 ± 1.6
	1	4.6 ± 1.6	5.2 ± 0.5	0	36 ± 2	0	9.4 ± 1.5
	2	3.4 ± 0.4	4.8 ± 0.6	0	39 ± 6	0	10.0 ± 0.8
	3	3.7 ± 0.8	4.8 ± 0.6	0	36 ± 3	0	10.8 ± 1.4
	4	3.1 ± 0.2	5.2 ± 0.7	0	32 ± 5	0	10.0 ± 0.7
	5	3.1 ± 0.2	5.7 ± 0.8	3 ± 3	39 ± 7	0.8 ± 0.8	10.4 ± 1.2
Pianch	0	30.0 ± 7.7	1.0 ± 0.0	26 ± 6	60 ± 9	7.0 ± 1.3	12.8 ± 1.1
	1	17.4 ± 1.9	1.0 ± 0.0	29 ± 3	60 ± 4	7.4 ± 0.5	12.2 ± 1.1
	2	11.0 ± 2.6	1.0 ± 0.0	24 ± 3	57 ± 4	7.8 ± 0.9	12.8 ± .07
	3	14.8 ± 2.6	1.0 ± 0.0	20 ± 4	50 ± 3	6.2 ± 1.1	11.6 ± 0.7
	4	16.2 ± 2.6	1.2 ± 0.2	19 ± 2	49 ± 3	6.2 ± 1.1	12.4 ± 0.8
	5	17.4 ± 2.8	1.5 ± 0.4	18 ± 4	49 ± 3	4.4 ± 1.5	13.0 ± 1.1

[a]In titration units.

The experimental model of neurogenic gastric achylia that we have established in hamadryas baboons represents the first methodological attempt to move the study of the etiology and pathogenesis of this widespread human disease to a new plane. Naturally, this short exposition of the experimental disorder in baboons leaves many questions unresolved. The complexity of this syndrome, as of neurogenic illness in general, demands further investigation by a variety of approaches. We hope that the experimental modeling of gastric disease in animals closely related to man can arouse the interest of physiologists, pathophysiologists, and physicians in the mechanisms whereby gastric achylia develops and is maintained for many years in human patients. The causes of many human illnesses are rooted in the living environment of the patient, in the effects of everyday stimuli activating different functional systems of the organism.

IV
Precancerous Gastric Lesions

One of the most clearcut and constant findings in the chronic neurogenic gastric achylia of hamadryas baboons is the formation of adenomatous polyps, principally in the pyloric antral area and along the transition zone to the body of the stomach.

PRECANCEROUS GASTRIC LESIONS IN MAN

In the opinion of many clinicians, achylia of many years duration is a relatively high-risk indicator for precancerous lesions of the stomach. An even higher risk indicator is gastric polyposis. This is explained by the great tendency of adenomatous gastric polyps to become malignant. Data regarding the frequency of malignancy in gastric polyps in man are presented in Tables 24 and 25.

In 70–85% of cases, polyps are located in the pyloric antral area (Fanardzhian & Danielian, 1961; Ziabbarov, 1961). Cancer of the stomach also occurs most frequently in this area, i.e., in 50–70% of cases (Sokolov & Petrov, 1961; Shevchenko, 1965).

As a rule, free hydrochloric acid is absent from the gastric juice of patients with gastric polyposis, or with malignant polyps and gastric ulcers. At the same

TABLE 24
Malignancy of Gastric Polyps in Man

Study	Frequency of malignancy (%)
Mel'nikov and Timofeev (1950)	40–60
Shevchenko (1955, 1965)	40–60
Bzynko (1955)	50
Elanskii (1963)	24
Arapov and Suslov (1963)	30

TABLE 25
Frequency of Different Stages of Polyp Development as Demonstrated by
Histochemical Techniques (Lisochkin, 1966)

Stage	Defining characteristic	No. of cases	Proportion of total cases (%)
I	Adenomatous polyps	113	54.4
II	Proliferative polyposis	14	6.4
III	Noninvasive carcinomatous polyps	5	2.4
IV	Invasive carcinomatous polyps	74	35.6
V	Advanced carinoma associated with polyposis	2	0.9
	Total:	208	100.0

time, however, the parietal cells of the fundus remain morphologically intact; i.e., the morphological substrate for hydrochloric acid secretion is not atrophied (Iudkovskaia, 1960; Lisochkin, 1966; and others).

Experiments in which neoplastic processes are induced or potentiated by the chronic application of various agents and other experimental conditions have special relevance for the problem of the pathogenesis of precancerous lesions.

ROLE OF THE NERVOUS SYSTEM IN TUMOROGENESIS

As early as 1910, the well-known Russian clinician G. A. Zakhar'in pointed out that "the two main signs that go along with cancer are old age and grief." He was convinced that "the percentage of cancer due to grief is as great as the percentage of marasmus due to syphilis."

It is to the great honor of Russian physiologists that they were responsible for elucidating the influence of disordered brain function on the development of neoplasms. It is no accident that the first work concerning the influence of chronic disturbances of higher nervous activity on the development of tumors came out of the laboratories of I. P. Pavlov.

The experimental induction of neoplasms in dogs was, at first, not a goal in itself but a serendipitous observation.

M. K. Petrova (1946), the colleague of Pavlov who initiated and carried through the most extensive investigations, systematically subjected seven dogs to neurogenic stressors and observed the development of a variety of benign and malignant tumors at different times after the onset of stress. The results, summarized in Table 26, were compared with those from dogs not subjected to neurogenic stress.

The same author conducted another experiment combining a carcinogenic agent (gaseous coal tar applied to the skin) with neurogenic stress, which functionally weakened the cerebral cortex and produced neurosis. For 2 years

TABLE 26
Development of Neoplasms in Dogs with Experimental Neurosis (Petrova, 1946)[a]

Subject	Age at death (years)	Type of neoplasm	Accompanying dystrophic signs
1	14	Cancer of the urinary bladder and lungs	
2	15	Papilloma of the skin; fibroma of the right kidney	Eczema
3	9–13	Papilloma about 4 cm in diameter on the skin of the back; fibroma of the upper gums (last 6 years before death); sarcoma near the left ear, the size of an apple (for 1.5 years to death); hypernephroma of the liver	Nonhealing ulcers on the skin of the back; eczema
4	?	Dense nodular tumors under the skin of the abdomen	Eczema
5	?	Thyroid carcinoma infiltrating adjacent tissues, adherent to the skin; metastasis to the liver, right lung, spleen and left kidney	Loss of hair; furunculosis; skin ulcerations
6	13	Papillomata on the skin of the head and trunk; dense tumor on the digits of the paw; adenoma of the urinary bladder	Nonhealing ulcers on the skin of the left shin and haunch

[a]Four control subjects observed to the 9–13th year of age did not show any of the dystrophic changes in skin or internal organs observed in the six experimental subjects described here.

coal tar was applied daily to a 10 × 10 cm area on the back of nine dogs (1–2 years old at beginning of experiment). Four of the dogs, the experimental animals, were subjected to experimental neurosis after the first year, whereas the other five, the control animals, did not undergo neurogenic stress. The stressed dogs showed papillomatosis at the site of chronic irritation. In addition, one of them developed a tumor near the parotid gland and another developed a sarcoma of the urinary bladder with metastasis to the kidneys, liver, intestine, and spleen. The control dogs developed papillomata at the site of coal tar application, but the lesions were only transient, subsequently disappearing without a trace.

Petrova's findings regarding the significance of functional disturbances of the nervous system in tumorogenesis were corroborated and developed further by

TABLE 27
Influence of Decerebration on the Development of Chicken Sarcoma in
Pigeons (Kavetskii, 1955)

Group	Number of subjects	Number with tumors	Number without tumors
Decerebrate	21	17	4
Control	31	1	30

other investigators. For example, A. P. Kalinin (1956), studying experimental neurosis in cats, demonstrated (in four of nine subjects) both gross and microscopic evidence of ulcers and polyps in the pyloric antrum of the stomach. In his study neurosis was induced by clashing alimentary and defensive response mechanisms using electroshock as the noxious stumulus.

The role of the cerebral cortex in the development of neoplasms was also substantiated in the work of R. R. Kavetskii (1955). Decortication in pigeons led to the loss of resistance to the development of tumors characteristic of fowl (Table 27).

Experimental material accumulated in the Soviet literature attests to the fact that disturbance of the functional state of the cerebral cortex by different means can accelerate the induction of benign and malignant neoplasms and induce "spontaneous" tumors as well. It is important to note, however, that current trends in oncological research give little place to the role of central nervous disturbances in affecting neoplastic processes.

SPONTANEOUS GASTRIC TUMORS IN BABOONS AND MONKEYS

The question of "spontaneous" tumors occurring in lower primates living in captivity has been dealt with in a number of works, both Soviet and foreign. According to Kent (1960) the world literature, up to the time of his writing, included descriptions of about 50 cases of malignant neoplasm in monkeys. Among these, 15 involved the alimentary tract. Carcinomas of the stomach had been reported in two baboons (Table 28). Benign gastric tumors were observed in monkeys with much greater frequency (Table 29). Among these were two cases of spontaneous gastric polyps in hamadryas baboons. Vadova and Gel'shtein (1960) reported gastric polyps in the pyloric area in only one of 256 hamadryas baboons autopsied.

Experimentally induced gastric tumors in baboons have not been reported previously and as a result the impression has arisen that, in contrast to man, the lower primates seldom develop gastric polyps. There is all the more reason, therefore, that our experiments, in which adenomatous proliferation of the gastric mucous membrane was found in almost all of the baboons subjected to

TABLE 28
Frequency of Spontaneous Gastric Tumors in Monkeys

Study	Number of animals autopsied	Frequency of tumors detected (%)
Zuckerman (1930)	530	0.19
Ratcliffe (1933)	971	0.10
Vadova and Gel'shtein (1956)	660	0.60
Lapin and Iakovleva (1960)	1179	0.34

experimental neurogenic gastric achylia, should attract the attention of investigators interested in tumors of the gastrointestinal tract.

DYSTROPHIC CHANGES OF THE GASTRIC MUCOSA IN NEUROGENIC GASTRIC ACHYLIA

Disturbance of pepsin formation accompanies and probably precedes adenomatous proliferation of the gastric mucosa in hamadryas baboons suffering from neurogenic gastric achylia. A number of investigators have studied decreases in the enzyme content of gastrointestinal secretions as indicators of dystrophic processes and as forerunners of degenerative changes in the glands of the gastrointestinal tract.

In our work the peptic activity of gastric juice was studied as an indicator of neurogenic functional disturbance of the gastric glands. We adopted Mett's optimal acidity method for determining the digestive activity of the secretions (1 cm^3 gastric juice with 30–60 titration units of free hydrochloric acid). Immobilization itself induces a marked decrease in the secretion of pepsin. Preliminary blockade of central nervous impulses by the use of the ganglionic blocking agent hexamethonium (1 mg/kg, subcutaneously) prevents this inhibition of pepsin formation for the entire period of immobilization (Figure 38). S. V. Anichkov and colleagues have demonstrated a corresponding normalizing effect of ganglionic blocking agents on the synthesis of protein in the gastric mucosa under conditions of pathologically intense neural influences from the central nervous system (Anichkov & Zavodskaia, 1965). The results of our experiments on baboons confirm their findings.

Chronic neurogenic gastric achylia in hamadryas baboons is sometimes accompanied by total apepsia, but hypopepsia is the more common finding. The digestive strength of gastric secretions is usually 5–7 Mett units rather than the normal 12–13 Mett units. The average peptic activity under various conditions is

TABLE 29
Spontaneous Benign Gastric Tumors in Baboons and Monkeys

Species	No. of cases	Ages	Description	Location	Study
Papio hamadryas	1	27 months	Papillary adenoma	–	Fox (1923)
Macaca mulatta	1	–	Adenoma	Anterior wall of the pyloric area	Hamerton (1930)
Macaca fascicularis	6	young	Papillomatous formations	Border of body and antral areas	Bonne and Sandground (1939)
Macaca mulatta	2	young	Polypoid growths	–	Lushbaugh (1947)
Papio hamadryas	1	4 years	Gastric polyp	Pyloric area	Vadova and Gel'shtein (1956)
Macaca mulatta	1	4 years	Multiple polyps, tubular adenoma	Entire surface of gastric mucosa	Vadova and Gel'shtein (1956)
Macaca nemestrina	1	4 years	Multiple polyps	Pyloric area	Vadova and Gel'shtein (1956)
Macaca mulatta	1	4 years	Tubular adenoma	Cardiac area	Vadova and Gel'shtein (1956)
Macaca mulatta	1	3.5 years	Multiple papillomata	Pyloric area	Kent and Pickering (1958)
Macaca mulatta	2	6 and 19 years	Tubular polyp	Fundal area	Lapin and Iakovleva (1960)
Macaca mulatta	2	young	Tubular polyp	Body and fundus	Lapin and Iakovleva (1960)

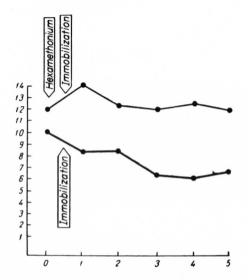

FIG. 38 Profound decrease in peptic activity of gastric juice from a Hamadryas baboon under conditions of fasting and immobilization and the preventive effect of hexamethonium (1 mg/kg, subcutaneous, 10 min before immobilization). Averages of five sessions. Abscissa, hour of session; ordinate, digestive strength (Mett units; 1 ml 0.36% HCl added to 1 ml of secretion).

presented in Figure 32. Column I represents pepsin content under normal conditions; columns II, IV, and VI show the effects of immobilization stress; and columns III, V, and VII show the normalizing effects of atropine, chlorpromazine, and hexamethonium, respectively. Because the neurotropic agents were introduced once a day after the zero sample of gastric juice was obtained and a total of five such sessions were conducted at 1- to 2-day intervals, the increase of peptic activity in the zero samples was presumed to have resulted from the indirect influence of these agents on the synthesis of enzyme in the chief cells of the stomach. To understand the normalizing influence of a drug administered 1 or 2 days earlier, one must assume that it has blocked the pathological central neural influences acting on the gastric glandular mechanisms for a prolonged period of time. During nocturnal sleep (Figure 32, VIII), when the pathological conditioned exteroceptive reflexes are inhibited, secretion of pepsin in baboons with neurogenic gastric achylia is also increased almost to normal levels. In one of the baboons the gastric juice eventually returned to normal. Both the enzyme content and the secretion of hydrochloric acid returned to a normal level.

These experiments demonstrated that (1) a CNS-mediated suppression of pepsin formation occurs in neurogenic gastric achylia; (2) by the use of pharmacological agents, one can obtain a sustained synthesis of enzyme by the chief cells of the stomach; (3) neurotropic agents, which usually are considered to suppress gastric secretion and which actually do inhibit it under normal conditions, have a normalizing influence on pepsin formation under conditions of neurogenic achylia; and (4) one can conjecture that the normalizing effects of atropine and hexamethonium on enzyme synthesis in neurogenic gastric achylia result from the blocking of efferent neural influences on the gastric glands, whereas those of chlorpromazine and sleep result from the disengaging or weakening of exteroceptive afferent influences on the alimentary centers of the brain.

The view that the suppression of pepsin formation in baboons with neurogenic gastric achylia is neurally mediated is further substantiated by comparing the peptic activity of secretions in the stomach with that of secretions in a Heidenhain pouch. In an experiment where this was done, the peptic activity of gastric juice from the stomach (with its connections to the central nervous system intact) was 1–2 Mett units; at the same time peptic activity in secretions from the pouch (with the vagi severed) was 12 Mett units (Figure 39). This observation, together with the previously noted restorative influence of atropine on pepsin secretion in baboons with achylia, leads us to conclude that the vagus nerve participates in chronic suppression of gastric juice secretion, at least insofar as pepsin formation is concerned. Moreover, these data demonstrate clearly that the suppression is neurally mediated and not a local or hormonally mediated inhibition of enzyme synthesis.

To illustrate the physiological significance of the degree of suppression of pepsin secretion seen in baboons with neurogenic gastric achylia Figure 40 presents the digestive strength of normal gastric juice in various dilutions; the acidity has been maintained at an optimal level for all determinations. It was evident that a digestive strength of 5–7 Mett units was recorded at a dilution of 64–256 times, whereas a digestive strength of 1–2 Mett units was obtained at dilutions of 1024 times. The reduction of digestive strength to 2–7 mm seen in baboons with achylia therefore represents an effective decrease in peptic activity by ten or even 100 times.

Because the peptic activity has been determined under conditions of optimal and constant acidity it can be readily noted that, whereas the gastric secretions

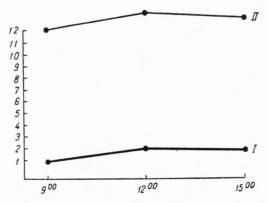

FIG. 39 Peptic activity of gastric secretions obtained from the main stomach (I) and the Heidenhain isolated pouch (II) in the baboon Vik with "spontaneous gastric achylia." Averages of ten sessions. Abscissa, hour of session; ordinate, peptic activity (Mett units; 1 ml 0.36% HCl added to 1 ml of secretion).

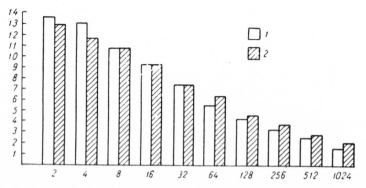

FIG. 40 Differences in digestive strength of gastric secretion in normal hamadryas baboons at different dilutions with acidity held constant and optimal. Abscissa, dilution; ordinate, peptic activity (Mett units). (1) Liquid portion of gastric secretion; (2) sediment of gastric secretion after standing 5 hr. Each column represents average of 28 samples.

of healthy hamadryas baboons show continuously intense digestive strength over long periods of time, those of baboons with neurogenic gastric achylia show marked fluctuations from session to session. It is possible that in gastric achylia one of the main properties of pepsin changes, viz., the ability of its proenzyme, pepsinogen, to be activated by hydrochloric acid (Figure 41). The reduction and variability of peptic activity seen in chronic neurogenic gastric achylia in baboons is similar to the findings of many authors that, with the development of cancer, one observes both a reduction, or a disappearance, of several specific proteins and changes in enzymatic activity (Kheddou, 1963).

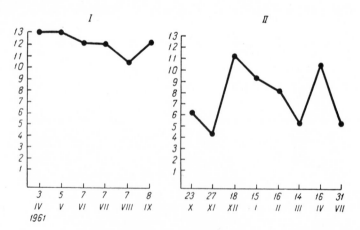

FIG. 41 Comparison of peptic activity of zero samples of gastric juice from the hamadryas baboon Zefir in the prestressor period (I) and during neurogenic gastric achylia (II). Abscissa, date of session; ordinate, digestive strength of gastric secretion (Mett units; 0.36% HCl added to 1 ml of secretion).

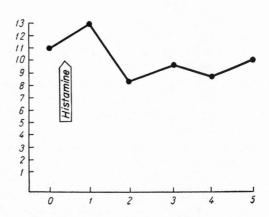

FIG. 42 Short-term stimulatory effect followed by prolonged suppressant effect of histamine on pepsin formation in a hamadryas baboon with neurogenic gastric achylia. Each point represents average of five experimental sessions. Abscissa, hour of session; ordinate, digestive strength (Mett units; 1 ml of 0.36% HCl added to 1 ml of secretion).

In some of the baboons with neurogenic gastric achylia, histamine, the direct stimulant of gastric gland secretion, failed to increase peptic activity of gastric secretion and, in fact, decreased it (Figure 42). The transient stimulatory effect of histamine during the first hour was followed by an inhibition of pepsin formation lasting for many hours. We obtained a similar result earlier in normal baboons when histamine was administered during negative emotional excitation elicited by the gastric probing procedure. Whereas the probing alone inhibited hydrochloric acid secretion, it did not depress the peptic activity of secretions. The joint effect of probing and histamine, however, was a profound decrease in peptic activity (Figure 43). Under conditions of chronic or acute inhibition of

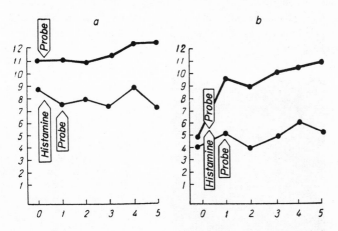

FIG. 43 Suppressant effect of histamine on pepsin formation in hamadryas baboons Pianch (a) and Zlak (b) during negative emotional excitation induced by the 10-min gastric probing procedure. Each point represents average of five sessions. Abscissa, hour of session; ordinate, peptic activity of gastric secretion (Mett units; 1 ml of 0.36% HCl added to 1 ml of secretion).

the gastric glands by the central nervous system, therefore, the reaction to the direct humoral stimulus of gastric secretion is distorted.

All of these findings point to a disturbance of pepsin synthesis in neurogenic gastric achylia. Furthermore, they indicate the central neural nature of this disturbance, which must be classified among the neural dystrophies. The disturbance takes on an even more clearcut form when it progresses to hyperplasia of the glandular epithelium of the gastric mucosa. The appearance of adenomatous polyps or of chronic ulcers in combination with adenomata becomes direct evidence for the development of precancerous lesions of the stomach.

ADENOMATOUS POLYPS IN EXPERIMENTAL NEUROGENIC GASTRIC ACHYLIA

The first signs of hyperplasia of the gastric glandular epithelium in hamadryas baboons with neurogenic gastric achylia were seen in the area of the gastric fistula. Massive glandular proliferation led eventually to evulsion of the fistula from the stomach and tamponade of the fistular opening (Figure 44). Testing of the secretions from these glandular proliferations revealed pepsin with an activity level of 4–5 Mett units, and morphological analysis revealed polypsis. Extrusion of the fistula from the stomach occurred in seven baboons. In three of these, Pianch, Zlak, and Zefir, the fistulas were established, evulsed, and replaced three times, and each time they were rejected again within 5 or 6 months. The presence of a fistula in the stomach was not necessary for the development of glandular hyperplasia, however. Four of the nine baboons in which neurogenic achylia was produced did not have fistulas implanted; yet they too developed hyperplasia following exposure to repeated prefeeding–immobilization sessions.

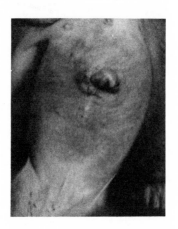

FIG. 44 Massive hyperplasia of the gastric mucous membrane around the gastric fistula as seen after evulsion of the fistula and plugging of the opening (baboon Azov).

Interestingly enough, the control animals in our studies, i.e., those with gastric fistulas which were not subjected to prefeeding–immobilization stress, were observed to secrete normal gastric juice for prolonged periods of time (6–16 months) without any signs of dislodgement of the fistula. [Figures 45 and 46 show normal gastric mucosa from two healthy baboons, Lazurnik (no fistula) and Antep (with fistula)].

In the baboons with gastric achylia, hyperplasia began to develop around the fistula within the first 2 or 3 months after the onset of achylia. Furthermore, autopsies on baboons with neurogenic gastric achylia that were sacrificed or that died in the course of the study revealed similar gastric lesions, often far from the site of the fistula (Figure 47). This finding, plus the fact that such changes were found in animals without fistulas, makes it unlikely that the polyposis was a result of the fistula on the gastric mucous membrane (Figures 48 and 49).

A summary of the data on benign tumors of the stomach in hamadryas baboons with neurogenic gastric achylia is presented in Table 30. In all nine of the baboons the tumors consisted of adenomatous polyps of different shapes

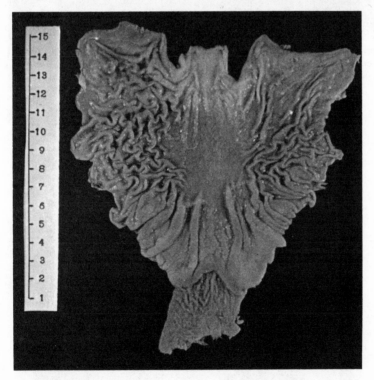

FIG. 45 Normal gastric mucosa from the healthy hamadryas baboon Lazurnik, sacrificed at $3\frac{1}{2}$ years of age (scale in centimeters).

FIG. 46 Normal gastric mucosa from the healthy baboon Antep with a fistula located at the most common site of implantation, in the anterior wall of the greater curvature of the stomach.

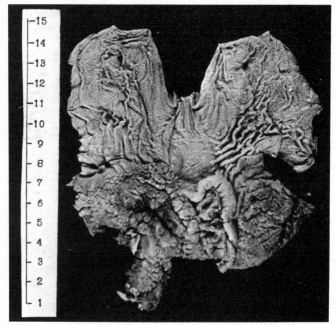

FIG. 47 Macroscopic gastric specimen from the hamadryas baboon Bakhmach who died 4 months after the onset of stressor sessions and 18 days after the onset of neurogenic gastric achylia. Note adenomatosis with two chronic ulcers in the pyloric antrum; the adenomatosis encroaches on the proximal portion of the body of the stomach.

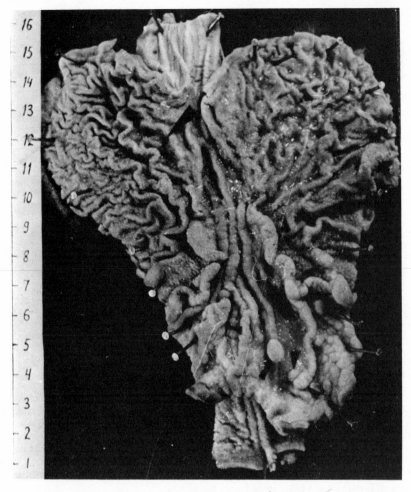

FIG. 48 Polyposis in the pyloric antrum of the stomach in Antil during chronic, experimentally induced neurogenic gastric achylia; this animal had no fistula.

and sizes (Fig. 50a–g). In a number of cases the same gastric specimen was found to contain polyps of different shapes and sizes, ranging from adenomatous changes in the gastric folds to polyps on pedicles and broad based adenomata. As a rule the polyps were multiple and were located in the pyloric antrum and in the intermediate zone of the body of the stomach. In several cases adenomatosis or polyposis occupied the whole surface of the antrum (Figures 47, 48, and 49). Less frequently, individual polyps were found in the fundus of the stomach (Figure 48).

In two animals (Bakhmach and Kleshchevina) adenomatosis occurred together with anacidity and chronic ulcers (Figures 47 and 50g). In Figure 50g, the base

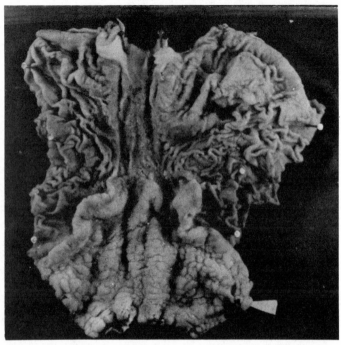

FIG. 49 Polyposis of pyloric antrum of the stomach in the baboon Izmail. This animal was exposed to food for long periods of time while in the restraint stand. He had no fistula.

of the ulcer is seen to consist of connective tissue; its smooth margin is eroded and covered over by adenomatous proliferation.

A summary of the histological findings is presented in Table 31. (This work was carried out in collaboration with M. T. Ivanov). The microscopic structure of the gastric mucosa in healthy hamadryas baboons was found to be not unlike that in healthy man (Figure 51).

Sometimes the polyps assumed the appearance of cystoadenomas (Figure 52). Regardless of their locations in various regions of the stomach the polyps and adenomatous growths were microscopically similar in structure. In addition to the tumors protruding into the lumen of the stomach (polyps and adenomas), areas of pylorization of the gastric glands were found in the body and the fundus. Here, as in the polyps, there occurred multiple cystically dilated glandular tubules and cystic nodules of various shapes and sizes lined with a single layer of undifferentiated, simple cuboidal, or columnar epithelium. In examining polyps microscopically one characteristically found that beneath the glandular tissue, which was composed primarily of undifferentiated epithelium (Figure 53), the pedicle was derived from a glandular ruga and contained parietal and chief cells of normal structure (Figure 54). Although most of the polyps were derived from glandular epithelium, some showed traces of fibrosis both

(text continues on page 121)

TABLE 30

Experimentally Induced Benign Tumors of the Stomach in Hamadryas Baboons With Neurogenic Gastric Achylia

Subject	Age at death	Time from beginning of stressor sessions	Type of tumor	Location
Larn (no fistula)	5 years	5 months	Adenomatosis	—
Antil (no fistula)	6 years, 4 months	1 year, 7 months	Polyposis	Pyloric antrum
Izmail (no fistula)	5 years	2 years, 7 months	Polyposis	Fundus, pyloric antrum
Kovboi (no fistula)	3 years, 4 months	10 months	Polyposis	Antrum
Pianch (fistula)	10 years	6 years, 8 months	Adenomatosis; single polyp	Pyloric antrum
Zefir (fistula)	4 years	9 months	Polyposis	Transition zone between body and antrum
Bakhmach (fistula)	3 years, 6 months	3.5 months	Adenomatosis; two chronic ulcers	Pyloric antrum
Kleshchevina (fistula)	6 years	1 year	Adenomatosis; chronic ulcer	Pyloric antrum
Lakmus (fistula)	3 years, 4 months	2.5 months	Adenomatosis	Pyloric antrum

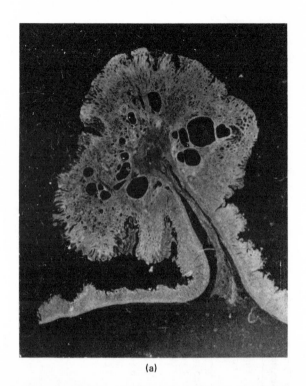

(a)

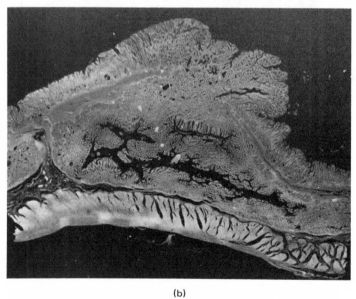

(b)

FIG. 50a and b (caption on page 118)

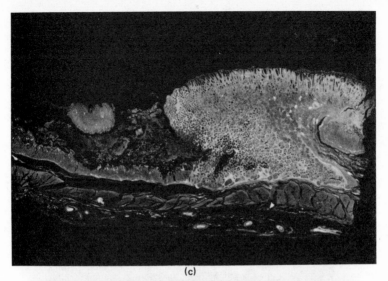

(c)

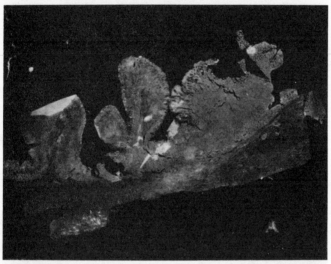

(d)

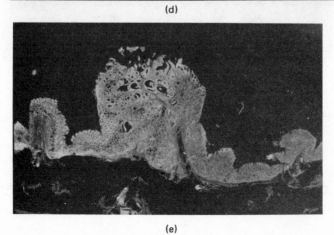

(e)

FIG. 50c, d, and e (caption on page 118)

(f)

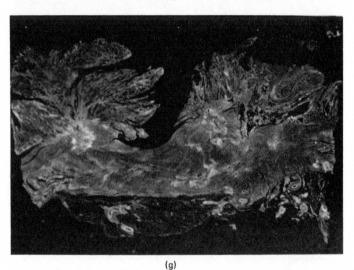

(g)

FIG. 50 f and g

FIG. 50 Different forms of adenomatous polyp in hamadryas baboons suffering from neurogenic gastric achylia. (a) Polyp on a pedicle from the intermediate zone (baboon Antil); (b) adenomatous polyp from the pyloric region (baboon Antil); (c) adenomatous polyp from the body of the stomach at its border with the intermediate zone in the lesser curvature (baboon Zagreb); (d) adenomatous polyp from the body of the stomach in the vicinity of the intermediate zone (biopsy from baboon Zefir); (e) adenomatous polyp from the fundus (baboon Izmail); (f) polyp and fold of polyposis from the pyloric antrum (baboon Kovboi); and (g) adenomatosis and ulcer from the pyloric antrum (baboon Bakhmach).

118

TABLE 31

General Characteristics of Adenomatous Polyps in Hamadryas Baboons with
Experimental Neurogenic Gastric Achylia

1. Large and small areas of pylorization in the regions ordinarily occupied
   by chief cell glands, i.e., lower portion of the fundus and, less often,
   body of the stomach.
2. Similar adenomatous polyps in the fundus, body and pyloric antrum.
3. Adenomatous polyposis covering the gastric rugae; pedunculated polyps;
   papillomatosis, and cystoadenomata.
4. Cystic dilatation of the glands and cystic nodules lined with a single
   layer of undifferentiated epithelium in polyps; areas of pylorization.
5. Brunnerization in adenomatous polyps in the pyloric antrum.
6. Fibrosis both within and on the surface of adenomatous polyps and in the
   areas of pylorization of the gastric glands.
7. Invasion of the submucosa by glandular formations at the base of adenomatous
   polyps.
8. Gross structural deformity.
9. Cellular dystrophy.
10. Proliferation of undifferentiated and, less frequently, of functional
    epithelium in adenomatous polyps.
11. Combination of adenomatosis and chronic ulcers.
12. Metaplasia of the glandular epithelium into different kinds of entodermal
    epithelium (enterolization, pylorization, Brunnerization); squamous cell
    metaplasia in polyps.
13. Combination of adenomatosis and polyposis with morphologically normal
    structure of the gastric glands.

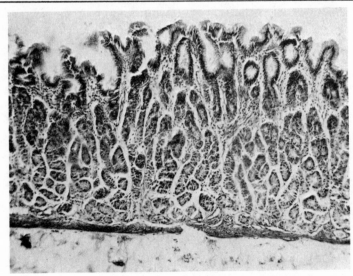

FIG. 51 Normal mucous membrane from the body of the stomach of hamadryas baboon
Takla. (Biopsy of mucosa obtained at the time the gastric fistula was implanted.) Stain: Van
Gieson; magnification: gamal' 2 × 10.

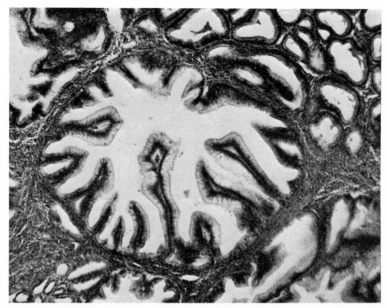

FIG. 52 Micropolyps (cystoadenomas) in the glandular portion of the polyp shown in Fig. 50b. Magnification: gamal' 2 × 8.

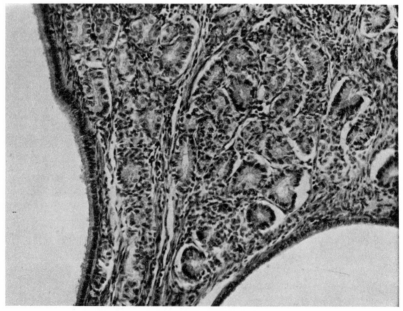

FIG. 53 Micrograph of glandular tissue from the tip of the polyp shown in Fig. 50a. Isolated parietal cells appear in otherwise undifferentiated epithelium and compacted glandular cells line cavities within the polyp. Magnification: gamal' 2 × 20.

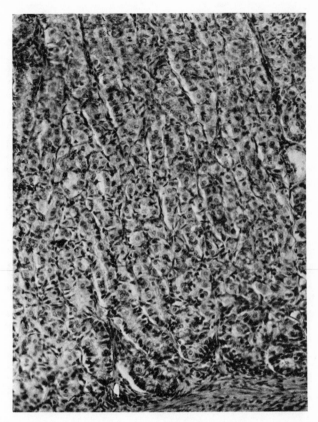

FIG. 54 Micrograph of a portion of mucous membrane at the base of the polyp shown in Fig. 50a. Hyperplasia of parietal cell origin is evident. Magnification: gamal' 2 × 20.

internally and on the surface (Figure 55). Fibrosis was also found in areas where pylorization of the gastric glands had occurred. For the most part, hyperplasia of the undifferentiated epithelium accounted for the development of adenomatous polyps, although sometimes marked hyperplasia of parietal and chief cell origin was seen as well (Figure 56). Squamous cell metaplasia was noted in one case (Figure 57). Often, one found glandular invasion of the submucosa at the base of a polyp, particularly in solitary follicles (Figure 58). These histological characteristics of the adenomatous polyps found in baboons are quite similar to benign tumors of the stomach seen in man (Lisochkin, 1966).

In all of the baboons studied, therefore, experimental neurogenic gastric achylia involved anacidity and was accompanied by polyposis and/or chronic ulcers developing over periods of many months. The combination of functional disorders of gastric secretion and pathological morphology in the form of adenomatous polyps is not inconsistent with a functional etiology. Despite the

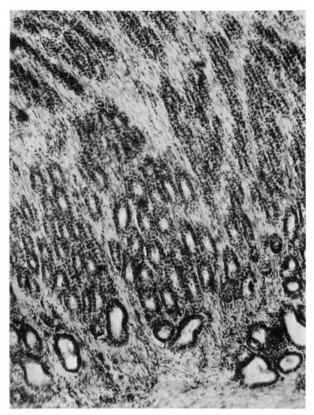

FIG. 55   Fibrosis at the base of an adenomatous polyp from the pyloric antral region of the stomach. Magnification: gamal' 2 × 10.

polyposis there remained in the gastric mucosa many gastric glands that were morphologically normal and capable of secreting hydrochloric acid and pepsin. It would therefore appear that the main reason for deficient secretion of hydrochloric acid and pepsin was not atrophy of the glands, but a functional inhibition of their activity. Apparently, morphological derangements in the form of adenomatous polyps can also occur as a result of the neural dysfunction that produces prolonged disturbances of gastric secretion.

It is possible that the glandular hyperplasia observed in the pyloric antrum in all cases and the pylorization of the gastric glands in several animals represented compensatory changes characteristic of neurogenic gastric achylia. Under conditions of chronic CNS inhibition of the parietal and chief cells of the fundus and body of the stomach (i.e., elimination of the first phase of gastric secretion), compensatory proliferation of glandular epithelium in the pyloric region takes place, enhancing the gastrin, humoral phase of gastric secretion. Under condi-

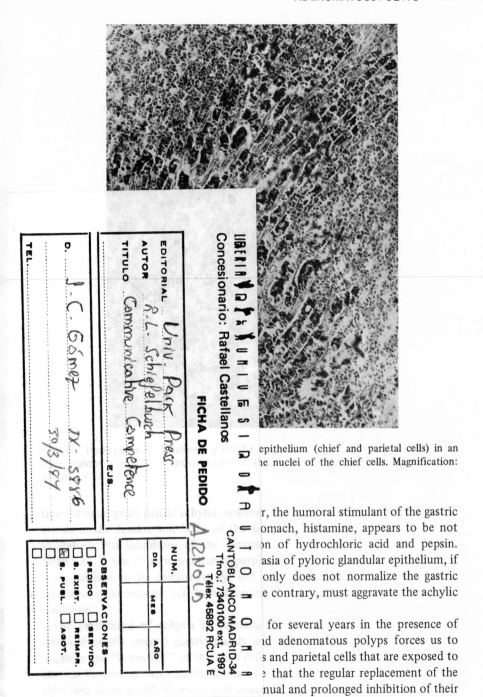

epithelium (chief and parietal cells) in an ... he nuclei of the chief cells. Magnification:

... r, the humoral stimulant of the gastric ... omach, histamine, appears to be not ... on of hydrochloric acid and pepsin. ... asia of pyloric glandular epithelium, if ... only does not normalize the gastric ... e contrary, must aggravate the achylic

... for several years in the presence of ... d adenomatous polyps forces us to ... s and parietal cells that are exposed to ... e that the regular replacement of the ... nual and prolonged inhibition of their

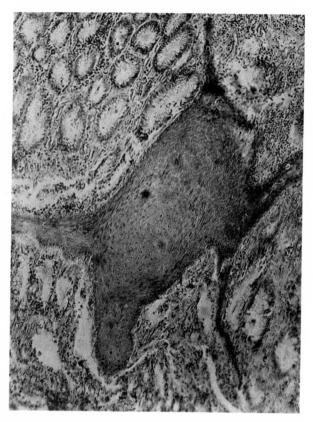

FIG. 57 Squamous cell metaplasia in an adenomatous polyp from the pyloric region of the stomach. Magnification: gamal' 2 X 10.

functions eventually leads to the emergence of cells of similar appearance, but with altered functional properties. The differentiation of functional elements in the gastric glands observed in baboons with neurogenic gastric achylia may be the result of gradual reorganization of the hereditary characteristics of the chief cells and parietal cells. This neurally mediated dystrophic influence, maintained by the CNS on the glandular elements for months or years and reinforced by hereditary selection, would eventually lead to the replacement of cells with normal functional properties by cells with the characteristics distinctive of tumor development. This hypothesis is consistent with the opinions and research findings of authors who have studied the preliminary phases of neoplasia. It is also supported by data regarding changes in the hereditary apparatus of the cell during carcinogenesis (Neiman, 1963; Kheddou, 1963; Khorsfol, 1963; Oilert, 1963).

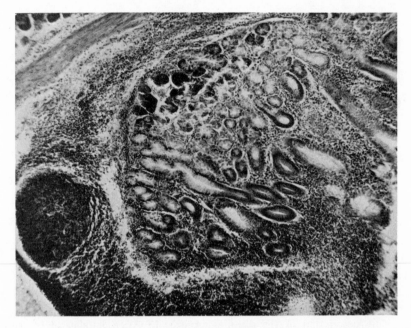

FIG. 58 Invasion of glandular structures into a solitary follicle in adenomatosis of the stomach. Magnification: gamal' 2 X 10.

Our observations on the development of gastric adenomatosis and polyposis in hamadryas baboons with experimental neurogenic gastric achylia both demonstrate the influence of the central nervous system on neoplastic processes in the stomach and provide future investigators with a highly reliable and relatively easily and quickly established model of precancerous lesions similar to those seen in man.

V
Functional Hyperkinesis and Paralysis in Hamadryas Baboons

Hysteria is one of the illnesses that man has recognized since ancient times. In 1827, Georget first suggested that it was a cerebral disorder, psychological in nature (Dotsenko & Pervomaiskii, 1964). In 1868, Charcot gave the classic scientific description of the disorder (Andre, 1898). A number of the early neuropathologists in this country considered hysteria to be a form of human neurosis (Bulatov & Stepanov, 1912; Dzerzhinskii, 1921; Astvatsaturov, 1927), and this view won general recognition in neuropathology and psychiatry with the work of I. P. Pavlov.

A major component in the extremely diverse symptomatology of hysteria is some form of motor disturbance. It may include hyperkinetic symptoms, such as convulsive fits, tremors, contractures, impairments of gait and posture, rapid muscular fatigue, paresis or paralysis, hysterical spasms, or paralysis of the smooth musculature of internal organs. According to E. Kretschmer (1960), the onset of any hysterical motor disorder is generally preceded by a period of "motor storm," which appears biologically to be nothing more nor less than an intense defensive reaction. Many authors emphasize the contributory roles of muscular tension, physical overexertion, and fatigue in conjunction with negative emotions (fear, pain, aversion, sorrow) in generating hysterical attacks (Astvatsaturov, 1927; Davidenkov, 1956; Kreindler, 1963).

As in other neuroses, the primary question in hysteria has to do with the mechanism that maintains the disorder in chronic form. The most widely accepted view has been that suggestion and autosuggestion are major factors (Andre, 1898; Babinsky, 1909; Khodos, 1948; Sepp, Tsuker, & Schmidt, 1954; and others). There is a risk in absolute adherence to this point of view, namely that everything not called "suggestion" or yielding to treatment by suggestion is referred back to the realm of organic pathology. The crux of the problem remains well concealed because acceptance of suggestion as the basic and unique cause of hysteria raises an impenetrable obstacle to the establishment in animals of an experimental syndrome deemed comparable to human hysteria. Many neurologists have therefore taken exception to the idea that suggestion plays an exclusive role in the pathogenesis of hysterical disorders in man (Blumenau, 1926; Dotsenko & Pervomaiskii, 1964). They argue that a number of hysterical symptoms cannot be induced voluntarily.

In considering the causal relationship between specific hysterical motor disorders and the organization of the motor system, the following observations regarding so-called "professional spasms" are of great interest. V. Dzerzhinskii (1921) pointed out that professional spasms develop only in the execution of specific movements (by writers, pianists, milkmaids, etc.). All other movements are executed accurately and easily, but those exercised in professional activity are impaired or lost because of tension or weakness in a particular group of muscles. Such disorders arise from overfatigue of the cortical motor centers controlling the professional movement. Medical treatment consists of complete rest from the task, after which work must be resumed gradually and with little energy expenditure. Sometimes a change of profession is required.

S. N. Davidenkov (1956) has pointed out that movement of the extremities can intensify hysterical cramps and spasms. For example, facial hemispasm is aggravated during eating, conversing, performing hard work, and excitement. According to Davidenkov's observations, "writer's cramp" occurs only during writing. He considers it a hysterical symptom and describes other professional spasms characteristically seen in typists, ballet dancers, violinists, barbers, etc. Stuttering pertains here, because in the stutterer nonverbal movements of the mouth are normal.

Intention spasms occur during attempts to reproduce some sort of new, unexpected movement. Pathophysiologically they can be interpreted as failure to establish a normal zone of inhibition around the excitatory focus. In addition to the required movement, for example, one sees superfluous movements caused by the excitation of neighboring sections of the cerebral cortex. According to Kretschmer (1960), treatment of convulsive conditions and contractures of the extremities is possible only after elimination of muscular tension in a recumbent position.

PHYSIOLOGICAL MECHANISM OF HYSTERIA

In 1929, V. M. Bekhterev attempted a physiological interpretation of hysteria by relating it to Vvedenskii's concept of parabiosis. Even earlier L. V. Blumenau (1926) attempted an interpretation in terms of I. P. Pavlov's concepts of higher nervous activity, in particular the concept of concentration of the inhibitory process in specific areas of the brain. He suggests that in hysteria one is dealing with inhibitions not of individual narrowly localized cerebral zones but of complex constellations of brain areas. That is why in hysteria one does not see such narrowly localized symptoms as hemianopsia, etc.

The study of experimental neuroses originated by Pavlov laid the groundwork for understanding the pathogenesis of hysteria. According to his findings (Pavlov, 1951), the pathophysiology of hysteria reduces to the following principles. Hysteria is a disease of the central nervous system characterized by a constitutional predominance of the subcortex over the cortex and, within the cortex, predominance of the first signal system over the second. Hysteria is seen most frequently in people with an "artistic" type of higher nervous activity and is characterized by a tendency toward hypnotic suggestibility. Susceptibility to suggestion and autosuggestion results from a capacity for intense concentration of excitation with strong negative induction, the physiological mechanism of hypnotic and posthypnotic suggestion. Hysteria is characterized by fear and a withdrawal into illness that is mediated by the laws governing conditioning of temporary connections. The diverse somatic symptoms of hysteria may originate in the cortex, e.g., the analgesias and paralyses appear as symptoms of cortical inhibition. The tendency toward an overflowing of inhibition in the cortex, by cutting off the second signal system, explains such symptoms as fantasy, dissociation from reality, and the twilight states of hysteria. Hysterical subjects lack coordination and balance in the functioning of three systems, the subcortical system and the two cortical signal systems; instead there is a vulnerability to breakdown in their interrelationships, which gives rise to symptoms of inhibition of "mental synthesis" and signs of split personality.

Physiologically, all hysterical syndromes are essentially the same. Against a background of cortical weakness one finds three physiological phenomena: (1) ready susceptibility to the hypnotic state; (2) extreme fixation and concentration of the neural processes in particular cortical zones because of domination by subcortical influence; and (3) excessive intensity and spread of negative induction (Maiorov, 1954).

Elaborating on the Pavlovian interpretation of hysteria, Davidenkov (1956) wrote that the hysterical hyperkineses include hysterical chorea, choreoathetosis, hysterical tremors of different rates and intensities, hysterical pseudotorsion dystonia, localized hysterical spasms, and chronic hysterical contractures of the extremities and trunk. From the point of view of mechanism, all of these syndromes reflect a persistent pathophysiological excitation in certain areas or dynamic constellations of the motor system that derive from the abnormal emotionality and suggestibility of such patients.

The cortical weakness characteristic of these patients, by positive induction of the subcortex, accounts for their marked emotionality and periodic emotional outbursts. At the same time, the hyperstimulation and chaotic activity of the subcortex can easily radiate into the weakened cortex, producing a pathological condition there. This excitatory irradiation in turn evokes strong negative induction, isolating these particular dynamic complexes from other cortical influences. As a result irreversible excitation or inhibition of particular functional constellations ensues. Thus, according to Davidenkov, is it possible to understand the phenomena of suggestion and autosuggestion, which earlier always seemed puzzling and mysterious. One and the same mechanism is capable of accounting for both the hysterical convulsive conditions and the hysterical anesthesias and paralyses.

FUNCTIONAL NEUROGENIC MOTOR DISTURBANCES IN ANIMALS

The question of whether it is possible to establish experimental models of hysteria in animals is complicated by the fact that, in addition to a variety of somatic symptoms, this disorder includes a number of peculiarly human mental aberrations—split personality, thought disorders, pathological hypnotic suggestibility, and autosuggestibility. Obviously one cannot speak in terms of complete reproduction in animals of the intricate psychopathological symptom complexes characteristic of human hysteria. Nevertheless, there remain many somatic hysterical symptoms in both man and animals so impressive as to suggest massive organic brain disease and yet characterized by such ready reversibility and exacerbation as to be unmistakably classifiable as functional illnesses of the central nervous system.

The literature contains a number of examples of functional motor disturbances in animals. P. N. Konovalov (1893), working in Pavlov's laboratory, reported motor agitation and temporary paresis in the limbs of swine restrained on a stand. The negative emotional reaction of the animal to immobilization manifested itself in inhibition of gastric secretions. In 1898 Cannon noted that cats held in physical restraint showed motor restlessness and depression of gastric movements. I. P. Pavlov and M. K. Petrova (1951) observed a temporary paralysis of the motor musculature, which ordinarily participates in the act of eating, in dogs exposed to conditioned stimuli for food while in a phasic hypnotic state. Hypnotic inhibition above all encompassed the areas of the motor system that were related to the most intensively involved muscle groups.

I. A. Vetiukov (1936), studying experimental neuroses in dogs, noted a number of symptoms including restlessness, motor excitement, shortness of breath, vomiting, digestive disorders, and motor incoordination. When defensive stimuli were presented, the dogs raised their heads with extreme extension of the forward extremities and loss of tonus of the posterior ones. Sexual stimulation of the males induced by the sight of females deepened the neurotic state even to complete paresis of the hindquarters. For a time, the animals became "invalids." However, a short pause in the conditioning trials without any special therapeutic procedures restored them to a normal state. N. I. Krasnogorskii (1939) succeeded in producing hyperkinesis in a dog by a conditioned reflex method. He noted two phases in the development of the conditioned motor disturbance: a phase of convulsive twitching of the muscles of the muzzle, extremities, and trunk lasting for several minutes, followed by a severe depressed state approaching stupor with apparent paralysis of the muscles of the tongue, neck, and extremities. K. M. Bykov (1953) observed a convulsive reaction, neurotic in nature, in a dog for which stimulation of gastric interoceptors was being used as a conditioned stimulus for noxious stimulation.

Such observations leave no doubt either as to the neurotic nature of experimental paralyses and hyperkinesis in animals or as to the role of conditioned reflex mechanisms in the development of functional motor disturbances.

From the time the Primate Center was established at Sukhumi in 1927, a particular kind of convulsive motor disorder has systematically been observed among the hamadryas baboons (Zel'geim, 1934; Voronin, Kanfor, Lakin, & Tikh, 1948). A. P. Zel'geim suggested that the seizures were epileptic in nature. L. G. Voronin and co-workers expressed the opinion that there was a connection between the convulsions and stress on the endocrine system. These authors considered it probable that pregnancy, delivery, and lactation unmasked a latent deficiency of parathyroid function, giving rise to hypocalcemic tetany in pregnant females and newborn infants.

Signs of motor disturbances in monkeys subjected to experimental neurosis have been repeatedly noted by various authors. S. D. Kaminskii observed negativism, stereotypy, and instability of conditioned motor response in anubis baboons; their usual motor activity gave way to sluggishness. L. A. Bam (1939) observed unsteady gait and muscular weakness in an ovariectomized female chacma baboon suffering from neurosis. D. I. Miminoshvili *et al.* (1960) observed body tremors, convulsive attacks, and adynamia in one hamadryas baboon with a neurogenic myocardial infarction. In 1962 we observed a convulsive fit with subsequent adynamia in a hamadryas baboon with experimental neurogenic gastric achylia (V. G. Startsev, 1964b). Schrier (1965) reported "cage paralysis" in one of eight rhesus monkeys housed under stressful conditions.

Our study has been the first directed specifically at testing the possibility that such motor disturbances in monkeys are functional and, in particular, neurogenic in nature.

SPONTANEOUS AND EXPERIMENTAL MOTOR DISORDERS IN HAMADRYAS BABOONS

In the years 1962–1967, as we were establishing an experimental model of neurogenic gastric achylia in hamadryas baboons, we observed several profound motor disturbances—convulsive attacks, paresis, paralysis, hyperkinesis, etc.—in our experimental animals. We began paying attention to the possible functional character of new motor disturbances in the baboons and made attempts to reproduce them. From Primate Center records it was possible to trace the history of development of the disease of the hamadryas baboons suffering from convulsive attacks. By comparing the conditions under which motor disorders developed spontaneously with the conditions intentionally designed to produce experimental neurosis, it was possible to work out common features of the events surrounding such disorders. The following is a description of the kinds of neurotic, hysteroid disorders observed and an attempt to analyze their physiological mechanisms.

In all, 49 hamadryas baboons were studied. In 32 the natural history of spontaneous convulsive disorders was followed from the time of onset until the animal died. Seventeen were used in experimental attempts to model such disturbances. The basic principle underlying the experiments was acutely or chronically to restrict movement and then to stress the motor system by evoking intense defensive activity.

Five of the 17 subjects (Azov, Takla, Zagreb, Ambarchik, and Kuzbass) were housed in groups for 2–4 years in small laboratory cages that considerably limited their daily motor activity. The immediate stimuli that were capable of eliciting motor disturbances (convulsive attacks, paralyses) were conditions that evoked extremely intense muscular activity accompanied by negative emotions (e.g., chasing at cage cleaning time, transfer to larger quarters next to unfamiliar adult animals, introduction into different living groups for several weeks).

Several kinds of neurotic, hysteroid motor impairments were observed. Two of the males, Zagreb and Ambarchik, both born May 23, 1961, had been removed from the troup at 2 years of age and housed together for 2 years in a laboratory cage without involvement in any kind of experimentation. Their motor activity and affiliative, defensive, and play behavior were well maintained in this setting. Their development as judged by size, sexual development, and hair distribution was somewhat retarded compared to that of baboons of the same age kept in open air compounds. Zagreb was the more dominant of the two.

On August 7, 1965 both males were simultaneously transferred to a larger cage, measuring 2 X 3 X 3 m. Outside the cage, separated by a transparent barrier, were several full grown males, who greeted their new young neighbors with threatening gestures and vocalizations. These novel surroundings evoked violent emotional motor activity on the part of the new animals. In the very first minutes both showed a gait disturbance characterized by incoordination and a posture with the knees half flexed, which made it impossible for them to jump onto a low shelf even though such leaps had never presented any kind of difficulty in their old home cage. Ambarchik's disorder did not progress beyond the impairment of gait. The more dominant animal, Zagreb, however, developed spasmodic quivering tremors in the lower extremities. During the subsequent 3 days his movements reflected a steadily progressive hypotonia; he sat continuously with arms extended and head sunk down between his knees. He ate slowly and his defensive activity appeared diminished. On August 10, 1965 he developed a right hemiparesis. When suddenly frightened, he jumped up on the shelf and immediately "froze" in a sitting position. On July 11, 1965 general paresis was noted; the adynamia was more pronounced. When one of the animal handlers attempted to catch him, he quickly climbed the bars of the cage to a height of about 1.5 m, but the muscular strength of his extremities was quickly exhausted and he fell to the floor, struggled a short time, and died. A careful autopsy revealed no anatomical lesion to which one could attribute such severe motor impairment.

Ambarchik continued to live in the same large cage alone, ate well, easily climbed the wire screen walls to the top of the 3-m high cage, jumped, and ran about without difficulty. On August 31, 1965 he was put into a group of 14 baboons, younger than he but of equal size. The abrupt change in social environment evoked an initial violent phase of emotional motor activity followed by a phase in which he moved about little, tended to isolate himself in a corner, and did not take part in the running and play of the other baboons. During feeding time on September 6, 1965, he was observed to have two attacks of tonic–clonic spasms in the space of 40 min, after which he got up but remained adynamic; he ate normally. He was removed from the compound to a small individual cage where he would not be exposed to the strong variegated social stimulation imposed by the group. A neuropathological consultation on September 7, 1965 yielded a diagnosis of upper motor neuron syndrome with paraparesis of the lower extremities. In the small cage his movements appeared undisturbed; his gait, aggressive behavior, and defensive responses were lively and appetite was normal. No gross motor disturbances were visible. On September 20, 1965 he was caught and subjected to a physical examination, following which he was released into a large cage for more thorough observation of his neurological status and motor activity. Examination at this time revealed hypodynamia and right hemiparesis, including the extremities, the face, and the masticatory muscles; furthermore, an intention tremor was noted. With the exception of the right patellar reflex, the deep tendon reflexes were absent. The plantar flexion and cremasteric reflexes were intact. General pain sensitivity was reduced. Muscle tone was increased in the right extremities.

After examination the baboon was again introduced into the group, where he withdrew to a corner. He vocalized and quivered but otherwise failed to move in response to playful and aggressive gestures on the part of the other baboons. On the morning of September 22, 1965 he was found in the cage lying prostrate after a convulsive attack. He was placed in a small cage, where he first sat with his back pressed against the wall and then collapsed. A neuropathological consultant noted 3 hr later that the animal had assumed an involuntary posture; only movements of the head were intact; the muscles of the tongue, face, and trunk fibrillated; the right corner of the mouth sagged; the pupils were dilated; the pupillary reflex to light was intact; deep tendon reflexes were diminished on the right and absent on the left; cutaneous reflexes were absent; pain sensitivity was markedly diminished; muscle tone was increased in the extremities bilaterally in an extrapyramidal pattern.

Two hours later the baboon sat up; vomiting set in, and he refused food. After a day his condition improved; he sat, walked, and took food with his hands. For the next 5 weeks he appeared normal. He was housed in a cage by himself. Between October 27 and November 5, 1965 other baboons housed within sight of Ambarchik were caught and removed from their cages periodically for a new, unrelated experiment. Often these events were accompanied by intense vocalization on the part of the other baboons and the animal handlers. On November 6, 1965 Ambarchik ate poorly and was sluggish. In the following days his condition worsened. On November 10 he sat inertly, apparently suffering from a paresis of both arms that prevented his taking food when it was offered to him. He took candy by mouth and leaped to the shelf and onto the window sill using only his legs and feet. Vomiting was noted. On November 11, 1965 he was found in the cage dead. Autopsy revealed a bloody mass in the stomach. No anatomical lesion was discovered that would have accounted for his motor disturbance.

In both Zagreb and Ambarchik the motor disturbances were transient and involved both hyperkinetic reactions, such as spasms, trembling, facial tics, and fibrillation, and paretic symptoms. Different muscular groups were alternately affected and not affected; when affected, they were alternately spastic and paretic. The symptoms were brought on by intense motor–emotional reactions, which occurred when the animals' stereotyped daily routine was acutely altered. When the animals were transferred from conditions that imposed long-term constraints on their mobility and that were monotonous and poor in biological stimulation to conditions of unaccustomed social interaction that placed intense and complex pressures on functioning of the motor system, they succumbed to a nervous breakdown with major disruption of functions in the motor sphere. Returning them to the previous conditions, poor in biological stimuli, eliminated or attenuated the profound motor disorders, again indicating their functional, neurotic character. The hysterical-like symptoms in this kind of experimental neurosis presumably derive from (1) weakness of the cortex, particularly of the motor areas and of special areas related to motor control of the extremities; in these cases, the weakness was caused by housing the animals in small cages that restricted their freedom of movement for a long period of time; (2) a predisposition of the cortical portion of the motor system to respond with a generalized inhibitory process when placed under unusually intense demands by the change of social environment; (3) the negative emotional stimulation associated with the defensive response mechanisms inevitably elicited by the change in social setting, particularly response mechanisms of the motor system under immediate challenge.

A hysterical motor disorder was produced in the baboon Azov (Figure 59a–c) under similar circumstances. He was transferred from a small home cage to a

(a)

(b)

FIG. 59a and b

FIG. 59 Hamadryas baboon Azov 3 hr after a convulsive attack. (a) Voluntary movements of the extremities are absent; movements of the head necessary for eating are intact and accompanied by synchronous flexing movements in the right hand and right foot. (b) Standing is impossible; when propped up, the animal rests on his back legs; his arms hang loose without movement. (c) The animal maintains an imposed posture with extremities extended, predominantly on the right.

larger cage, which contained a female and was located within view of several other mature males. He had shown brief spasmodic attacks previously under the stress of being driven from one side of the home cage to the other; but now he developed frequent and prolonged convulsive attacks with paresis and paralysis of quite a different character.

The baboon Takla also developed disturbances of motor activity on being transferred to a troup of baboons in an open air compound. She showed tremors of the trunk and extremities, a gait disorder, and progressive sluggishness. She also manifested infantile fear behavior in that at moments of danger she, a fully mature female, clasped another animal in the ventral—ventral position characteristic of a young monkey clasping its mother. The other animal was a young male who watched after her and carried her to safety. The motor disorders were eliminated by removing her from the troup and returning her to the small familiar home cage.

The baboon Kuzbass developed spasms in the extremities lasting 5–20 sec each time he was caught and pulled from his cage. No motor disturbance of any kind was ever noted when he was free and unchallenged in the cage.

In these cases as well, therefore, hyperkinetic and paretic or paralytic symptoms appeared in the context of gross muscular stress with a strong negative emotional component.

Two other baboons (Vismut and Amulet) lived continuously for many months in restraint chairs that enforced immobilization of the body with relative freedom of movement in the extremities. These animals, Vismut in particular, developed severe motor disturbances when attempts were begun to condition food-reinforced motor responses. After a 30-min period of conditioning trials and at the moment when discrimination trials were begun, Vismut suffered a convulsive attack consisting of more than a hundred spasmodic movements; the right hand, which had been used to press the response lever, was primarily involved. Later, when that hand was accidentally wounded, the left became the working hand and the spasmodic symptoms were more noticeable in the left hand. Still later, he developed spasms of both arms and legs that were accompanied by an involuntary cry. These symptoms were rarely observed outside the experimental setting. With further conditioning sessions, as the differential response became well established, the spasms disappeared and outside the experimental situation they were not observed for a year. Then 2 years after the onset of experiments in the restraint chair, the animal developed a generalized muscular weakness and sluggishness, which progressed rapidly to death. The other baboon maintained in a chair developed a variety of fixed movement patterns.

Nine hamadryas baboons (Bakhmach, Abo, Antil, Lolium, Kleshchevina, Pianch, Zlak, Dramor, and Zestafon) were subjected to repeated periods of immobilization in a restraint stand for 5 hr at a time (Figure 1). Five of them developed motor disturbances at various times after the immobilization sessions in association with negative emotions related to the activation of defensive response mechanisms. Abo and Antil exhibited motor disturbances under the combined effects of immobilization and chlorpromazine, whereas it was clear that neither alone produced the disorder. Abo developed an unmistakable paresis of the right hand which persisted for $1\frac{1}{2}$ months. Stimuli that elicited defensive excitation intensified the paresis so that the hand hung limp. When tested in the conditioning chamber, he pressed the response lever with his right hand, but the pressure exerted was very weak (Figure 60). The paresis gradually disappeared and did not recur in 3 years of observation.

Dramor and Zestafon developed paralyses of the extremities and died after fixation in the immobilization stand during treatment with the cholinolytic

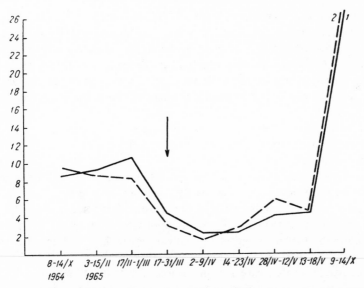

FIG. 60 Abrupt drop in strength of conditioned lever press responses by the right hand in the baboon Abo during the development of a functional paresis of that hand. Abscissa, dates designating the beginning and end of experiments which consisted of five sessions each. Ordinate, pressure on the lever in millimeters excursion of the recording pen. (1) pressure in response to auditory CSs; (2) pressure in response to light CSs; arrow, experimental sessions in which immobilization was imposed after eating and treatment with chlorpromazine (2.5 mg/kg, intramuscular).

agent benactyzine (1 mg/kg). Pianch and Zlak met similar fates when submitted to immobilization stress under the influence of metamizil (2–5 mg/kg). When baboons were given the drugs in these dosages under conditions of nonrestraint, they showed only a 1- to 4-hr inhibition of the conditioned motor responses and a mild, transient ataxia. The combination of the defensive excitation elicited by immobilization and the pharmacological blockade of central muscarinic cholinergic mechanisms (Denisenko, 1966) produced an abrupt derangement of function of the motor system and its relationship with subcortical motor centers, which led to a profound motor disorder ending in death.

As indicated above, a review of the medical records of hamadryas baboons at the Sukhumi Primate Center yielded reports of a total of 49 animals with convulsive and paralytic disorders. Of these, 30 were males and 19 females. The majority (41) were born at Sukhumi. The disorders occurred most frequently among sexually mature animals (17 in the age range 6–20 years; 26 in the range 3–6 years; five in the range 1–3 years; and only one less than 1 year of age). The duration of illness, i.e., the time from the first spasmodic attacks to death, was highly variable. Fourteen died during the first known attack. The remaining 35 were observed to have repeated spasmodic attacks or other motor disorders that alternated with periods of normal function. Twelve were affected for 1–15 days; 11 for 1–12 months; nine for 2–6 years; and three from 7–11 years. The majority of the baboons (41 of the 49) participated in experiments of one kind or another. All of the females were examined regularly with regard to pregnancies, deliveries, and spontaneous abortions. Twenty-six of the animals were transferred from the open compound to small cage housing and back an average of 12 times.

The illnesses were characterized by convulsive attacks, hyperkineses, paralyses and pareses, impairment of posture and gait, disruptions of sensations, and vegetative disorders.

The convulsive attacks were always associated with a stressful situation and were preceded by motor excitement; they did not develop during sleep. They lasted from several seconds to 5 min. The spasms were tonic in character with tremor, adduction of the extremities, and opisthotonos or rigidity of the nuchal musculature. Sometimes tonic–clonic convulsions with a predominance of the tonic component were observed (Figure 61).

The convulsions often gave the impression of a "protest" reaction, i.e., they occurred when the animal resisted being caught in a squeeze cage or fought to escape a "persecutor." They were seen in one baboon that became paralyzed

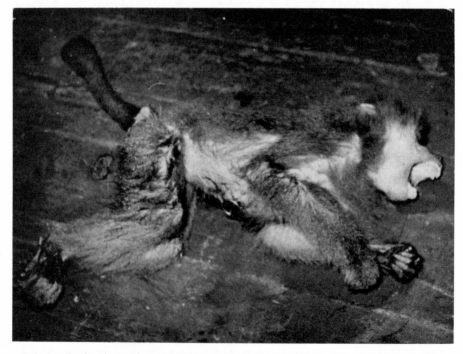

FIG. 61   Tonic phase of a convulsive attack in the hamadryas baboon Bakhmach. The disorder was brought on by immobilization stress; within an hour, the animal was able to move about and eat.

whenever it was unable to escape an animal handler or other baboons or to respond motorically to cries of the baboon troup.

During such convulsions, the corneal and pupillary reflexes are often intact. As a rule, the attacks are not followed by sleep. Social, alimentary, parental, and sexual reflexes are markedly inhibited. The spasmodic attacks are often reduced by morphine; administration of calcium is ineffective. Serum calcium during the spasmodic attacks is 9.41 ± 0.32 mg % (average of 28 determinations from 11 baboons), i.e., within the normal range for baboons (Asatiani, 1960) and for humans during hysteria (Dotsenko & Pervomaiskii, 1964). Serum potassium was 18.84 ± 0.39 mg % (average of 18 determinations from seven baboons).

Among the phenomena classified as hyperkineses were tremors of the head, body, and extremities, especially the fingers and toes, and fibrillary twitching of the muscles; nystagmus and concordant movements were also noted (Figure 59a). These symptoms occurred at rest and intensified during movement.

The paralyses and pareses always developed in connection with stress, defensive motor excitation, and negative emotions; usually, but not necessarily, they occurred after convulsive attacks. (It is possible that in some cases a preceding convulsion occurred but was not observed.) Negative emotions (concomitant to defensive, social, sexual, or alimentary reflexes) aggravated the paralyses or pareses. However, returning the baboon to more peaceful surroundings with a minimum of external stimulation reduced or eliminated these symptoms.

Paralyses and pareses took the form of transient mono-, hemi-, para-, and quadriplegias. Sometimes paresis of the tongue and masticatory musculature was observed. The right hand was more frequently affected than the left, an observation of distinct interest in view of the fact that hamadryas baboons tend to be right handed (Voitonis & Tikh, 1949). Both spastic and flaccid paralyses were observed. With tetraplegia, movements of the head, eyes, pharynx, trunk, and tail were preserved; micturition and defecation were not disturbed. Sudden auditory, tactile, or painful stimuli characteristically elicited tremors throughout the body. The pareses affected only voluntary movements; automatic movements, such as sucking and grasping, were preserved.

If one lifted a paralyzed baboon in this state and placed him on the floor, he collapsed either prone or lying on one side like a dead body; at the same time he was capable of grasping at the hands of the experimenter or for the support of the cage. When one attempted to examine him for muscular strength he resisted at first but this reaction quickly subsided. Eating, emotional stress, or any kind of gross body movement led to rapid exhaustion of motor activity.

Paralysis of one muscle of a synergistic group was not observed. Deep tendon reflexes were ordinarily intact and testing them elicited generalized trembling. The intensity of the cutaneous reflexes might be either exaggerated or diminished.

Disturbances of gait were a component of many of the motor disorders. In some cases, the animals moved about with knees half flexed, even though when sitting or lying down they tended to extend the legs completely. In other cases the animal moved about with legs unusually extended in a stilted gait. In some instances a baboon locomoted in normal fashion except that he dragged one leg or arm. Animals with such a monoplegia, or a hemiplegia, showed generalized trembling of the other extremities, the head and body during locomotion. Defensive excitation intensified the paralysis, making walking that much more difficult.

A striking form of motor disorganization is seen in baboons unable to stand or walk. Usually they move about in a sitting position, resting on the buttocks. In some cases a baboon unable to rise from a lying position is able to perform automatic or involuntary movements and voluntarily move the head.

The disorders of sensation included analgesia of the paralyzed extremity. Two baboons developed amaurosis. In one of them the blindness was reversible and intermittent.

The vegetative disturbances seen in baboons suffering from spasmodic attacks and paralysis included anorexia, vomiting, hematemesis, constipation, diarrhea, gastric anacidity, and coronary insufficiency (Figure 62).

Insofar as baboons lack the second signal system, language, one cannot consider their psychological disturbances entirely analogous to hysteria in man. Still, a number of factors attest to the development of primitive forms of psychological disorders in these animals. We have already mentioned a unique instance of infantile response to threat in a fully mature female. In some cases one can identify socially conditioned biological response mechanisms triggering or mediating certain of the motor disorders. For example, convulsive symptoms

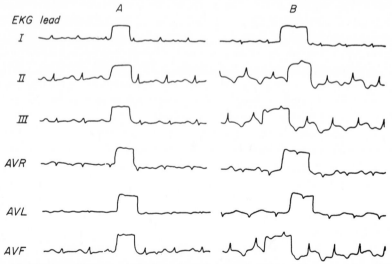

FIG. 62 Electrocardiogram of the hamadryas baboon Antil (A) under normal conditions; (B) during quadriplegia induced by repeated experiments with immobilization stress following activation of alimentary response mechanisms; the animal had received chlorpromazine (2.5 mg/kg; intramuscular). Note transitory signs of coronary insufficiency.

developed in a dominant male when he was housed with a female in view of other powerful, threatening males. The same was observed when two adolescent males were placed in a new cage together under similar conditions; the more dominant of the two developed motor disturbances.

In a third case, a dominant male died of a convulsive disorder within a week after the death of his subordinate male cagemate of several years, who himself died during a convulsive attack; alone for a week, the dominant male died in a quite similar convulsive episode. Although both animals had suffered from motor disturbances for more than 6 months, the death of one and the resultant disruption of familiar social relations stimulated the onset of convulsive attacks leading to the death of the second.

In three instances we observed what appeared to be hereditary illness in the offspring of mothers with convulsive motor disorders. On one occasion the young animal developed a spasmodic attack immediately after a spasmodic attack in the mother.

The symptoms of the illness in hamadryas baboons, therefore, are in many respects reminiscent of hysteria in man. Table 32 presents in summary form the neuropathological symptoms of spontaneous hysteroid motor disorders seen in hamadryas baboons (compiled with the assistance of G. A. Kuraev, neuro-pathologist).

Very likely age is an important factor in the development of motor disturbances in baboons. This is not so likely to derive from some flaw in development of the organism as from the significant qualitative shifts in social relationships of the mature animals when they encounter a multitude of conflicts between stimuli releasing various social, sexual, parental, and alimentary response mechanisms in connection with life in captivity. These conflicting situations give rise to the nervous stress out of which various disorders, including the motor disorders, emerge. The neurotic reorganization of higher nervous activity progresses gradually with age until a wide variety of factors become capable of triggering the spasmodic attacks or paralyses.

The young baboon, from the moment of birth until 6–12 months of age, is in the immediate custody of the mother and under the protection of other mature members of the troup. The constant conflicts that arise among mature individuals in small home cages, and to a lesser degree in the open compounds, affect him little. Between 1 and 3 years of age, i.e., until the onset of sexual maturity, the young baboons are often maintained separately from the more mature animals in cages or open compounds. Play dominates the interrelationships of the adolescent animals; fights are relatively rare and considerably less violent than among the mature animals. The highly active life, especially in the outdoor compounds, assures a high degree of development and exercise of the motor system in the young baboons. If they do not become sick or become involved in an experiment, they are seldom subjected to clinical procedures that inevitably stress the cortical representation of the defensive response mechanism.

TABLE 32

Neuropathological Symptoms in Hamadryas Baboons with Spontaneous
Hysteroid Motor Disorders[a]

Cranial nerve signs	Pupillary dilatation during convulsion (6); intermittent blindness (1); facial hypesthesia (1); weak pupillary reflex to light (1); nystagmus (3); strabismus (1); sagging of the lower jaw (1); salivation (1); choreic symptoms of the musculature of the face (1); facial paresis (1)
Motor symptoms: active movements	Inability to get up after convulsion (3); paresis of the legs (8); quadriplegia (1); movements hampered by weakness, paresis or rigidity (6); no active movements (3); uncoordinated movements (2)
Passive movements and muscle tonus	Hypotonia in the lower extremities (5); hypertonia (7); tonus intermittently different in muscles of the upper and lower extremities (4); extrapyramidal hypertonia (3)
Hyperkinesis	Intention spasms (4); tremor (10); fibrillary twitching of the muscles (11); myorhythms (9)
Epileptic seizures	Tonic seizures (13); clonic-tonic seizures (15); Jacksonian seizures (3)
Synkinesis	None
Hypokinesis and akinesia	Adynamia after and between attacks (14); hyperkinesia (3)
Gait	Failure to walk (2); walking with knees half flexed (1); with legs unusually extended (1); paretic (1); uncoordinated (1)
Deep tendon reflexes	Hyperactive (1); hypoactive (1)
Cutaneous reflexes	Absent (1)
Sensation	Hyperesthesia (painful face) (1); reduced pain sensitivity (2)
General CNS symptoms	Vomiting (14); loss of consciousness (1)

[a]Based on veterinary records reflecting course of the disease in 39 animals; numbers in parentheses represent number of animals with given symptoms.

At about 3 years of age, the baboons are transferred from the compounds and large open air cages to other quarters, where they are held for examination for pregnancies, deliveries, and spontaneous abortions. At this point a large proportion of them become subjects for different kinds of experiments.

The onset of sexual maturity is attended by great changes in the behavior of baboons, especially under conditions of captivity. They become less active. Play response mechanisms almost disappear with age. Because most of the mature baboons, particularly those involved in experiments, are housed in relatively small cages, their movement is still further restricted. In the natural habitat, normal locomotion from place to place in search of food and frequent tree climbing compensates for the tendency to decreased activity with age. In captivity, however, the animals live for years in cages, never making any particular exertion to obtain food or defend themselves against natural enemies; long-term restriction of movement of mature baboons is unavoidable in many circumstances.

At times, e.g., when such animals must be caught for examination or an experiment or during fights with other baboons in the same cages, they engage in extreme motor activity. They defend themselves fiercely against their baboon antagonists or the animal handlers. Even when catching the animal in a squeeze cage, one man on each arm and leg is barely sufficient to control a mature baboon. During such extreme muscular activity the motor system comes under singular functional stress. Parts of it, particularly those mediating movements of the extremities, must undergo extremely intense excitation.

One important feature of this excitation is that it occurs in the part of the nervous system that controls motor activity, the requirements for which have been satisfied for years by relatively weak, routine muscular activity. Housing a baboon for long periods of time in a small laboratory cage or a restraint chair and depriving it of normal social relationships reduces and limits activity of the motor system. Another important feature of the excitation of the motor system that occurs under the abrupt muscular stress of furious running and climbing about the walls and ceiling of the cage to escape the teeth of a baboon antagonist or to avoid being driven into a transfer cage and of the excitation elicited by immobilization on the restraint stand, in a chair, or on the board is that it is surely accompanied by stimulation of the strongest possible negative emotions. These negative emotions paired with the extreme muscular stress very quickly acquire the character of conditioned reflex defensive dominants. Thereby, according to the principles of classical conditioning (Pavlov, 1951), the conditions are met for establishing continual emotional excitation of the subcortex, inductive inhibition of the cortex, and the development of isolated foci of excitation and inhibition in the motor area of the cortex.

The observations described here suggest that the motor disturbances seen in hamadryas baboons and the functional, neurotic character of their onset and progression are pathophysiologically similar to hysterical phenomena seen in man. The analogy is also supported by a comparison of etiological factors predisposing to hysteria in man and baboons (Table 33).

The hyperkineses and paralyses observed in the baboon can therefore serve as models of similar hysterical motor disorders characteristic of man. The mechanism whereby experimental hyperkinesis or paralysis develops in baboons involves the formation of a defensive dominant. The latter emerges under condi-

TABLE 33

Comparison of Factors Predisposing to Hysteria in Man and Hamadryas
Baboons

In man	In hamadryas baboons
Overprotected childhood and adolescence	Prolonged housing in cages with deprivation of social interaction
Complex and conflicting life situations as a basis for psychological trauma (hysteria of war time and peace time)	Complex and conflicting social and sexual relations in captivity
Psychotraumatic factor (psychological reaction to physical trauma)	Neurotraumatic factor (conditioned and unconditioned reactions to aggression by other baboons)
Exhausting physical labor, acute and chronic physical overexertion, attendant negative emotions	Forced muscular stress, attended by negative emotions (running and clambering about the cage under attack by other baboons, or during catching for an experiment; resisting immobilization in the squeeze cage, at the hands of the animal handlers, on restraint stands or in chairs)
Chilling	Chilling
Age; physiologically and socially maturation forces transition to new, more complex conditions of life from simpler conditions of childhood (development of hysteria between the ages of 15 and 25 years)	Age; maturation produces changes in sexual and social life which (along with new duties vis-à-vis caring for the young) complicates the activity of the central nervous system and increases the number of conflict situations
Hysterical imitation of illness of others	Imitation of convulsive attacks of another baboon
Relatively voluntary manifestation of hysterical symptoms	Conditioned reflex character of the onset of hysterical attacks

tions of excessive muscular stress of a defensive nature and the attendant negative emotions. Total restraint of the extremities or chronic limitation of movement contributes to the emergence of a defensive dominant with pathological motor activity. When the defensive dominant develops in the motor sphere of a nonhuman primate, one sees an example of experimental pathology of motor activity. The motor disturbances in hysteria are system specific, i.e., of the motor system, not only in the sense that the neuromuscular apparatus that executes a variety of motor reactions is impaired but, more importantly from a causal point of view, these disorders (hyperkinesis and paralysis) come to be triggered by otherwise normal activity of the muscular apparatus. Every movement produces feedback signals from the muscle and joint capsule receptors.

These signals enter the central motor system where repeated neurogenic stress has established a defensive dominant. The kinetic sensations associated with natural movements therefore become signals, conditioned stimuli for excitation of the defensive dominant with all of the ensuing pathological reactions of the motor apparatus. Of course, not just any movement attains such significance, but primarily the tense motor activity associated with defensive responses and accompanied by emotions of pain and fear. The motor disruptions are not observed except when the animal moves. Motor responses of the animal provoke and intensify the motor disruptions. Weakness of the motor system, caused by chronic restriction of movement, predisposes to the formation of a pathological defensive dominant and the consequent tendency toward motor disturbances.

To the extent that the basic forms of hysterical motor disorders seen in man are modeled experimentally in baboons, one must recognize a certain independence of these phenomena from the hypnotic suggestion and autosuggestion, to which animals are presumably not susceptible. This, however, does not negate the general similarity of hysteroid hyperkineses and paralyses between the lower primates and man. Clarification of the fundamental etiologic and pathogenetic mechanism of these disorders can very likely facilitate the development of new modes of prevention and therapy.

VI
Experimental Neurogenic Disorders of the Sexual Cycle in Hamadryas Baboons

The major biological feature that differentiates the sexual cycle of primates from that of other mammals is its multicyclicity, a characteristic that presumably has particular survival value for the species. At the same time, if one considers vulnerability of the female sexual cycle to neurogenic stress, such cyclicity increases the likelihood of neurogenic sexual disturbances because the possibility of important phases of the sexual cycle coinciding with different stressful conflict situations acquires greater significance than in animals without cycles or with cycles of longer duration. In this regard, experimental studies of disturbances of the sexual cycle in nonhuman primates with sexual cycles of approximately the same duration as in the human female are of particular interest.

NORMAL NEUROHORMONAL REGULATION OF THE SEXUAL CYCLE IN PRIMATES

The sexual activity of primates is regulated by neural and hormonal mechanisms that under healthy conditions produce a regular cyclicity. Normal sexual cycles in all mammals, including primates, are biphasic.

According to E. I. Kvater (1961), changes in cerebral cortical activity arising in response to internal and external stimuli regulate the sexual system largely through the hypothalamus. All primates exhibit an ovarian–menstrual cycle different from the estrus of other animals, an outward manifestation of ovulation.

Experiments on lower animals have demonstrated that the moment of ovulation is accompanied by abrupt changes in the electrical activity of the frontal cortex, limbic cortex, and lateral preoptic areas of the hypothalamus. Noting the prominent affective features of the sexual act, Kvater writes that: "Different

146

emotions can evoke functional changes in the hypothalamus and thence in the hypophysis, which may be accompanied by massive output of the gonadotrophic hormones." These hormones, follicle-stimulating hormone (FSH) and luteinizing hormone (LH), trigger ovulation.

Ovulation can be blocked by such drugs as reserpine and chlorpromazine, which suppress cortical activity. The ovulatory blocking effect of such pharmacological preparations as nembutal, morphine, chlorpromazine, and reserpine is ascribed to the fact that these preparations disturb the excitability of the reticular formation and hypothalamus. Ovulation may fail to occur following damage to anterior areas of the hypothalamus, but in such cases it can still be triggered by direct stimulation of the hypophysis. The ovulatory process triggered by FSH and LH from the hypophysis is inhibited by atropine and dibenamine. Atropine apparently acts on the early stages and more central components of the neural mechanism mediating gonadotrophic hormone secretion. Dibenamine probably influences the terminal hypothalamic link but may also act directly to block the secretion of hormone by the hypophysis.

Normal menstruation sets in with the sloughing of the transformed mucous membrane of the uterus. Transformation of the membrane is governed by a hormone produced in the corpus luteum of the ovary, and hence ovulation is a necessary condition for menstruation; without ovulation the corpus luteum does not develop and transformation of the endometrium is not initiated. There are situations, however, in which ovulation takes place but menstruation fails to occur. Sympathomimetic substances, e.g., ephedrine and amphetamine, inhibit menstrual bleeding, whereas parasympathomimetic substances, e.g., acetylcholine and prostigmine, enhance it. P. V. Bochkarev and K. N. Pavlova (1937) have cited data to show that the vaginal cycle, which is also controlled by ovarian endocrine stimuli, parallels the menstrual cycle both in women and female baboons; it is not seen during pregnancy or menopause.

L. V. Alekseeva (1961, 1963), studying sexual cycles in the hamadryas baboon, observed regular fluctuations in the urinary estrogens, estrone, estradiol, and estriol. The excretion of estrogens increases in the middle of the first phase of the cycle, on the day of ovulation, and before menstruation. Three similar peaks of estrogen secretion are described for women with normal menstrual cycles. In anovulatory cycles the overall excretion is reduced and the typical shape of the curve is altered.

Urinary pregnanediol also shows regular changes with different phases of the sexual cycle in hamadryas baboons and in women. In the first phase of the female baboon's cycle the quantity of pregnanediol in urine is insignificant; after ovulation it noticeably increases and then decreases again before menstruation (Alekseeva & Grigorenko, 1965).

In experiments on mature female monkeys (*Macaca mulatta*) it has been demonstrated that the quantities of FSH and LH in the hypophysis increase toward the middle of the menstrual cycle and decrease after ovulation. Females also show increases in adrenocorticotropic hormone (ACTH) and somatotropic hormone (SH) in the anterior lobe of the hypophysis in midcycle, whereas the quantity of thyrotropic hormone decreases at this point (Simpson, van Wagenen, & Carter, 1956).

RELATIONSHIP OF THE SEXUAL CYCLE
TO OTHER BIOLOGICAL FUNCTIONS IN HAMADRYAS BABOONS

The periodic swellings of the "sex skin" and menstruation serve as two outward manifestations of the sexual cycle in baboons. The swelling of the sex skin is a particularly distinct and useful index of the stage of the cycle in this species.

The normal sexual cycle among hamadryas baboons is comprised of four phases: (1) the prefollicular quiescent phase, or pause, from the end of menstrual bleeding to the beginning of swelling of the sex skin; (2) the follicular phase, from the first day of swelling of the sex skin to ovulation; (3) the luteal phase, from the day of ovulation to menstruation; and (4) menstruation. The mean duration of the cycle is 36 days. Mean durations of the individual phases are 3.9, 13.6, 16.2, and 2.5 days, respectively.

According to findings by L. V. Alekseeva (1949, 1963) based on the analysis of 1684 sexual cycles in hamadryas baboons, prolongation of the cycle usually is caused by extension of the prefollicular phase. This quiescent phase of sexual function in primates appears homologous to the diestrus pause of rodents. If it persists for more than 32 days then it is best interpreted as a missed cycle. Among healthy female baboons the quiescent phase often has no significance; it lengthens under a variety of adverse conditions.

Amenorrheic cycles, i.e., cycles without menstrual flow, are also seen in hamadryas baboons (Bochkarev, 1935). These are characterized by the usual swelling of the sex skin, which attests to the maturation and growth of the ovarian follicles, but ovulation probably fails to occur and menstruation does not follow.

The sex skin is an important secondary sex characteristic in baboons. The degree of swelling strongly influences the relationship between the sexes. Maximum mutual interest coincides with maximum swelling, which in turn correlates with the day of ovulation.

The two-phased aspect of sexual function in primates is associated with many other cyclical changes. Baboon females, in different phases of the sexual cycle, show differences in higher nervous activity, emotion, pupillary reaction, muscular strength, arterial pressure, heart rate, blood morphology, body temperature, metabolic rate, gas exchange, respiration, vital capacity, intestinal and gastric peristalsis, etc. Information regarding cyclical changes in physiological indices that correlate with phases of the sexual cycle is to be found in the works of a number of authors (Alekseeva & Avdzhiian, 1961; Startsev & Ianson, 1968). The majority of such indices show a biphasic fluctuation, which is interpretable in terms of interaction of the sympathetic and parasympathetic divisions of the nervous system.

The hemoglobin concentration in the blood increases in the middle of the cycle to 18–20 mg %. Also, the red and white cell counts fluctuate with particular phases of the cycle (Alekseeva, 1954). Regular fluctuations in daytime rectal temperature are readily traced through the phases of the cycle. Low in the first phase, body temperature increases rapidly toward the beginning of the second phase (the day of ovulation) and remains elevated during the second phase of the cycle. The shift at ovulation can amount to $2°$ or more (Alekseeva, 1963). Arterial pressure also changes markedly with different phases of the cycle. In a given female, arterial pressure can range in the first half of the cycle from 110/60 to 120/80 mm Hg and in the second half increase to 150/90 mm Hg and higher. Heart rate and respiration show small but reliable fluctuations through the phases of the cycle (Alekseeva, 1961, 1963). Blood sugar also changes, increasing toward the middle of the cycle and decreasing in the second phase (Alekseeva, 1963).

Oxygen consumption is lower in the first phase of the cycle; it then increases and remains at a high level in the second phase (Alekseeva & Avdzhian, 1961). Twenty-four hour urine excretion is lower in the first phase of normal menstrual cycles than in the second phase. In anovulatory, amenorrheic cycles this regularity is absent. The specific gravity of the urine is inversely proportional to its volume; it is higher in the first and lower in the second phase of the cycle. Body weight tends to increase in the first phase and decrease in the second; this relationship does not always hold, however (Figure 63).

Our data indicate that not all functional systems of the female organism are equally involved in the fluctuations of the sexual cycle. Gastric secretion in particular has proved to be relatively stable and independent of change through the different phases of the sexual cycle.

Ontogenetically the organs of digestion undergo their full development before the onset of sexual maturity. It is possible that fluctuations of function of the gastric glands are controlled by independent central regulatory mechanisms such that the cyclical sexual mechanism does not exert any significant effect. We found that gastric secretion in hamadryas baboons, however, is subject to the central regulatory mechanisms governing the diurnal rhythm. It is excited in the morning and daylight hours and is inhibited at night. This further attests to an independence of the physiological rhythms of gastric secretion and the sexual cycle in baboons and may help to explain the absence of correlation between the two.

According to data obtained by L. V. Alekseeva, there is a close relationship between higher nervous activity and the phases of the sexual cycle. The propor-

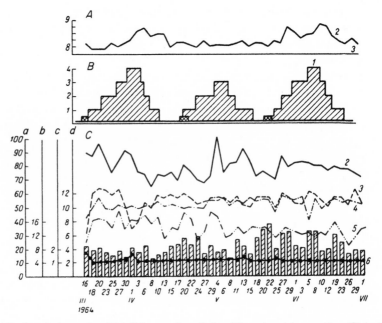

FIG. 63 Correlations of weight (A), sexual cyclicity (B), and gastric secretion (C) in the mature female hamadryas baboon Nochnitsa. Abscissa, dates of weighing and of gastric secretion determinations. Stage of the sexual cycle was recorded daily on the basis of degree of swelling of the sex skin and menstruation. Ordinate: (A) weight (kg); (B) degree of swelling of the sex skin (four-point scale); (C) indices of gastric secretion in zero samples: (a) acidity in titration units, (b) digestive strength (Mett units), (c) pH, (d) volume (ml). (1) Volume; (2) total acid; (3) free acid; (4) control (digestive strength of 1 ml of secretion combined with 1 ml 0.36% HCl); (5) digestive strength; (6) pH. Sexual cycle comprises prefollicular phase (not observed in the baboon tested), follicular phase (from onset of swelling to maximum), luteal phase (from maximum swelling to menstrual phase), and menstrual phase.

tion of correct motor responses in a food-reinforced conditioning paradigm increased to 80–100% in the first phase of the cycle and decreased to 0–20% in the second phase of the cycle.

SPONTANEOUS AND EXPERIMENTALLY INDUCED DISTURBANCES OF THE SEXUAL CYCLE IN BABOONS

Alekseeva found that the average 35- to 36-day duration of the sexual cycle in hamadryas baboons could change significantly and that most frequently this was caused by prolongation of the prefollicular phase, or quiescent stage. Bochkarev (1935) described three types of sexual cycle in the hamadryas baboon: menstrual, anovulatory, and pregravid. The swelling of the sex skin in anovulatory cycles does not differ either in duration or in intensity from that seen in the menstrual cycle. Most likely, follicular maturation progresses as in the menstrual cycle but ovulation does not occur. In connection with this, the second phase of the cycle is shortened and menstruation is not observed. Anovulatory cycles are observed often in young females, which have less opportunity for copulation than the stronger adult females that continuously surround the male. Such cycles are also observed in aged females when the sexual cycle is fading, and among mature healthy females during hot summer months and cold winter months and during pregnancy and lactation. They are noted primarily in newly imported baboons or in the first generations born in the Sukhumi breeding colony. Pregravid cycles (proceeding to pregnancy) are characterized by shortened time of swelling of the sex skin (20.4 days on an average). Of 1684 cycles recorded, only 316 ended in pregnancy (Alekseeva, 1963).

Alekseeva (1957) observed experimentally induced disturbances of sexual cyclicity in three hamadryas baboon females subjected to stress. The methods of inducing stress involved the establishment of "conflict situations" as devised by D. I. Miminoshvili. The animals were subjected to continual clashes of natural social, sexual, and alimentary response mechanisms. As the imposition of stressors continued, the general behavior of the baboons changed; it acquired a defensive character. The animals lost weight and hair. Conditioned alimentary motor responses were inhibited and paradoxical and ultraparadoxical patterns of response to signal stimuli appeared. The changes in higher nervous activity typical of the normal phases of the cycle disappeared.

Changes in the sexual cycle occurred in all three animals but they varied from individual to individual. Among the abnormalities observed were irregularities in the duration of particular phases (arrhythmia), fusion of two cycles into one, disappearance of the menstrual phase, breakthrough bleeding, and cycles with two peaks of sex skin swelling.

In our investigation of two hamadryas baboon females, changes in sexual cyclicity were obtained in response to two different kinds of stressor. The first occurred as a result of surgical and anesthetic trauma during the implantation of a gastric fistula under morphine and ether anesthesia. The results are illustrated in Figure 64. The operation performed on the baboon Kleshchevina (Figure 64A) coincided with the conclusion of the menstrual phase and beginning of the follicular phase of the next cycle. This cycle did not begin at once, however. The onset of swelling was delayed by about 2 months. The pause between cycles was therefore prolonged to the equivalent of two full cycles. Once the new cycle began, it and the subsequent cycle proceeded normally.

In the second baboon, the operation coincided with onset of the follicular phase (Figure 64B). The very day after the operation, swelling of the sex skin suddenly subsided and 12 days later, i.e., unusually early, there began a protracted course of menstrual bleeding. Except for some prolongation of the following prefollicular phase, the cycles proceeded normally thereafter.

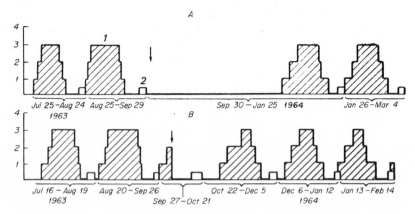

FIG. 64 Influence of the trauma of abdominal surgery on sexual cyclicity in two hamadryas baboons, Kleshchevina (A) and Nochnitsa (B). Abscissa, beginning and ending date of individual menstrual cycles; ordinate, magnitude of swelling of the sex skin (four-point scale). (1) Degree of swelling; (2) menstruation. Arrow: day of surgery (gastric fistula implanted under general anesthesia). Otherwise legend same as in Fig. 63.

Therefore, abdominal surgery can significantly disrupt the sexual cyclicity in hamadryas baboon females. The kind of disturbance probably depends on the phase of the sexual cycle in which the stressful event occurs. The disturbance is largely restricted to that sexual cycle during which the nervous stress is imposed, whereas the subsequent cycles remain for all practical purposes normal. If the stress is imposed before the onset of a cycle (before the follicular phase) that cycle is essentially postponed, whereas stress imposed after the onset interrupts the cycle.

The same animals were subjected to other stressors, viz., repeated immobilization on the stand under fasting conditions (Figure 65, I) and after eating apples in the home cage (Figure 65, II, III). Repeated immobilizations in which the extremities were fixed for 5 hr at a time had a greater effect on the sexual cycles of Nochnitsa than of Kleshchevina (Figure 65, B and A, respectively). In Nochnitsa the first series of immobilization experiments coincided with the menstrual phase; menstruation was prolonged to 7 days, and the prefollicular phase extended to 14 days. Both of the next two series of immobilizations coincided with the beginning of the follicular phase. Under these conditions the swelling of the sex skin subsided temporarily and then resumed to produce a two-peaked pattern; the cycles were markedly prolonged. In Kleshchevina, immobilization stress produced a distinct prefollicular phase that she did not show under normal conditions. In both baboons the stress influenced most strongly the cycle during which it was incurred. Subsequent cycles were usually normal. Perhaps the mechanisms that generate the new sexual cycle simulta-

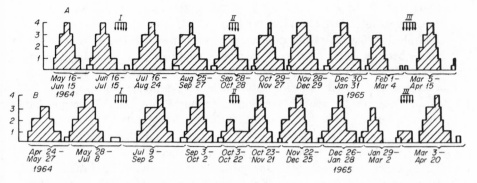

FIG. 65 Influence of immobilization stress on sexual cycles of the baboon females Klesh-chevina (A) and Nochnitsa (B). (I) Five-hour immobilization in fasting stage; (II and III) 5-hr immobilization after eating in the home cage. Arrows: days of sessions involving immobilization. Otherwise legend same as in Fig. 63.

neously establish a unique "physiological barrier" against further influence of neural stress mechanisms set in motion by earlier stressors.

One of the most frequent disturbances of sexual cyclicity observed under stressful conditions is prolongation of the prefollicular phase, or pause. The fact that this pause is almost a vestigial phase in the normal menstrual cycle, appearing primarily under various unfavorable conditions (Alekseeva, 1963), suggests that it may be the primate homolog of diestrus in rodents. Perhaps, when it occurs in baboons under stress it represents "regression" to a bio-logically more primitive, phylogenetically older mechanism for regulating sexual cyclicity.

EXPERIMENTAL NEUROGENIC AMENORRHEA
IN HAMADRYAS BABOONS

There is only one report in the literature of experimental neurogenic amenorrhea in female hamadryas baboons (Alekseeva, 1957, 1959b). The conditions under which experimental neurosis was induced were as follows. Three females were placed in individual living cages next to wire screen enclosed compounds housing males of the same species. The males strenuously attempted to join them and, failing, climbed the walls of the compound threatening the females and each other, dashed about the cage, etc. The females also lived in a continual state of motor excitation and vocalized incessantly. To potentiate the conflict, the females were rotated from one cage to another every 2 or 3 days. This intensified the waves of motor and emotional excitation. The situation was made most stressful at feeding time by feeding the females first. Abandoning the males as unattainable they ate directly in front of the unfed males, who would ordinarily eat first. Such experiments lasted about 2 months.

Individual menstrual phases dropped out in all three females, and one of the animals became amenorreic for 5 months. Clearly, an experimental paradigm capable of inducing amenorrhea lasting the equivalent of five menstrual cycles in the baboon might serve as a reasonable model of neurogenic amenorrhea in the human. The disorder seen in the female baboon is not readily interpretable purely in terms of the humoral regulatory mechanisms that control female sexual function in lower mammals. The mechanism of these disorders must involve the regulatory role of the central nervous system.

In our experiments neurogenic amenorrhea was observed in the female hamadryas baboon, Takla (Figure 66). This animal had lived for a long time in a small cage with a male of about the same age. Her menarche occurred at the age of 4 years 2 months and she went through two quite normal sexual cycles. At about this time her submissive and sexual behavior toward the male increased. The beginning of mature sexual activity coincided with the winter months, when the mature male hamadryas baboons were also housed indoors. The threatening gestures and vocalizations of the mature males had a double effect. The female developed neurogenic amenorrhea and her male companion developed neurogenic impotence. The female failed to menstruate for a period of time equivalent to four full cycles. During copulatory activity, the male developed erections, which subsided abruptly before intromission. The repeated failures to carry copulation to conclusion gave way to aggression on the part of the male toward the female, including fighting and biting. With the advent of summer, when the

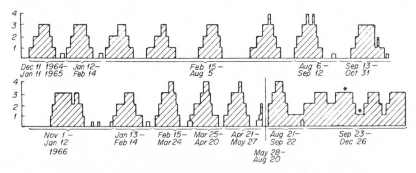

FIG. 66 Neurogenic amenorrhea in the female hamadryas baboon Takla consisting of cycles of swelling of the sex skin alternating with protracted quiescent periods (Feb. 15 to Aug. 5, 1965) and later a breakdown in the cyclical pattern itself (Aug. 21 to Dec. 26, 1966). Arrhythmia, two-peaked swellings, prolonged prefollicular phases, and intermittent bleeding are apparent. Menstrual bleeding is indicated by open rectangles. Asterisks represent times when the photographs appearing in Figs. 67 and 68 were taken. Otherwise legend same as in Fig. 63.

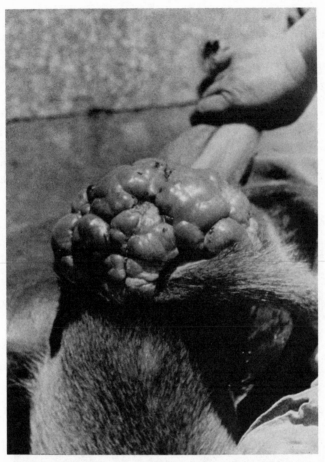

FIG. 67 Maximal abnormal sex skin swelling as seen in the hamadryas female baboon Takla; this animal was subject to chronic neurogenic amenorrhea.

other males were returned to the outdoor compound, the sexual relationship of the pair remained inadequate. Distorted sexual reactions were observed whenever the animal handlers or experimenters appeared. The male showed elements of "protective" behavior toward the female at the beginning of copulatory activity, but these gave way to aggression at the end. Subsequently, when the pair was housed in a large home cage in view by the mature males, the male partner developed acute, severe motor disturbances and died. The female was placed in a troup of baboons, but she too developed hysteroid motor disorders (adynamia and tremors of the body and extremities). She was returned to a small individual home cage, and these disorders quickly disappeared. Later on she was housed with a normal female baboon. After a period of amenorrhea

(February 15 to August 5, 1965), the menstrual phase reappeared in her sexual cycles but there were still serious deviations from the norm: varied duration or arrhythmia of cycles, two-peaked cycles, protracted prefollicular phases, intermittent bleeding (November 1 to December 1, 1966), and, again, absence of menses (March 25 to April 20, 1966).

Beginning August 21, 1966 the amenorrhea was complicated by a new disturbance of the cyclicity of sex skin changes; the quiescent phase disappeared. Two periods of maximal and minimal swelling (indicated by asterisks, in Figure 66) are illustrated by the photographs in Figures 67 and 68. They show that along with disappearance of the quiescent phase, the nature of the swelling began to deviate significantly from normal (Figure 69); instead of the smooth

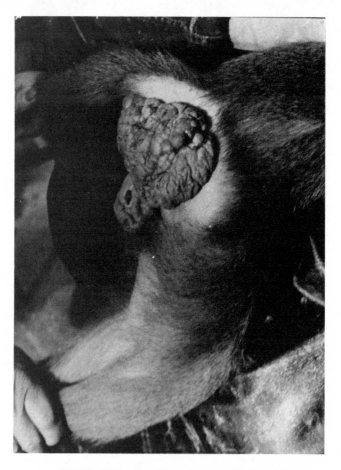

FIG. 68   Minimal swelling of the sex skin in Takla.

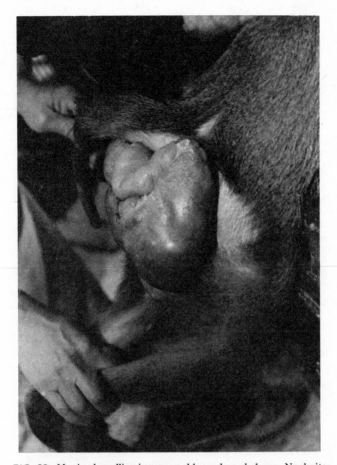

FIG. 69   Maximal swelling in a normal hamadryas baboon, Nochnitsa.

appearance of the normally tumescent perineum, the sex skin became crenulated with numerous lobulations of variable size.

On December 15, 1966 Takla was transferred to a new cage to live with the normal female Nochnitsa and a 9-year-old male. (The male, Zefir, had been suffering for 7 years from experimental neurogenic gastric achylia.)

As seen in Figure 70B Takla's amenorrhea, absence of the quiescent phase, and gross disturbance of sexual cyclicity lasted for 11 months. Menses were reestablished only after the male was removed. Figure 70A shows that disturbances of sexual cyclicity also have occurred in the previously normal female, Nochnitsa, during the time she is housed with the male; she shows prolonged menstruation (December 15, 1966, to January 15, 1967 cycle), absence of menstrual bleeding (January 16 to February 16 cycle), and four cycles with no quiescent phase as

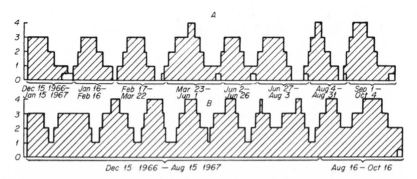

FIG. 70 Disturbance of sexual cyclicity in the normal hamadryas baboon female Nochnitsa (A) and combination of amenorrhea with loss of the quiescent phase in Takla (B) during the period in which they were housed with a male suffering from neurogenic impotence. Menstrual phase denoted by open rectangles.

seen in Takla. In all probability, these changes resulted from the impotence of the male. Tests of higher nervous activity had revealed symptoms of neurosis before he was housed with the females (unstable positive conditioned responses and frequent discrimination deficits in conditioning experiments). He was unusually disturbed during the 10 months he lived with the females (Figure 71). During this time he was in a constant state of sexual excitation; he had a continuous erection, which subsided at once whenever he approached one of the females. His sexual advances were often accompanied by aggression toward the female. The females were stressed by any sexual activity on the part of the male and also by the furor that arose every time the male was caught for the conditioning experiments. The latter was achieved with great difficulty and was traumatic to the male and females alike.

Our experiments therefore corroberate the findings of L. V. Alekseeva (1957, 1959b) regarding the neurogenic nature of amenorrhea in female hamadryas baboons. It is possible to establish experimental models of neurogenic amenorrhea in hamadryas baboons either by exposing them to powerful visual and auditory social stimuli without opportunity to consummate the sexual response patterns thus set in motion or by otherwise disrupting the sexual relationships of males and females living together. Under the latter conditions, we found that sexual disturbances emerged both in the females (amenorrhea, disturbances of cyclicity) and in the male (psychogenic impotence). Whereas amenorrhea and disruption of sexual cyclicity in the females could be traced to sexual incompetence and aggressivity in the male, the cause of the male's impotence could not be attributed directly to the females' sexual disorders, because despite their amenorrhea and acyclicity their sexual receptivity was not detectably reduced.

The sexual impotence of the male was related primarily to the fact that his first sexual relations with the females occurred under circumstances where his

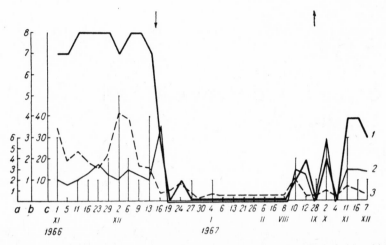

FIG. 71 Neurotic state of the male hamadryas baboon Zefir during the period in which he was housed with the females under conditions in which defensive response mechanisms were continually activated. Arrows indicate the beginning and end of communal housing. Otherwise legend same as in Fig. 6.

defensive response mechanisms were mobilized. Subsequently, normal sexual stimuli gradually became signals of the defensive dominant. In this male, the previous neurotic condition induced by chronic restraint and immobilization contributed greatly to this conversion. Animals that have survived experiments involving immobilization stress commonly exhibit hysterical-like reactions to many stimuli, including sexual stimuli. This is true of both male and female hamadryas baboons.

Our observations regarding neurogenic amenorrhea and impotence in hamadryas baboons supports the views of leading Soviet sexologists regarding the psychogenic nature of amenorrhea in the human female (Kvater, 1961) and sexual incompetence in the human male (Mil'man, 1965; Ivanov, 1966).

We are confident that further investigations along these lines in baboons can establish a reliable model of human psychogenic sexual disorders and also lead to more rational and effective therapy of such disorders.

VII
A Conditioned Reflex Model
of Chronic Hyperglycemia

Diseases similar to diabetes mellitus were mentioned in medical writings as early as 1500–3000 B.C. (Ebbell, 1937). The first experimental investigations of this illness, however, did not occur until Claude Bernard's work in the middle 1800s. Bernard (1813–1878) was a scientist who contributed greatly to our knowledge of carbohydrate metabolism in general and its disturbances in diabetes in particular (Best, 1960).

Among the major early achievements in the experimental study of diabetes mellitus were the clarification of the role of the liver in regulating blood sugar levels (Bernard, 1872), the relating of diabetes to disturbance of the organism's ability to utilize carbohydrates, and the discovery that the pancreatic hormone, insulin, reduces the concentration of sugar in the blood and increases the penetration of glucose from the blood into muscle cells.

Primary credit goes to Claude Bernard for establishing the role of the central nervous system in the development of hyperglycemia and glucosuria. He found in animal experiments that puncturing the floor of the fourth ventricle of the brain with a needle induced a temporary diabetic condition. The mechanism of the hyperglycemia produced by this procedure has not been fully elucidated to this day.

NEUROGENIC DIABETES MELLITUS IN HUMANS

According to L. G. Leibson (1962), the brain participates in the normal regulation of blood sugar levels, and clinicians have long recognized the possibility that diabetic disease may be initiated or exacerbated by severe emotional shocks. Claude Bernard wrote (1872): "I know of cases in which a single emotional upset was enough to induce the temporary appearance of sugar in the urine."

Professor S. V. Levashov (1904), analyzing the cause of illness in 238 cases of diabetes, indicated that very often patients related the onset of the illness to nervous stress, grief, anxieties, or head trauma. K. M. Bykov (1944) wrote that diabetes was a frequent clinical finding in stock brokers, in whom it was apparently caused by shocks to the central nervous system.

Knowles (1960) has suggested that diabetes can arise under the influence of extremely intensive emotional excitation and that living under severe emotional tension for long periods of time can induce a rather stable hyperglycemia which, in people with a predisposition to diabetes, can develop into the disease itself. Many investigators, however, have failed to corroborate this hypothesis. Hinkle and Wolf (1952) registered a decrease rather than an increase in blood sugar levels during acute emotional reactions. (The only exceptions were intense fear or horror, which were accompanied by increased epinephrine secretion.) Further investigations are therefore necessary to confirm or rule out the role of the nervous system in the regulation of blood sugar and in the pathogenesis of diabetes mellitus.

SPONTANEOUS AND EXPERIMENTAL DIABETES IN ANIMALS

I. M. Sokoloverova (1960) described the only case in the literature of spontaneously occurring diabetes of pancreatic origin in a baboon. This female hamadryas baboon showed classic signs of diabetes mellitus: hyperglycemia, glucosuria, polydipsia, polyuria, and polyphagia. Further investigation disclosed the disturbances of carbohydrate, protein, fat, water, and gas metabolism typical of diabetes. The animal also showed a chronic disturbance of sexual cyclicity that, in light of the preceding chapter, would be consistent with a disorder of neurogenic origin.

A thorough review of methods used to provoke or potentiate glucosuria in experimental animals has been published by D. J. Ingle (1960). Among the methods he describes are (1) dietetic manipulations (excessive feeding, malnutrition, rapid transition from a diet rich in fat to one rich in carbohydrates); (2) methods producing insulin deficiency (pancreatectomy, administration of alloxan or related compounds, parenteral administration of great quantities of glucose to normal animals or animals with subtotal pancreatectomy, sudden discontinuation of insulin after long-term administration); (3) hormonal manipulations (growth hormone; prolactin; ACTH; such adrenocortocosteroids as hydrocortisone, cortisone, corticosterone, 11-dehydrocorticosterone, and several synthetic derivatives of hydrocortisone; 11-oxygenated derivatives of progesterone; estrogens; thyroxin; epinephrine; pitressin; glucagon); (4) stressors eliciting acute glycogenolytic response (piqûre, emotional stimulation, asphyxia, physical trauma, toxins, pharmacological agents); (5) stressors eliciting chronic hyperglycemic responses (infections, fractures, drugs); (6) phlorrhizin and related compounds, uranium salts, and other renal poisons. According to Ingle, none of these methods has produced an entirely satisfactory model of diabetes mellitus as seen in man.

It is possible that the initiating factor in clinical diabetes is no longer apparent at the time the patient presents for medical attention. In considering the role of the nervous system in the origin of diabetes Ingle (1960) writes: "Efferent discharges from the sympathetic system can cause release of epinephrine and hence of glucose from the liver. This response can be elicited by various stimuli. The nervous system probably affects carbohydrate metabolism by other mechanisms, but there is little relevant information."

There have been reports in the literature regarding the establishment of hyperglycemia in dogs. When an indifferent stimulus (a whistle) is paired repeatedly with injections of epinephrine, presentation of the stimulus with an empty syringe or the injection of physiological saline come to elicit the same kind of increase in blood sugar (Fishchenko & Beliaev, 1939) or may evoke glucosuria (Savchenko, 1940). Other investigators, however, have been unable to establish conditioned reflex hyperglycemia using epinephrine as the unconditioned stimulus (Gantt, 1935; Savchenko, 1946).

Some investigators have observed an increase in blood sugar level in people ingesting saccharine solution and have explained this finding in terms of a conditioned hyperglycemic response elicited by saccharine's stimulation of the oral cavity (Kosiakov, 1952; Kanfor, 1959). In all of the studies where hyperglycemia has appeared to be elicited by a conditioned reflex mechanism, the reflex has been unstable and of extremely short duration.

HYPERGLYCEMIC RESPONSES TO IMMOBILIZATION
IN CATS AND BABOONS

Boehm and Hoffman (1878) first reported glucosuria in cats tied to a restraint stand; they referred to the phenomenon as "*Fesselungs*-diabetes." They did not, however, discuss the significance of this finding from the point of view of brain mechanisms of emotion.

Cannon, Shohl, and Wright (1911) replicated the experiments of Boehm and Hoffman, excluding the element of pain. They tied the cats to a stand for various periods of time ranging from 30 min to 5 hr. The males, especially young males, reacted strongly to this procedure, the females less so. Glucosuria developed in all 12 animals. In most it appeared within 30–40 min, although in several animals the latency of onset was 5 hr. Urine samples collected on a subsequent day showed no trace of sugar. Adrenalectomy abolished the glucosuric response, even though the duration of the fixation was increased by two or three times. On the basis of these experiments Cannon (1929) concluded that negative emotions contribute to the maximal mobilization of the energy resources of the organism. Muscle contractility is enhanced; cardiac function is intensified; the vessels of the heart, lungs, and brain dilate; arterial pressure increases; and hyperglycemia develops because of increased secretion of epinephrine into the blood stream and by direct breakdown of liver glycogen.

Hyperglycemia of sudden onset has also been reported for rhesus monkeys subjected to 4-hr immobilization in a supine position (Poirier, Ayotte, Lemire, Ganther, & Cordeau, 1955). These authors did not comment on possible long-term effects of immobilization on blood sugar level.

Low levels of hyperglycemia (100–120 mg %) have been reported in monkeys of various species (hamadryas baboons, green marmosets, and rhesus monkeys) when first subjected to a new experiment (Iu. P. Butnev, 1957, 1961a, b). Butnev explained this finding in terms of the influence of defensive and orienting response mechanisms on carbohydrate metabolism. With repetition of the experiments, the reaction of the animals to the experimental situation extinguished and blood sugar levels diminished to 70–90 mg %. It should be noted that the factor of physical restraint inevitably contributes to the initial hyperglycemia seen in the experimental setting.

In the experiments designed to model neurogenic gastric achylia in hamadryas baboons, we noted increases in blood sugar averaging up to 150 mg % during immobilization of the baboons, whether on an empty stomach or after eating (Figure 72). In individual experiments the concentration of sugar in the blood increased to 190 mg %. This hyperglycemia did not persist, however, beyond the duration of the immobilization session. Repeated immobilizations were attended by a decrease in the hyperglycemic response. Furthermore, after a series of sessions with 5 hr of immobilization, the animals suffering from chronic neurogenic gastric achylia developed a hypoglycemic condition (Figure 36). In these experiments, the animals had been fed before immobilization, so that their blood sugar levels were presumably elevated at the time of stress. It therefore appears that immobilization stress after eating is inadequate for the generation of chronic hyperglycemia in hamadryas baboons.

CHRONIC EXPERIMENTAL NEUROGENIC HYPERGLYCEMIA IN RHESUS MONKEYS

Up to the present time no one has succeeded in establishing a reliable animal model of diabetes mellitus (or its primary symptom, hyperglycemia) altogether on the basis of nervous stress. The hyperglycemic reactions that have been studied in various animals, including monkeys, have not as yet conclusively elucidated the diabetic state. This may be because once diabetes mellitus has been induced by brain mechanisms involving emotional stress, such stress is not

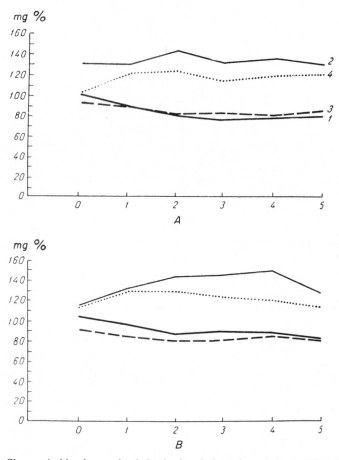

FIG. 72 Changes in blood sugar levels in the female hamadryas baboons Kleshchevina (A) and Nochnitsa (B) under different experimental conditions (mean data from five sessions). Abscissa, time from onset of experiment; ordinate, blood sugar concentration (mg %) under conditions of (1) free behavior in the home cage; (2) immobilization on a restraint stand in the fasting state; (3) free behavior in the home cage after completion of sessions with immobilization in the fasting state; (4) immobilization after eating apples in the home cage.

necessary to sustain it. It is therefore possible that the most appropriate animal model of human diabetes is one in which the neurogenic hyperglycemia is a chronic illness greatly outlasting the stressor events that has initiated it.

What mechanisms might generate a neurogenic hyperglycemic condition of this kind? Our work, of course, has not solved the extremely complex questions of pathogenic mechanisms in diabetes mellitus. It has been primarily an attempt to test by experiment the hypothesis that conditioning defensive behavior to fluctuations in blood sugar level may lead to pathological functioning of the system which regulates that level, i.e., the system which controls carbohydrate metabolism. To this end, experiments were carried out to establish elevated blood sugar level as an interoceptive conditioned signal of a defensive dominant.

The investigations were conducted on five imported female rhesus monkeys 5–7 years old that had participated in other experiments at the Primate Center. All of them were known to have developed functional gastric anacidity during their life in captivity. Otherwise, they were healthy. They were housed together in a large outdoor wire net cage measuring 3 × 3 × 2 m and within view of other monkeys in similar cages. The outdoor cage communicated through a small door with a similar but smaller indoor cage from which they were caught for experimental purposes in transport cages or squeeze cages. On experimental days parallel blood samples were obtained from incisions of the two ear lobes at 9:00, 10:00, 11:00 and 12:00 o'clock noon. The procedure for taking blood samples required 2–3 min per animal. Blood sugar was determined by the Hagedorn–Jensen method. The investigation, carried out between May 6 and December 28, 1963, consisted of nine experimental series of five sessions each. The sessions were separated by 1–4 days so that each series lasted 10–15 days. Data from each experimental series were subjected to statistical analysis. In addition, the data were analyzed for changes in blood sugar levels within and between experiments over the entire course of the investigation. In all, 1190 blood sugar analyses were carried out.

In the first series the sugar level in peripheral blood was determined at 9:00, 10:00, 11:00, and 12:00 o'clock with the animals unfed and free, between the taking of blood samples, to interact in normal fashion in the outdoor home cage. It was presumed that these four samples represented the normal glucose levels under the animals' accustomed living conditions; the animals were caught and blood taken as rapidly as possible to limit the effect that this procedure might have had on the blood sugar level. Results of the first series of sessions are presented in Tables 34 and 35.

TABLE 34

Concentration (mg %) of Sugar in The Peripheral Blood of Rhesus Monkeys on an Empty Stomach and under Free Behavioral Conditions[a]

Subject No.	Time			
	9:00	10:00	11:00	12:00
5311	100 ± 2	99 ± 4	103 ± 1	106 ± 2
5314	101 ± 4	101 ± 1	102 ± 1	102 ± 2
5369	100 ± 5	103 ± 2	103 ± 1	102 ± 1
5371	99 ± 5	101 ± 3	103 ± 2	106 ± 3

[a]Experimental Series #1: dates of sessions: May 6, 8, 10, 13 and 15, 1963.

TABLE 35
Changes in Blood Sugar Levels of One Subject
(No. 5369) across Sessions[a]

	Time			
Date	9:00	10:00	11:00	12:00
May 6, 1963	81	94	103	100
May 8, 1963	107	106	112	103
May 10, 1963	100	106	99	100
May 13, 1963	108	100	100	103
May 15, 1963	103	107	100	104

[a]Stomach empty, free behavior between blood samples.
Experimental Series #1.

It is apparent that the blood sugar levels of fasting female rhesus monkeys under free behavioral conditions was relatively constant both among subjects and within the same subject from hour to hour and across days.

The concentrations of blood sugar reported here agree closely with values reported elsewhere for healthy rhesus monkeys (Butnev, 1957) and for man (Predtechenskii, 1960).

In the second experiment, all conditions were the same as in the first series of sessions, except that the animals were administered glucose intravenously in doses of 2 g/kg hourly after the 9:00, 10:00, and 11:00 o'clock blood samples were taken. The first (9:00) sample served as a control with the other three (10:00, 11:00, 12:00) reflecting the organism's handling of glucose loads 1 hr after administration. Monkeys have been noted for their high tolerance to carbohydrate loading, so that intravenous injections of glucose produce hyperglycemia only in samples drawn 5, 20, and 30 min after administration, following which the initial level is reestablished (Butnev, 1961b). Our data corroborate such reports. They indicate that, in the healthy monkey, the tissues have a high capacity to utilize intravenous glucose loads and reflect prompt regulatory activity on the part of the systems that control blood sugar concentration (Tables 36 and 37).

The third experimental series was carried out to determine the effects of strong defensive excitation and negative emotions on blood sugar levels. In this series the monkeys were immobilized in a supine position on wooden stands (Figure 73), which were set up in the home cage. During the time they were fixed to the stands, the animals struggled constantly to free themselves. Although they attracted the attention of monkeys in neighboring cages, the activities of the latter continued to include the usual mixture of playing, running, climbing on the wire net walls, eating, etc. For the restrained monkeys, all of these familiar everyday events were paired with the unfamiliar, acutely

TABLE 36

Influence of Intravenous Glucose Loading on Sugar Levels
(mg %) in Peripheral Blood of *Macaca mulatta* with Animals
Released between Capture for Hourly Samples[a]

Subject No.	Time			
	9:00	10:00	11:00	12:00
5311	114 ± 5	120 ± 9	115 ± 4	109 ± 4
5314	106 ± 3	112 ± 5	113 ± 6	114 ± 5
5369	115 ± 6	114 ± 6	115 ± 5	109 ± 3
5371	109 ± 4	116 ± 7	114 ± 8	111 ± 3

[a]Experimental Series #2; dates of sessions: May 17, 20, 22,
24 and 27, 1963.

disturbing physical restraint. The point of these experiments was not only to
show that immobilization was an adequate stimulus to evoke hyperglycemia but
also to create a defensive dominant in the central nervous system under natural,
familiar stimulus conditions. It was postulated that through such a process it
would be possible to establish a hyperglycemic dysfunction of chronic nature.

The repeated and extended immobilization of the monkeys where they could
view one another, their own cage, other monkeys nearby engaged in their usual
daily activities, and the attending staff should unite these natural stimuli into a
complex of signal stimuli for the defensive dominant. Because immobilization
was imposed under conditions of hunger, extreme muscular activity, and emo-
tionally induced, epinephrine-mediated high blood sugar, these phenomena
could also become interoceptive signals for the defensive dominant.

One monkey died in the second hour of the first immobilization experiment.

TABLE 37

Changes in Blood Sugar Levels (mg %) of *Macaca mulatta*
(No. 5369) during Baseline Intravenous Glucose
Loading Experiments[a]

Date	Time			
	9:00	10:00	11:00	12:00
May 17, 1963	96	100	108	101
May 20, 1963	111	101	111	105
May 22, 1963	113	130	114	116
May 24, 1963	115	124	107	110
May 27, 1963	142	116	135	116

[a]Experimental Series #2.

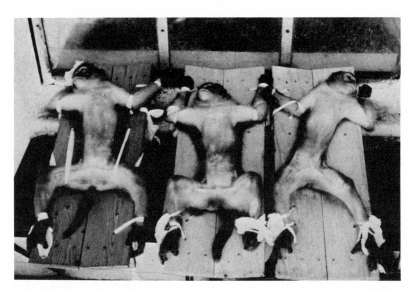

FIG. 73 Immobilization of rhesus monkeys on restraint stands placed in the home cage.

Autopsy disclosed only multiple punctate hemorrhages in the viscera. The remaining monkeys showed no significant increase in blood sugar in the first experiment. The hyperglycemia emerged only gradually with repeated immobilizations, and the extent of rise was relatively limited; blood sugar concentration did not rise much above 160 mg %. The fact that on successive days the 9:00 preimmobilization blood sample showed elevated sugar levels suggested that the hyperglycemia was mediated by a conditioned reflex mechanism. The first fixations of fasting animals in the stand yielded mean blood sugar levels of 150 mg %. After two or three sessions this concentration was seen in the first sample of the day, and even higher concentrations were registered after the animal was immobilized (Tables 38 and 39). [Interestingly, the monkey that died early in the first experiment showed a drop in blood sugar level to 98 mg % just before death (Table 38).]

After the series of immobilization sessions, the behavior of the monkeys in the home cage changed drastically. Aggressive behavior predominated both in their relations with one another and toward the monkeys in adjacent cages. Whenever the animal handlers or experimenter appeared, the animals withdrew to a corner or to the ceiling of the cage.

The fourth experiment was an exact repetition of the first: blood samples were taken from the animals, fasting and under conditions of free behavior in the home cage.

The purpose now was to evaluate longer term aftereffects of the repeated immobilizations. Contrary to expectation, the average level of sugar in the blood

TABLE 38
Blood Sugar Levels (mg %) in Fasting Rhesus Monkeys with
Immobilization on the Restraint Stand between
Blood Samples[a]

Subject No.	Time			
	9:00	10:00	11:00	12:00
5311	139 ± 10	150 ± 6	149 ± 9	150 ± 9
5314	123	138	98 (died)	
5369	140 ± 8	147 ± 6	146 ± 6	149 ± 8
5371	136 ± 9	149 ± 3	147 ± 8	145 ± 8

[a]Experimental Series #3; dates of sessions: May 29, June 1, 4, 7 and 10, 1963.

did not subside rapidly but proved to be even higher than during the immobilization experiments (Tables 40 and 41). The mean values now corresponded to the maximal values observed at the time the animals were immobilized, and they were surprisingly constant both within and across subjects (ranging from 159 ± 1 to 164 ± 0.5 mg %).

Experiment 5 demonstrated that this conditioned reflex hyperglycemia was also observed under conditions of more prolonged hunger and when blood was drawn at different times of day (Tables 42 and 43). Therefore, the hyperglycemia seen in rhesus monkeys after repeated immobilization is resistant to prolonged food deprivation and is not a simple reflex to the time of day when immobilization occurred. It evidently represents a chronic and stable neurogenic disruption of carbohydrate metabolism. Compared to the experimental monkeys, the control animal (No. 5310) continued to show lower blood sugar levels.

TABLE 39
Changes in Blood Sugar Level (mg %) in One Fasting Subject
(No. 5369) during Repeated Sessions with
Immobilization Stress[a]

Date	Time			
	9:00	10:00	11:00	12:00
May 29, 1963	116	126	123	120
June 1, 1963	132	144	147	149
June 4, 1963	146	155	156	160
June 7, 1963	147	149	150	160
June 10, 1963	160	160	156	156

[a]Experimental Series #3.

TABLE 40

Conditioned Reflex Hyperglycemia in Fasting Rhesus
Monkeys after Sessions Involving Immobilization Stress[a]

	Time			
Subject No.	9:00	10:00	11:00	12:00
	Sugar (mg %)			
5311	161 ± 1	161 ± 1	163 ± 1	164 ± 1
5369	159 ± 1	162 ± 1	162 ± 1	162 ± 1
5371	161 ± 1	161 ± 1	162 ± 1	161 ± 1

[a]Experimental Series #4; dates of sessions: June 13, 15, 17,
19 and 21, 1963.

In fact, in this animal the blood sugar concentration gradually decreased as the study progressed. The aggression of the monkeys that had been subjected to immobilization was directed mainly toward this animal.

The concentration of sugar in the peripheral blood was still about 160 mg % in all of the experimental monkeys a month after the immobilizations had been discontinued. Against this background of continued disturbance of the mechanisms regulating blood sugar, an attempt was undertaken further to potentiate the hyperglycemia by pairing intravenously administered sugar loads with immobilization. In this, the sixth experimental series, the first daily blood sample was drawn with the animal fasting; then it was fixed to the restraint stand as before, except that at 1-hr intervals it received glucose intravenously (2 g/kg). Blood for analysis was drawn every hour just before administration of the next glucose load. The purpose was to evaluate the functional limits of the combined regulatory mechanisms—pancreatic, hepatic, and muscular—in the context of

TABLE 41

Changes in Blood Sugar Levels (mg %) of Subject
No. 5369, Fasting, during the Development of Conditioned
Reflex Hyperglycemia[a]

	Time			
Date	9:00	10:00	11:00	12:00
June 13, 1963	159	162	163	160
June 15, 1963	155	164	160	162
June 17, 1963	162	160	160	161
June 19, 1963	159	161	164	165
June 21, 1963	160	161	162	162

[a]Experimental Series #4.

TABLE 42

Conditioned Reflex Hyperglycemia in Rhesus Monkeys
under Conditions of Extended Food Deprivation and
Shifting Time of Experimental Sessions to Different Hours
of the Day[a]

	Time			
Subject No.	12:00	13:00	14:00	15:00
	Sugar (mg %)			
5310 (control)	133	126	121	119
5311	159 ± 1	159 ± 1	159 ± 1	161 ± 1
5369	160 ± 1	159 ± 2	159 ± 1	160 ± 1
5371	159 ± 1	160 ± 1	160 ± 1	161 ± 1

[a]Experimental Series #5; dates of sessions: June 25, 27, 29
and July 2 and 4, 1963.

conditioned reflex hyperglycemia. One monkey became sick during this series. It developed polyphagia, polydipsia, diarrhea, weight loss, and temporary paresis initially of the arms and then of the legs. Stool examinations for dysentery were negative. All subjects developed blood glucose levels of 180 ± 2 mg % and higher. The first daily samples also showed increases to 170 ± 5 mg %.

Extreme hyperglycemia failed to develop, however, The blood glucose level rose to the renal clearance threshold, 180 mg %, but exceeded this threshold by very little (Tables 44 and 45).

The seventh and eighth experiments were analogous to the first. The blood sugar levels fluctuated between 183 ± 0.3 and 175 ± 1.5 mg %, and by the time these two series were completed the duration of the experimental conditioned reflex hyperglycemia had reached almost 4 months (Tables 46 and 47).

In the interval between these two experiments one subject (No. 5311) died

TABLE 43

Changes in Blood Sugar Concentration (mg %) in Subject
No. 5369 with Time of Sessions Shifted to Later Hours
of the Day

	Time			
Date	12:00	13:00	14:00	15:00
June 25, 1963	156	155	155	156
June 27, 1963	158	156	156	159
June 29, 1963	162	158	158	160
July 2, 1963	162	164	162	163
July 4, 1963	160	161	161	161

TABLE 44

Influence of Intravenous Loads of Glucose on Sugar
Concentration (mg %) in the Peripheral Blood of Fasting
Rhesus Monkeys Subjected to Immobilization Stress[a]

Subject No.	Time			
	9:00	10:00	11:00	12:00
5311	170 ± 4	175 ± 2	179 ± 2	182 ± 2
5369	170 ± 5	174 ± 3	176 ± 3	180 ± 2
5371[b]	167	175	180	181

[a]Experimental Series #6; dates of sessions: July 9, 12, 15, 19, and 22, 1963.
[b]Subject 5371 became ill after the third time.

with symptoms of polyphagia, polydipsia, and hyperglycemia; autopsy revealed marked adiposity, fatty degeneration of the liver, and multiple hemorrhages in the internal organs.

The ninth and last experimental series was conducted 3 months after discontinuation of the monkeys' involvement in any kind of experimental procedure. The blood sugar level of the two remaining experimental animals matched that of the control animal, i.e., had returned to normal levels (Table 48).

The experimental conditioned reflex hyperglycemia of many months duration therefore disappeared within 6 months after the termination of experiments involving immobilization stress. One of the remaining experimental monkeys died in 1964 and the other in 1966. The latter, No. 5369, was housed in a breeding colony where she became pregnant. The fetus died *in utero* and the mother died a short time later. Autopsies of the last two experimental subjects

TABLE 45

Changes in Blood Sugar Concentration (mg %) in Monkey
No. 5369 with Repeated Experiments in Which Intravenous
Loads of Glucose Were Paired with Immobilization

Date	Time			
	9:00	10:00	11:00	12:00
July 9, 1963	155	165	172	182
July 12, 1963	163	172	169	171
July 15, 1963	172	175	177	179
July 19, 1963	176	177	180	181
July 22, 1963	182	181	183	183

[a]Experimental Series #6.

TABLE 46
Conditioned Reflex Hyperglycemia in Rhesus Monkeys in the
First Weeks after Intravenous Loads of Glucose
Administered during Immobilization Stress[a]

Subject No.	Time			
	9:00	10:00	11:00	12:00
	Sugar (mg %)			
5310 (control)	129 ± 3	126 ± 2	124 ± 1	122 ± 1
5311	182 ± 1	182 ± 1	182 ± 1	183 ± L
5369	181 ± 1	182 ± 1	183 ± 0	183 ± 0
5371	181 ± 1	182 ± 1	183 ± 0	183 ± 0.5

[a]Experimental Series #7; dates: July 24, 26, 30 and August
1 and 3, 1963.

both revealed fatty degeneration of the liver and multiple punctate hemorrhages in the internal organs.

To summarize, the experimental illnesses produced in rhesus monkeys by repeated immobilization in combination with intravenous loads of glucose included a variety of pathological phenomena, such as marked defensive behavior, polyphagia, polydipsia, adiposity or abrupt weight loss, chronic hyperglycemia, temporary paresis of the extremities, pathological pregnancy and intrauterine death of the fetus, and early death either at the climax of hyperglycemia or after reversion to normal glucose levels. At autopsy all of the monkeys showed fatty degeneration of the liver and petechial hemorrhages in the gastrointestinal tract, heart, lungs, and other parenchymatous organs.

Most of these signs and symptoms are seen with greater or lesser frequency in

TABLE 47
Persistence of Conditioned Reflex Hyperglycemia in Rhesus
Monkeys after a 40-day Pause in the Experiments[a]

Subject No.	Time			
	9:00	10:00	11:00	12:00
	Sugar (mg %)			
5310 (control)	129 ± 3	127 ± 1	128 ± 0.3	127 ± 1
5311		DIED		
5369	173 ± 4	176 ± 1	178 ± 0	177 ± 1
5371	175 ± 1	178 ± 0	179 ± 1	178 ± 1

[a]Experimental Series #8, dates: September 10, 12, 16, 18
and 21, 1963.

TABLE 48

Reestablishment of Initial Blood Sugar Levels (mg %) after a
Three-Month Pause between Experiments[a]

Subject No.	Time			
	9:00	10:00	11:00	12:00
5310 (control)	102 ± 4	89 ± 6	93 ± 1	96 ± 4
5369	102 ± 7	88 ± 4	91 ± 3	92 ± 1
5371	94 ± 4	95 ± 4	91 ± 1	91 ± 1

[a]Experimental Series #9; dates of sessions: December 18, 20, 23, 26 and 28, 1963.

diabetes mellitus in man. For example, Plum (1960) and White (1960) reported that vascular disease accompanies diabetes in up to 94% of cases. Ingle (1960) recognizing that vascular lesions are commonly encountered in diabetes mellitus in humans, has found no reference to such lesions in the literature on experimental diabetes mellitus in animals. He suggested the cause of this deviation might be differences in the duration of clinical diabetes in the human and animal models of diabetes that had been studied.

Pathology of pregnancy and childbirth in diabetes mellitus is encountered in almost 50% of human cases (Kvater, 1961). Muscular weakness, rapid fatigability, and even paralysis have been recorded by different authors (Bernard, 1872; Levashov, 1904; Plum, 1960). Increased muscular fatigability in diabetes mellitus is probably related to the fact that a deficiency of circulating insulin impairs the transport of glucose into muscle cells (Stetten & Mortimer, 1960). Plum (1960) has also suggested that a disturbance of neuromuscular transmission may underlie the motor disruptions seen in diabetes mellitus.

In the present study experimental hyperglycemia, with blood glucose levels reaching the renal clearance threshold (180 mg %) and outlasting the stressor events by several months, attests to a profound disturbance of the mechanisms that regulate the concentration of sugar in peripheral blood in rhesus monkeys subjected repeatedly to immobilization stress. In the rhesus monkey immobilization of the body and extremities not only led to the simultaneous development of a defensive dominant in the motor system, but also to massive transfer of glucose into the bloodstream, thus further potentiating the behaviorally induced stress on muscular functioning.

Inasmuch as any muscular activity of biological significance presupposes a coordination of function between the motor centers of the brain and the mechanisms that supply the muscles with glucose, it is reasonable to presume that it involves either neural or humoral excitation of the pancreatic insulin releasing mechanism. Insulin secretion during muscular activity assures the delivery of glucose to the muscle cells and enhances the deposition of glucose from the blood into the liver when muscular activity ceases. This is why, under normal conditions, the concentration of sugar in the blood quickly returns to the normal range after muscular exertion.

Because insulin is the only known factor that reduces blood sugar concentration, it is quite likely that the prolonged hyperglycemia induced by immobilization was mediated not only by elevated epinephrine levels but also by a reduction of insulin activity. The intermittent weakness of the extremities seen during immobilization of several of the animals and the paralysis of the extremities and cardiac arrest that occurred in one of them could all be explained by an insulin deficit during immobilization stress. If one considers that the epinephrine response must have been most intense in the first hours of the first immobilization sessions, then one might have expected the most pronounced hyperglycemia to have accompanied the most intense defensive excitation that occurred at those times. To the contrary, however, marked hyperglycemia was not seen in the first sessions in any of the subjects, even the one who died in the very first session. It is possible that in this first session the central mechanisms of motor excitation operated as usual, coordinating an influx of insulin into the bloodstream. The hyperglycemia emerged with repeated imposition of the immobilization stress. It is possible that with forced immobilization the failure of the motor acts of the animal to achieve the accustomed result not only induces a pathologically persistent focus of excitation in the motor system but also disrupts the coordinated reciprocity of mechanisms governing muscular output and the release of insulin, which would ordinarily guarantee an adequate carbohydrate energy source to the muscles.

The chronic hyperglycemic condition induced by immobilization can hardly be explained in terms of the epinephrine mechanism alone. An increase in blood sugar levels to 160–180 mg % is impossible with normal levels of insulin release into the bloodstream. Under nonstressful conditions, intravenous glucose loads of 2 g/kg in normal monkeys established an initial extremely high concentration of sugar in the blood but, nevertheless, after 1 hr the hyperglycemia had disappeared. The chronic hyperglycemia is therefore more likely attributable to reduced insulin output or to an elevated threshold of the pancreatic mechanism that ordinarily releases insulin as a function of blood sugar level. There is some evidence for hepatic involvement in this syndrome of chronic neurogenic hyperglycemia in monkeys, in that all subjects have shown fatty degeneration of the liver at autopsy.

The reversibility of the experimental neurogenic hyperglycemia after several months of rest suggests that it is functional in character. The immobilization stress was situational in that it occurred in the home cage setting where the animals continued to live after the stressor episodes had ceased. The defensive dominant and the hyperglycemia accompanying it could thus become conditioned to a complex of exteroceptive stimuli, including all of the animals' familiar life events, and environmental stimuli, cage, monkeys, etc. An alternate mechanism that might account for the chronic hyperglycemia would be the conditioning of elevated blood sugar as a pathological interoceptive stimulus for the defensive dominant. Once the defensive response mechanism was conditioned to elevations of blood sugar, other physiological increases of sugar concentration in the blood (e.g., with normal muscular exertion, by ingestion of sugar, by emotional response) would also excite the defensive dominant and thus reestablish directly, through its regulatory role in carbohydrate metabolism, the physiological state that occurred during immobilization. Very likely, this mechanism also contributed to the chronic neurogenic hyperglycemia that we produced experimentally.

Regardless of how one explains the mechanism of neurogenic experimental hyperglycemia in rhesus monkeys, it is clear that it develops in the context of immobilization stress and that it can be potentiated by immobilization with intravenous administration of a glucose load. In these experiments hyperglycemia induced by endogenous and exogenous mechanisms coincided repeatedly and for extended periods of time with the most intense defensive excitation. Such simultaneity of occurrence is sufficient for the development of a temporary pathological connection through which hyperglycemia of any origin can come to activate the defensive dominant.

VIII
Neurogenic Ischemic Heart Disease in Hamadryas Baboons[1]

Several investigators have attempted to produce coronary insufficiency and myocardial infarctions in the baboon by imposing excessive strain on, or clashing, alimentary, sexual, social, and defensive reflexes. (Magakian, *et al.,* 1956; Magakian, 1965, 1967; Miminoshvili *et al.,* 1960; Miminoshvili, 1957) In addition, examinations at the Sukhumi Primate Center of baboons that had not been subjected to special stress detected a number of cases of coronary insufficiency which apparently developed under the conditions of living in captivity (Kokaia, 1954, 1958; Magakian *et al.,* 1956; Magakian, 1967).

Our previous studies, in which a variety of systemic disorders were produced by immobilization stress, led to the theory that the physiological system that suffered disruption during experimental neurosis was the system that happened to be particularly active at the time the stressor was imposed. This chapter describes a study designed to produce chronic cardiovascular disorders by imposing the immobilization stressor at times when the cardiovascular system was intensely activated. Our prediction was that cardiac activation would thus become a conditioned signal of impending defensive excitation elicited by immobilization. Once this connection was established, the scene would be set for the long-term disruption of cardiovascular function, because any naturally occurring activation of the heart would activate the defensive dominant, which in turn would feed back to derange cardiovascular function.

The subjects for the investigation were four healthy male hamadryas baboons 2 years of age (Numbers 9337, 9361, 9382, and 9383). The experiments were carried out with the subjects in the fasting state. The electrocardiograms (EKG) were recorded in 12 leads; arterial blood pressure (BP) was recorded by sphyg-

---

[1] This chapter, originally published as a research article (Startsev, Repsin, & Shestopalova, 1972), was not included in the original volume.

momanometer and inflatable arm cuff. The experiment consisted of five phases. In Phase I the EKG and BP were recorded at rest; in Phase II they were recorded after the cardiovascular system had been activated by 5 min of running in the cage (the baboons were chased by an animal handler, who pretended he was attempting to catch them). In Phase III the measurements were taken 1 hr after the beginning of immobilization (fixation of the extremities and trunk of the animal in a supine position on a restraint board). In Phase IV the animals were chased for 5 min and then fixed to the restraint board and the EKG and BP were recorded after 1 hr of immobilization. Phases I–IV each consisted of a series of five daily sessions. Phase V consisted of a series of measurements of EKG and BP made at various periods of time after cessation of the stressor phase (IV) of the experiment.

When the EKG was recorded under resting conditions (Phase I), it was found to be normal in all subjects except for variable depression or slight inversion of the T wave in leads III and AVF, which occurred in three of the animals. In animal No. 9337 the EKG was entirely normal. In sessions where the EKG was recorded after exercise without immobilization (Phase II), baboon No. 9383 continued to show variable T-wave inversion in leads III and AVF; in the other three animals the EKG was entirely normal.

In Phases III and IV, which involved immobilization alone or immobilization preceded by exercise, all of the subjects except No. 9337 began to show gradual

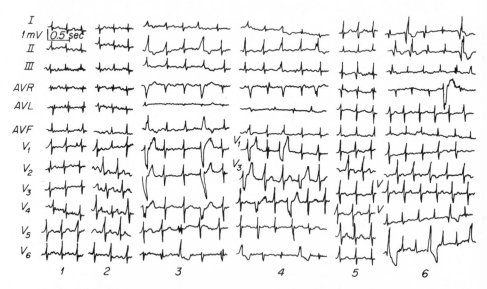

FIG. 74   EKG of baboon No. 9361: leads from top to bottom, I, II, III, AVR, AVL, AVF, and V 1–6 (1) at rest; (2) after exercise; (3) 1 hr after onset of immobilization; (4) 1 hr after onset of immobilization preceded by exercise; (5) 1 month after stressor sessions; (6) 80 days after stressor sessions.

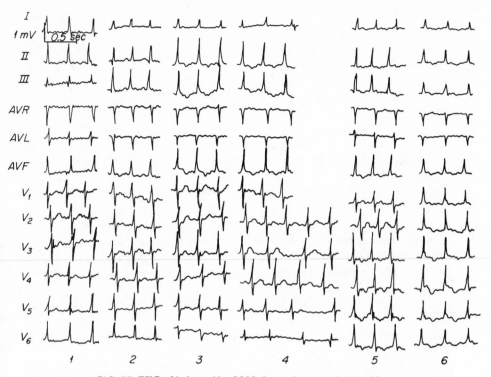

FIG. 75 EKG of baboon No. 9383. Legend same as in Fig. 74.

EKG changes characteristic of ischemia. During the first immobilization session No. 9361's EKG showed pathological ventricular complexes occurring irregularly every two to four cardiac cycles (Figure 74). This gave way to a picture of intermittent left bundle branch block, which persisted throughout the period of immobilization. One week after cessation of the stressor sessions, the conduction block was accompanied by an abnormal Q wave in III, inverted T in III and AVF, and, after a month, in chest leads V_1, V_2, and V_3 as well. At this time, elevation of the ST segment was noted. Eighty days after the stressor phases, T-wave inversion in II and Q-wave abnormalities in I and II were added to this picture.

In baboon No. 9382 immobilization was accompanied by negative T waves in III and AVF with ST elevation. When the immobilization was preceded by exercise, T-wave inversion was noted in lead II as well. One week, 1 month, and 80 days after cessation of the immobilization sessions all of these changes persisted with the addition of T-wave changes (depressed, biphasic, or inverted) in the precordial chest leads.

The EKG changes seen in baboon No. 9383 (Figure 75) during the immobilization sessions consisted in disappearance of the T wave in I and AVL; negative T waves in II, III, AVR, and AVF; and elevation of the ST segment; in addition the R–R interval intermittently increased by 40–60%. One week after cessation of the immobilization sessions, T-wave inversion and elevation of the ST segment were also seen in chest leads V_3-V_6. After 80 days, negative T-waves and elevated ST segments were evident in all leads except AVL.

The EKG of baboon No. 9337 remained normal throughout all phases of the experiment.

In summary, in three of the four subjects, the combination of physiological activation of the heart with immobilization stress led to ischemic EKG changes that became progressively more severe for at least 3 months after cessation of the stressor sessions.

The changes in BP observed in this study were similar in all subjects. There was a diminution of pulse pressure caused by increased diastolic pressure during immobilization, with stabilization of diastolic pressure at 100 mm Hg or higher in the poststressor phase (V). The systolic pressure was essentially unchanged.

We have shown in previous investigations that pathological EKG changes can be induced by immobilization alone, but if the immobilization is not combined with cardiac activation by intense exercise the EKG changes are not as pronounced and they do not progress in severity after the immobilization stress is discontinued.

The results of this study corroborated the concept that chronic pathological changes occur in those functional systems in which activation has become a conditioned signal for the pathological defensive dominant. In our opinion this model of ischemic heart disease most appropriately simulates both the clinical picture and basic mechanisms of stress-induced ischemic heart disease in man.

Conclusion

The modeling of human neurogenic disorders in animals presents a very difficult and complex challenge in that no one experimental model can be expected to match exactly its human counterpart. If one is to obtain data relevant to the etiology and pathogenesis of neurotic conditions in man, however, the first important step is to select an appropriate species for study. There are many important physiological questions that are usefully studied in such animals as dogs, cats, and rats. However, when one is concerned about the pathophysiology of neurogenic disorders, even in as seemingly straightforward a system as the gastrointestinal system such animals often prove not to be appropriate. Man's neuroses are highly conditioned by social factors and, to this extent, the neurotic states produced in nonhuman primates by the manipulation of the social environment are more comparable to the human syndromes than are those studied in other laboratory animals.

The experimental literature on simulating human diseases in nonhuman primates leaves no doubt as to the advantages of the primate model. At the same time, disorders of higher nervous activity and visceral pathology have not received the serious attention they deserve either in the Soviet Union or abroad. Perhaps recognition of the inadequacy of our understanding of the basic processes underlying pathology of the cardiovascular system, the gastrointestinal tract, the hormonal systems, and neoplasia account for the overwhelming tendency for biomedical researchers to restrict their investigations and theoretical constructs to the simplest possible laboratory models. Still, in our time the monkey is not a rare, difficult to obtain object of study for investigations that merit it.

Worthwhile biomedical experimentation with primates demands of the investigator maximal attention to the goals of the experiment and expert consideration of the biological characteristics of the species, particularly of the high level of development of the central nervous system. The various neurogenic disorders described in this volume grew out of our theoretical principles regarding system-specific disorders attending immobilization neurosis in nonhuman primates. One such principle was that the motor system was extremely important in the primate. Stressing this system in such a way as to produce a qualitative change in its function would be expected to establish in it a pathological dominance over other functional systems.

The method we selected to stress the motor system and establish pathological dominance in the motor areas of the brain was short- or long-term fixation of the body and extremities such that, despite every physical effort, the animal was unable to move. An important feature of the technique was the extreme mismatch it produced between the previously experienced appropriateness and effectiveness of intense motor exertions and their abrupt and total futility in the experimental situation. In terms of "feedback afferentation" (Anokhin, 1968), the pathological defensive dominant can be thought of as the consequence of a particular kind of mismatch between "resultative" and "nonresultative" feedback within the motor system. Second, in order to establish selective influence of the pathological defensive dominant on a specific functional system, we used the principles of classical conditioning; i.e., we transformed activation of the target system into a signal for the defensive dominant. By transforming such natural and vital functions as eating sexual arousal, cardiovascular exercise, and interoceptive chemical stimulation into conditioned stimuli for the pathological dominant, it was possible to produce disorders that were limited primarily to the corresponding functional systems: alimentary, sexual, cardiovascular, or metabolic. The conditioning process required repeated experimental sessions in which the activation of the target system was followed by imposition of the immobilization stressor. The development of stable chronic disorders was guaranteed, for the conditioned stimuli were naturally recurring, vital functions of the organism.

This new approach to the induction of neurogenic system-specific disorders in nonhuman primates has proved useful in producing experimental disruption of food-reinforced conditioned behavior, gastric achylia (with polyposis, chronic ulcers, and precancerous lesions of the stomach), hysteroid motor disorders, amenorrhea, a prediabetic state, and coronary insufficiency. Very likely it can be employed to simulate a variety of other human psychosomatic disorders as well.

The aim of the present work has been to draw the attention of the medical world to the development of a new experimental model of neurosis in monkeys and to accomplishments of Soviet primatology in general.

References

Afanas'ev, A. N. *Klinischeskaia Meditsina,* 1934, **12**(6), 904–910.

Alekseeva, L. V. In *Referaty nauchno-issledovatel'skikh rabot za 1947g, OMBN AMN SSSR.* Moscow, 1949. P. 7.

Alekseeva, L. V. *Biulliten' Eksperimental'noi Biologii i Meditsiny,* 1954 **37**(1), 54–58.

Alekseeva, L. V. Opyt polucheniia narushenii polovoi funktsii u samok obez'ian v usloviiakh eksperimental'nogo nevroza. *Rasshirennoe Zasedanie Biuro Otdeleniia Mediko-Biologicheskikh Nauk AMN SSSR.* Sukhumi: Tezisy Dokladov, 1957. Pp. 23–25. (a)

Alekseeva, L. V. K voprosu o vzaimootnoshenii polovoi funktsii i vysshei nervnoi deiatel'nosti u samok obez'ian. *Desiatyi vsesiuyznyi s'ezd akusherov i ginekologov.* Moscow: Tezisy Dokladov, 1957. (b)

Alekseeva, L. V. *Problemy Endokrinologii i Gormonoterapii,* 1959, **5**(3), 11–16. (a)

Alekseeva, L. V. *Problemy Endokrinologii i Gormonoterapii,* 1959, **5**(1), 55–62. (b)

Alekseeva, L. V. In *Voprosy fiziologii i patologii obez'ian.* Sukhumi, 1961. Pp. 261–272.

Alekseeva, L. V. In *Obez'iana-ob'ekt meditsinskikh i biologicheskikh eksperimentov.* Sukhumi, 1963. Pp. 157–185.

Alekseeva, L. V., & Avdzhian, M. V. In *Voprosy fiziologii i patologii obez'ian.* Sukhumi, 1961. Pp. 273–281.

Alekseeva, L. V., & Grigorenko, V. E. In *Voprosy fiziologii, eksperimental'noi patologii i radiobiologii.* Sukhumi, 1965. Pp. 110–112.

Andre, Zh. *Klinicheskii obzor boleznei nervnoi sistemy.* (Translated from French.) St. Petersburg, 1898.

Anichkov, S. V., & Zavodskaia, I. S. *Farmakoterapiia iazvennoi bolezni.* Leningrad, 1965.

Anokhin, P. K. *Biologiia i neirofiziologiia uslovnogo refleksa.* Moscow, 1968.

Anokhin, P. K. Cybernetics and the integrative activity of the brain. In M. Cole & I. Maltzman (Ed.), *A handbook of contemporary Soviet psychology.* New York: Basic Books, 1969. Pp. 830–856.

Arapov, D. A., & Suslov, A. M. Rak zheludka. In *Trudy VIII mezhdunarodnogo protivorakovogo kongressa, 5. Voprosy Klin. Onkolog.* Moscow-Leningrad, 1963. Pp. 160–162.

Asatiani, V. S. *Biologicheskie tablitsy.* Tbilisi, 1960. Chapter 1.

Astvatsaturov, M. I. *Kratkii uchebnik nervnykh boleznei.* Moscow-Leningrad, 1927.

Atkinson, A. J., & Ivy, A. C. *American Journal of Digestive Disease,* 1938, **5**(1), 30–35.

Babinski, J. *Semaine Medicale* (Paris), 1909, **29**, 3–8.

Babkin, B. P. *Sekretornyi mekhanizm pishchevaritel'nykh zhelez.* Leningrad, 1960.

Bam, L. A. *Biulliten' VIEM,* 1936, no. 3/4, 95–98.

Bam, L. A. *Fiziologicheskii Zhurnal SSSR,* 1939, **27(1),** 31–40.

Bam, L. A., & Kaminskii, S. D. *Biulliten' Eksperimental'noi Biologii i Meditsiny,* 1942, **14(3),** 47–51.

Beier, V. A. *Vnutrennie bolezni rukovodstvo dlia vrachei.* Leningrad, 1963.

Bekhterev, V. M. In G. F. Lang & D. D. Pletnev (Eds.), *Chastnaia patologiia i terapiia.* Leningrad, 1929.

Bernard, C. *Leçons de pathologie expérimentale.* Paris: Baillière, 1872.

Best, C. H. Epochs in the history of diabetes. In R. H. Williams (Ed.), *Diabetes.* New York: Hoeber, 1960. Pp. 1–13.

Blumenau, L. V. *Isteriia i ee patogenez.* Leningrad, 1926.

Bochkarev, P. V. *Arkhiv Biologicheskikh Nauk,* 1935, **40(2),** 101–120.

Bochkarev, P. V., & Pavlova, K. N. *Akusherstvo i Ginekologiia,* 1937, **9–10,** 7–16.

Boehm, R., & Hoffman, F. A. *Arkhiv Eksperimental'noi Patologii i Pharmakologii,* 1878, **8,** 271–308.

Bonne, C., & Sandground, J. H. *American Journal of Cancer,* 1939, **37,** 173–185.

Bosheniatova, N. E. Mekhanicheskii faktor kak vozbuditel' zheludochnoi sekretsii u obez'ian *Macacus rhesus.* Sukhumi, 1938 (manuscript).

Bosheniatova, N. E., & Voronin, L. G. *Izvestiia AN SSSR, Seria Biologii,* 1943, No. 6, 361–370.

Brodie, D. A., & Marshall, R. W. *American Journal of Physiology,* 1963, 204, No. 4, 681–685. (a)

Brodie, D. A., & Marshall, R. W. *Science,* 1963, **141(3576),** 174–175. (b)

Brooks, F. S., Ridley, P., Attinger, F., & Neff, K. *American Journal of Physiology,* 1963, **205(6),** 1093–1095. (a)

Brooks, F. S., Ridley, P., Attinger, F., Bjovedt, G., & Neff, K. American *Journal of Physiology,* 1963, **206(6),** 1096–1098. (b)

Brugsh, & Shittengel'm, (sic.). *Rukovodstvo po klinicheskim metodam issledovaniia dlia studentov i vrachei.* Berlin, 1921.

Bulatov, P. N., & Stepanov, N. I. *Kratkii uchebnik nervnykh i dushevnykh boleznei.* St. Petersburg, 1912.

Bussabarger, R. A., & Ivy, A. C. *Proceedings of the Society of Experimental Biology and Medicine* (New York), 1936, **34(2),** 151–152.

Butnev, Iu. P. *Biulliten' Eksperimental'noi Biologii i Meditisiny,* 1957, **44(9),** 27–30.

Butnev, Iu. P. In *Voprosy fiziologii i patologii obez'ian.* Sukhumi, 1961. Pp. 9–14. (a)

Butnev, Iu. P. In *Voprosy fiziologii i patologii obez'ian.* Sukhumi, 1961. Pp. 15–23. (b)

Bykov, K. M. *Kora golovnogo mozga i vnutrennie organy.* Moscow-Leningrad, 1944.

Bykov, K. M. *Interoretseptory. Izbrannye proizvedeniia,* Moscow, 1953, **1,** 197–200.

Bykov, K. M., & Kurtsin, I. T. *Kortiko-vistseral'naia teoriia patogeneza iazvennoi bolezni.* Moscow, 1952.

Bykov, K. M., & Kurtsin, I. T. *Kortiko-vistseral'naia patologiia.* Leningrad, 1960.

Bzynko, V. F. In *Predrak, ranniaia diagnostika i profilaktika raka. Uchenye Zapiski KRROI, Kiev,* 1955, **5,** 174–183.

Cannon, W. B. *American Journal of Physiology,* 1898, **1,** 359–382.

Cannon, W. B. *Bodily changes in pain, hunger, fear, and rage.* (2nd ed.) New York: Appleton, 1929.

Cannon, W. B., Shohl, A. T., & Wright, W. S. *American Journal of Physiology,* 1911, **29,** 280–287.

Chechulin, A. S. K voprosy o patofiziologicheskikh mekhanizmakh narushenii sekretornoi deiatel'nosti zheludka (i nekotorykh drugikh, funktsii organizma) v usloviiakh kortikal'nogo i subkortikal'nogo nevroza, *Tezisy dokladov konferentsii, fiziologiia i Patologiia pishchevareniia i voprosy kurortologii i fiziologii.* Tbilisi, 1963. Pp. 188–189.

Cherkovich, G. M. Opyt polucheniia nevrozov u obez'ian pri eksperimental'nom izmenenii sutochnogo ritma. *Soveshchanie po voprosam evoliutsii fiziologii nervnoi sistemy.* Leningrad: Tezisy i Referaty Dokladov, Pp. 178–179.

Cherkovich, G. M. *Rasshirennoe zasedanie Biuro Otdeleniia Mediko-Biologicheskikh Nauk AMN SSSR.* Sukhumi: Tezisy Dokladov, 1957. Pp. 48–49.

Cherkovich, G. M. *Patologicheskaia Fiziologiia i Eksperimental'naia Terapiia,* 1959, 6, 22.

Cherkovich, G. M. In *Fiziologiia i patologiia vysshei nervnoi deiatel'nosti.* Sukhumi, 1960. Pp. 123–132. (English transl. in *Soviet Psychology,* 1969–70, 8(2), 119–136.

Chireikin, V. Kh. *Vrachebnaia Gazeta,* 1931, 3, 177–185.

Davidenkov, S. N. *Klinicheskie lektsii po nervnym bolezniam.* Leningrad, 1956.

Davidenkov, S. N. *Nevrozy.* Leningrad, 1963.

De Los Santos, M. A., Bucaille, M., Delgado, J. M. R., & Spiro, H. M. *Gastroenterology,* 1962, 42(5), 595–598.

Denisenko, P. P. *Gangiolitiki: Farmakologiia i klinicheskoe primenenie.* Leningrad, 1959.

Denisenko, P. P. *Tsentocal'nye kholinolitiki.* Leningrad, 1966.

Dolin, A. O. *Patologiia vysshei nervnoi deiatel'nosti.* Moscow, 1962.

Dotsenko, S. N., & Pervomaiskii, B. Ia. *Nevrozy.* Leningrad, 1964.

Dzerzhinskii, V. *Kratkii uchebnik nervnykh boleznei.* Ekaterinoslav, 1921.

Dzhalagoniia, Sh. L. In *Fiziologiia i patologiia vysshei nervnoi deiatel'nosti obez'ian.* Sukhumi, 1960. Pp. 133–141.

Dzhalagoniia, Sh. L. *Zhurnal Vysshei Nervnoi Deiatel'nosti,* 1962, 12(3), 472–480.

Dzhalagoniia, Sh. L. In *Meditsinskaia primatologiia.* Tbilisi, 1967. Pp. 97–106.

Dzhikidze, E. K., Gvazava, I. S., Stasilevich, Z. K., Kavtaradze, K. N., Pekerman, S. M., Gasparian, G. S., Ivanov, M. T., & Bondar', L. I. In *Materialy nauchnoi konferentsii Instituta Eksperimental'noi Patologii i Terapii AMN SSSR.* Sukhumi, 1963. Pp. 25–26.

Ebbell, B. (transl.) *The papyrus Ebers.* Copenhagen: Levin and Munksgaard-Ejnar Munksgaard, 1937.

Einhorn, M. On achylia gastrica. *Medical Record,* 1892, 41, 650–654.

Elanskii, N. N. *Trudy, 5 Voprosy Klinicheskoi Onkologii, Moscow-Leningrad,* 1963, 162–165.

Fanardzhian, V. A., & Danielian, G. A. *Trudy VII vsesoiuznogo s'ezda rentgenologov i radiologov.* Moscow, 1961. Pp. 58–64.

Ferguson, J. H. *Proceedings of the Society of Experimental Biology* (New York), 1932, 30(3), 328–330.

Ferguson, J. H., McGavran, J., & Smith, E. R. B. *Journal of Physiology,* 1934, 82(1), 1–10.

Ferguson, J. H., & Smith, E. R. B. *Journal of Physiology,* 1935, 83(4), 455–458.

Fishchenko, G. A., & Beliaev, P. M. *Trudy Vitebskogo Gosudarstvennogo Instituta,* 1939, 2, 7.

Fox, H. *Disease in captive wild mammals and birds: Incidence, description, comparisons.* Philadelphia: Lippincott, 1923.

Funt, I. M. *Klinicheskaia Meditsina,* 1947, 25(2), 23–32.

Gantt, W. H. *XV Meshdunarodnyi fiziologicheskii kongress.* Moscow-Leningrad: Tezisy, 1935. P. 88.

Gavlichek, V. *Uslovnaia oboronitel'naia dominanta kak model' gipertonicheskogo sostoianiia organizma.* Moscow, 1962.

Gordon, O. L., Motrenko, V. D., & Peredel'skii, S. A. *Klinicheskaia Meditsina,* 1935, 13(2), 283–289.

Gordon, O. L., & Zlatopol'skii, A. R. *Klinicheskaia Meditsina,* 1937, 15(10–11), 1293–1301.

Gukasian, A. G. *Vnutrennie bolezni.* Moscow, 1958.

Hamerton, A. E. *Proceedings of Zoological Society of London,* 1930, 1, 357–380.

Hinkle, L. E., & Wolf, S. The effects of stressful life situations on the concentration of blood glucose in diabetic and nondiabetic humans. *Diabetes,* 1952, 1, 383–392.

Iakovleva, E. A. *Eksperimental'nye nevrozy.* Moscow, 1967.

Ingle, D. J. Experimental diabetes. In R. H. Williams (Ed.), *Diabetes.* New York: Hoeber, 1960. Pp. 297–308.

Iudkovskaia, I. L. *Slizistaia obolochka zheludka pri iazve i pri rake iz iazvy.* Leningrad: Avtoreferat kandidatskoi dissertatsii, 1960.

Ivanov, N. V. *Voprosy psikhoterapii funktsional'nykh seksual'nykh rasstroistv.* Moscow, 1966.

Ivanov-Smolenskii, A. G. *Ocherki patofiziologii vysshei nervnoi deiatel'nosti.* Moscow: Medgiz, 1952.

Kalinin, A. P. *Sbornik avtoreferatov i tezisov nauchnykh rabot.* Kazan', 1956. Pp. 57–60.

Kaminskii, S. D. *Biulliten' VIEM,* 1935, 9–10, 12–13.

Kaminskii, S. D. *Biulliten' VIEM,* 1936, 3–4, 88–95.

Kaminskii, S. D. In *Soveshchanie po probleme vysshei nervnoi deiatel'nosti, sozyvaemoe v sviaze s pervoi godovshchinoi so dnia smerti I. P. Pavlova.* Moscow-Leningrad: Tezisy Dokladov, 1937. Pp. 10–12. (a)

Kaminskii, S. D. Sbornik *dokladov 6-go vsesoiuznogo s'ezda fiziologov, biokhimikov i farmakologov.* Tbilisi, 1937. Pp. 182–185.

Kaminskii, S. D. *Arkhiv Biologicheskikh Nauk,* 1939, 53(2–3), 69–88. (a)

Kaminskii, S. D. *Arkhiv Biologicheskikh Nauk,* 1939, 53(2–3), 89–100. (b)

Kaminskii, S. D. *Arkhiv Biologicheskikh Nauk,* 1939, 54(1), 59–69. (c)

Kanfor, I. S. O slozhnoreflektornoi reguliatsii uglevodnogo obmena. Avtoreferat dissertatsii, Moscow, 1959.

Kavetskii, R. E. In *Vysshaia nervnaia deiatel'nost' i kortiko-vistseral'nye vzaimootnosheniia v norme i patologii.* Kiev, 1965. Pp. 84–98.

Kazanskii, N. P. Materialy k eksperimental'noe patologii i eksperimental'noi terapii zheludochnykh zhelez sobaki. Dissertatsiia, St. Petersburg, 1901.

Kent, S. P. Spontaneous and induced malignant neoplasms in monkeys. *Annals of the New York Academy of Sciences,* 1960, 85(3), 819–827.

Kent, S. P., & Pickering, J. E. Neoplasms in monkeys (*Macaca mulatta*): Spontaneous and irradiation induced. *Cancer,* 1958, 11, 138–147.

Kheddou, A. Uspekhi v izuchenii protsessov kantserogeneza za 1958–1962. VIII. *Mezhdunarodnyi protivorakovyi kongress. Voprosi biokhimii raka, i kantserogeneza. Trudy 2.* Moscow-Leningrad, 1963. Pp. 267–272.

Khorsfol, F. *VIII Mezhdunarodnyi protivorakovyi kongress. Voprosy biokhimii raka, kantserogeneza. Trudy 2.* Moscow-Leningrad, 1963. Pp. 288–289.

Khodos, Kh, G. *Uchebnik nervnykh boleznei.* Moscow, 1948.

Kipiani, T. I., & Miminoshvili, D. *II Soveshchanie po voprosam evoliutsii fiziologii nervnoi sistemy.* Tbilisi: Tezisy Dokladov, 1956. Pp. 132–133. (a)

Kipiani, T. I., & Miminoshvili, D. I. *Soveshchanie po voprosam evoliutsii fiziologii nervnoi sistemy.* Leningrad: Tezisy Dokladov, 1956. P. 82. (b)

Knowles, H. C. The incidence and development of diabetes mellitus. In R. H. Williams (Ed.), *Diabetes.* New York: Hoeber, 1960. Pp. 360–369.

Kokaia, G. Ia. *Biulliten' Eksperimental'noi Biologii,* 1954, No. 12, 23.

Kokaia, G. Ia. Elektrokardiogramma zdorovykh obez'ian razlichnykh vidov i vozrastov. Kandidatskaia dissertatsiia, Sukhumi, 1958.

Konchalovskii, M. P. Zheludochnaia akhiliia. Dissertatsiia, Moscow, 1911.

Konovalov, P. N. Prodazhnye pepsiny v sravnenii s normal'nym zheludochnym sokom. Dissertatsiia, St. Petersburg, 1893.

Kosiakov, K. S. *Zhurnal Vysshei Nervnoi Deiatel'nosti,* 1952, **5**, 709.

Krasnogorskii, N. I. *Razvitie ucheniia o fiziologicheskoi deiatel'nosti mozga u detei.* Leningrad, 1939.

Kreindler, A. *Astenicheskii nevroz.* Bucharest: Izdatel'stvo Akademii Rumynskoi Narodnoi Respubliki, 1963.

Kretschmer, E. *Hysteria, reflex, and instinct.* New York: Philosophical Library, 1960. (English translation from the German.)

Kriazhev, V. Ia. *Fiziologicheskii Zhurnal SSSR,* 1945, **31**(5–6), 236–259.

Kriazhev, V. Ia. *Vysshaia nervnaia deiatel'nost' zhivotnykh v usloviiakh obshcheniia.* Moscow, 1955.

Kudrevetskii, V. V. Achylia gastrica simplex. *Arkhiv Biologicheskikh Nauk.* Vol. 2 (supplement). St. Petersburg, 1904. Pp. 97–111.

Kuksova, M. I. O nekotorykh osobennostiakh dinamiki kartiny krovi u nizshikh obez'ian. Dissertatsiia, Sukhumi, 1956.

Kurtsin, I. T. *Nauchnye soveshchaniia po probleme fiziologii i patologii pishchevareniia.* Leningrad: Tezisy Dokladov, 1951. Vol. 1. P. 36.

Kurtsin, I. T. *Zhurnal Vysshei Nervnoi Deiatel'nosti,* 1965, **15**(2), 414–423.

Kurtsin, I. T., Physiological mechanisms of behavior disturbances and corticovisceral interrelations in animals. In M. W. Fox (Ed.), *Abnormal behavior in animals.* Philadelphia: Saunders, 1968. Pp. 107–116.

Kurtsin, I. T., & Slutsskii, N. E. In *Nervno-gumoral'nye reguliatsii v deiatel'nosti pishchevaritel'nogo apparata cheloveka.* Moscow, 1935, Vol. 2. Pp. 7–44.

Kuznetsov, N. V. *Sovetskii Vrachebnyi Zhurnal,* 1937, **23**, 1763–1772.

Kvater, E. I. *Gormonal'naia diagnostika i terapiia v akusherstve i ginekologii.* Moscow, 1961.

Lagutina, N. I. In *Materialy nauchnoi konferentsii IEPIT AMN SSSR.* Sukhumi, 1963. Pp. 45–46.

Lagutina, N. I., Norkina, L. N., Dzhalagoniia, Sh. L., Sysoeva, A. F., & Panina, P. S. Eksperimental'nye nevrozy u obez'ian—itogi i perspektivy. Biologiia i patologiia obez'ian, izuchenie boleznei cheloveka v eksperimente na obez'ianakh, *Materialy Mezhdunarodnogo Simpoziuma v Sukhumi 17–22 Oktiabria, 1966,* Tbilisi, 1967, 64–70.

Lang, G. F. *Gipertonicheskaia bolezn'.* Moscow. 1950.

Lapin, B. A., & Yakovleva, L. A. *Comparative pathology in monkeys.* Springfield, Illinois: Charles C Thomas, 1963.

Leibson, L. G. *Sakhar v krovi.* Moscow-Leningrad, 1962.

Levashov, S. V. Iz nabliodenii nad diabetes mellitus. *Arkhiv Biologicheskikh Nauk,* 1904, **11**(supplement), 55–67.

Levenson, I. A., & Agol, M. I. *Klinicheskaia Meditsina,* 1936, **14**(5), 681–686.

Lisochkin, B. G. Adenomatoznye polipy zheludka. Avtoreferat kandidatskoi dissertatsii, Leningrad, 1966.

Luriia, R. A. *Bolezni pishchevoda i zheludka.* Moscow-Leningrad, 1935.

Magakian, G. O. *Gipertoniia u obez'ian kak eksperimental'no—biologicheskaia model' gipertonicheskoi bolezni cheloveka.* Moscow: Tezisy Dokladov, 1953. Pp. 13–14. (a)

Magakian, G. O. *Biulliten' Eksperimental'noi Biologii i Meditsiny,* 1953, **35**(2), 44. (b)

Magakian, G. O. Eksperimental'naia terapiia gipertonii i koronarnoi nedostatochnosti u obez'ian. *Rasshirennoe zasedanie Biuro Otdeleniia Mediko-Biologicheskikh Nauk AMN SSSR.* Sukhumi: Tezisy Dokladov, 1957. Pp. 30–31.

Magakian, G. O. Issledovanie patogeneza gipertonii, koronarnoi nedostato-chnosti i infarkta miokarda v eksperimente na obez'ianakh. Doktorskaia dissertatsiia, Sukhumi, 1965.

Magakian, G. O. In *Biologiia i patologiia obez'ian, izuchenie boleznei cheloveka v eksperimente na obez'ianakh,* Tbilisi, 1966. Pp. 77–81.

Magakian, G. O. In *Meditsinskaia primatologiia.* Tbilisi, 1967. Pp. 190–200.

Magakian, G. O. *Voprosi fiziologii i eksperimental'noi patologii, sbornik trudov Instituta Eksperimental'noi Patologii i Terapii.* Sukhumi, 1968, Pp. 370–376. (Translated as Neurogenous hypotension in apes as a model of neurocirculatory hypotension. *Soviet Psychology,* 1969–70, 8(2, winter), 161–168.

Magakian, G. O., Miminoshvili, D. I., & Kokaia, G. Ia. *Eksperimental'nye narusheniia reguliatsii krovianogo davleniia i koronarnogo krovoobrashcheniia u obez'ian.* Moscow: Tezisy Dokladov, 1953. Pp. 14–16.

Magakian, G. O., Miminoshvili, D. I., & Kokaia, G. Ia. *Klinicheskaia Meditsina,* 1956, **34**, No. 7, 30.

Maiorov, F. P. *Istoriia ucheniia ob uslovnykh refleksakh.* Moscow-Leningrad, 1954.

Manina, A. A., Khananashvili, M. M., & Lazuko, N. N. *Zhurnal Vysshei Nervnoi Deiatel' nosti,* 1971, 21(4), 686–691.

Markov, Kh. M. *Rasshirennoe zasedanie Biuro Otdeleniia Mediko-Biologicheskikh Nauk.* Sukhumi: Tezisy Dokladov, 1957. Pp. 31–35.

Markov, Kh. M. *Zhurnal Nevropatologii i Psikhiatrii,* 1959, 59(10), 1184–1192.

Martius. *Achylia gastrica, ihre Ursachen und ihre Folgen, mit einem anatomischen Bietrage von O. Lubarsch.* Leipzig und Wien: F. Deuticke, 1897.

Martsinskovskii, B. I. *Vrachebnaia Gazeta,* 1931, **22**, 1671–1675.

Masserman, J. H., & Pechtel, C. *Annals of the New York Academy of Science,* 1953, 56(2), 253–265.

Mel'nikov, A. V., & Timofeev, N. S. Predrakovye zabolevaniia zheludka, ikh diagnostika profilaktika, i lechenie. In *Voprosy Onkologii.* Moscow, 1950. Pp. 190–200.

Miasnikov, A. L. *Propedevtika* (diagnostika i chastnaia patologiia vnutrennikh boleznei). Moscow, 1956.

Miasnikov, A. L. *Trudy IX vsesoiuznoi konferentsii terapevtov 23–25 Oktiabria, 1957.* Moscow, 1958. P. 32.

Mil'man, L. Ia. *Impotentsiia.* Leningrad, 1965.

Miminoshvili, D. I. Funktsional'nye narusheniia vysshei nervnoi deiatel'nosti pri stolknovenii protsessov vobkuzhdeniia v kore golovnogo mozga. In *Tezisy Dokladov na rasshirennom zasedanii Biuro Otdeleniia Mediko-Biologicheskikh Nauk, AMN SSSR, Posviashch. 25-Letii sukhumskoi mediko-biologicheskoi stantsii.* Moscow, 1953. Pp. 6–7. (a)

Miminoshvili, D. I. *Opyt polucheniia nevroticheskikh sostoianni u obez'ian. in 16-e soveshchanie po problemam vysshei nervoi deiatel'nosti.* Leningrad: Tezisy i Referaty Dokladov. 1953. Pp. 144–145. (b)

Miminoshvili, D. I. Tezisy Dokladov, Sukhumi, 1957. Pp. 36–37.

Miminoshvili, D. I. In I. A. Utkin (Ed.), *Problems of medicine and biology in experiments on monkeys.* New York: Pergamon, 1960. Pp. 53–68.

Miminoshvili, D. I., & Dzhikidze, E. K. *Biulliten' Eksperimental'noi Biologii i Meditsiny,* 1955, **39(3)**, 29–33.

Miminoshvili, D. I., Magakian, G. O., & Kokaia, G. Ia. In *Fiziologiia i patologiia serdechno-sosudistoi sistemy.* Moscow: Tezisy Dokladov, 1954. Pp. 43–44.

Miminoshvili, D. I., Magakian, G. O., & Kokaia, G. Ia. In I. A. Utkin (Ed.), *Problems of medicine and biology in experiments on monkeys.* New York: Pergamon, 1960. Pp. 103–122.

Miminoshvili, D. I., Magakian, G. O., & Kokaia, G. Ia. In *Voprosy fiziologii i patologii obez'ian.* Sukhumi, 1961. Pp. 173–181.

Neiman, I. M. *VIII Mezhdunarodnyi protivorakovyi kongress. Trudy, Vol. 4. Voprosy biologii opukholevoi kletki, radiobiologii, luchevoi terapii predraka.* Moscow-Leningrad, 1963. Pp. 375–377.

Nguen Tkhyong. In *Meditsinskaia primatologiia.* Tbilisi, 1967. Pp. 50–57.

Norkina, L. N. *Poluchenie nevroticheskikh sostoianii u obez'ian pri narusheniiakh v stereotipe signalov.* Sukhumi: Tezisy Dokladov, 1957. Pp. 41–42.

Norkina, L. N. *Zhurnal Vysshei Nervnoi Deiatel'nosti*, 1958, 8(1), 56–63.

Oilert, V. *VIII Mezhdunarodnyi protivorakovyi Kongress. Trudy, Vol. 2. Voprosy biokhimii raka i kantserogeneza.* Moscow-Leningrad, 1963. Pp. 289–291.

Orbeli, L. A. *Arkhiv Biologicheskikh Nauk*, 1905, 12(1), 68–100.

Orlik, V. A. *Sovetskaia Meditsina*, 1950, 10, 10–11.

Osler, W. *The principles and practice of medicine.* New York: Appleton, 1928.

Panina, P. S. In *Voprosy fiziologii, Eksperimental'noi patologii, i radiobiologii.* Sukhumi, 1965. Pp. 39–43.

Panina, P. S. In *Meditsinskaia primatologiia.* Tbilisi, 1967. Pp. 140–147.

Pavlov, I. P. Proba fiziologicheskogo ponimaniia simptomatologii isterii (1932). In *I. P. Pavlov polnoe sobranie sochinenii.* Vol. 3, Book 2. Moscow-Leningrad, 1951. Pp. 195–218.

Pavlov, I. P., & Petrova, M. K. K fiziologii gipertonicheskogo sostoianiia sobaki (1932). In *I. P. Pavlov, polnoe sobranie sochinenii.* Vol. 3, Book 2. Moscow-Leningrad, 1951. Pp. 133–146.

Petrova, M. K. *Trudy Fiziologicheskikh Laboratorii im Akademika I. P. Pavlova*, 1945, 12(1), 5–32.

Petrova, M. K. *O roli funktsional'no oslablennoi kory golovnogo mozga v vozniknovenii razlichnykh patologicheskikh protsessov v organizme. Moscow, 1946.*

Plum, F. The neurologic complications of diabetes. In R. H. Williams (Ed.), *Diabetes.* New York: Hoeber, 1960. Pp. 602–622.

Poirier, L. J., Ayotte, R. A., Lemire, A., Ganthier, C., & Cordeau, J. P. *Revue Canadienne de Biologie*, 1955, 14(2), 129–143.

Porter, R. W., Brady, J. V., Conrad, D. G., & Mason, J. W. *Federation of American Societies for Experimental Biology*, 1957, 16(1), 101–102.

Porter, R. W., Brady, J. V., Conrad, D. G., Mason, J. W., Galambos, R., & McRioch, D. *Psychosomatic Medicine*, 1958, 20(5), 379–394.

Porubel', L. A., Prokhorova, I. A., Sergeev, A. H., & Slavin, Iu. M. *Pervaia otchetnaia nauchnaia konferentsiia moskovskogo N.–Issled, in-ta preparatov protiv poliomielita.* Moscow: Tezisy i Referaty Dokladov, 1958. P. 41.

Pospelov, S. A., & Maslennikov, A. P. *Klinicheskaia Meditsina*, 1936, 14(9), 1318–1323.

Predtechenskii, V. N. *Rukovodstvo po klinicheskim laboratornym issledovaniiam.* Moscow, 1960.

Rakhman, V. I. *Russkaia Klinika*, 1929, 11(58), 213–220.

Rakov, A. I., Shemiakina, T. V., & Ol'shanskii, A. S. *Klinicheskaia Meditsina*, 1954, 32(4), 54–58.

Rasmussen, R. A., & Brunschwig, A. *Proceedings of the Society of Experimental Biology and Medicine* (New York), 1941, 46(2), 298–300.

Ratcliffe, H. L. *American Journal of Cancer*, 1933 1(17), 116–135.

Reizel'man, S. D., & Govorchuk, R. Iu. *Vrachebnoe Delo.*, 1935, 3, 243–250.

Savchenko, V. A. *Biulliten' Eksperimental'noi Biologii i Meditsiny*, 1940, 9(5), 293–295.

Savchenko, V. A. *K mekhanizmu deistviia insulina i adrenalina.* Leningrad, 1946.

Sazontov, V. I., & Dobrolet, L. M. *Sovetskaia Meditsina*, 1957, 2, 73–78.

Schnedorf, J. G., & Ivy, A. C. *Proceedings of the Society of Experimental Biology and Medicine* (New York), 1937, 36, 192–193. (a)

Schnedorf, J. G., & Ivy, A. C. *American Journal of Digestive Disease and Nutrition*, 1937, 4(7), 429–432. (b)

Schrier, A. M. *Journal of Comparative and Physiological Psychology*, 1965, 59(3), 378–384.

Sepp, E. K., Tsuker, M. B., & Schmidt, E. V. *Nervnye bolezni.* Moscow, 1954.

Sergeeva, I. V. Znachenie predvaritel'noi travmatizatsii v preimushchestvennom porazhenii sosudistoi sistemy pri eksperimental'noi nevroze. In *Kortical'nye mekhanizmy reguliatsii deiatel'nosti vnutrennykh organov.* Moscow-Leningrad: Nauka, 1966. Pp. 135–141.

Shenger-Krestovnikova, N. R. *Izdaniia Petrogradskogo Instituta im. P. F. Lesgafta,* 1921, **3,** 1–42.

Shestopalova, S. K., & Startsev, V. G. In *Voprosy fiziologii i eksperimental'noi patologii.* Sukhumi, 1968. Pp. 92–96.

Shevchenko, I. T. In *Predrak, ranniaia diagnostika i profilaktika raka. Uchenye Zapiski KRROI, 5.* Kiev, 1955. Pp. 5–14.

Shevchenko, I. T. *Zlokachestvennye opukholi i predshestvuiushchie zabolevaniia.* Kiev, 1965.

Shul'tsev, G. P., & Bondar', Z. A. *Sovetskaia Meditsina,* 1941, **4,** 27–29.

Simpson, M. E., van Wagenen, G., & Carter, F. Hormone content of anterior pituitary of monkey (*Macaca mulatta* with special reference to gonadotrophins). *Proceedings of the Society of Experimental Biology and Medicine,* 1956, **91,** 6–11.

Smith, G. P., Brooks, F. P., Davis, R. A., & Rothman, S. S. *American Journal of Physiology,* 1960, **199(5),** 889–892.

Soborov, I. K. Izolirovannyi zheludok pri patologicheskikh sostoianiiakh pishchevaritel'nogo kanala. Dissertatsiia, St. Petersburg, 1899.

Sokolov, Iu. N., & Petrov, V. I. *Trudy VII vsesoiuznogo s'ezda rentgenologov i radiologov.* Moscow, 1961. Pp. 52–58.

Sokoloverova, I. M. In I. A. Utkin (Ed.), *Problems of medicine and biology in experiments on monkeys.* New York: Pergamon, 1960. Pp. 171–186.

Startsev, V. G. *K sravnitel'no-fiziologicheskoi kharakteristike zheludochnoi sekretsii u obez'ian. III nauchnoe soveshchanie po evoliutsii fiziologii, posviashchennoe pamiati Akademika L. A. Orbeli.* Leningrad: Tezisy Dokladov, 1961. Pp. 182–184.   (a)

Startsev, V. G. *Fiziologicheskii i farmakologicheskii analiz sekretornoi raboty zheludka obez'ian.* Leningrad: Tezisy Dokladov, 1961. Pp. 36–38.   (b)

Startsev, V. G. *Nauchnaia konferentsiia* (eksperimental'nye i klinicheskie obosnovaniia primeneniia neirotropnykh sredstv). Leningrad: Tezisy Dokladov, 1963. Pp. 167–168.

Startsev, V. G. *X S''ezd Vsesoiuznogo Fiziologicheskogo Obshchestva im. I. P. Pavlova,* 1964, **2(2),** 292.   (a)

Startsev, V. G. Nevrogennaia zheludochnaia akhiliia u obez'ian. Doktorskaia dissertatsiia, Sukhumi, 1964.   (b)

Startsev, V. G. *Fiziologicheskii Zhurnal SSSR,* 1964, **50(9),** 1169–1176.   (c)

Startsev, V. G. *Fiziologicheskii Zhurnal SSSR,* 1965, **51(2),** 243–250.

Startsev, V. G. In *Biologiia i patologiia obez'ian, izuchenie boleznei cheloveka v eksperimente na obez'ianakh. Materialy mezhdunarodnogo simpoziuma v Sukhumi.* Sukhumi, 1966. Pp. 114–118.   (a)

Startsev, V. G. *Materialy dokladov k nauchnoi konferentsii. Deistvie neirotropnykh sredstv na troficheskie protsessy i tkanevoi obmen.* Leningrad, 1966. Pp. 81–82.   (b)

Startsev, V. G. Uslovnoreflektornaia giperglikemiia na obez'ianakh. In *Voprosy fiziologii i eksperimental'noi patologii.* Sukhumi, 1968. Pp. 219–228.   (a)

Startsev, V. G. Modelirovanie nevrogennoi zheludochnoi akhilii na obez'ianakh i ee farmakoterapiia. In *Voprosy fiziologii i eksperimental'noi patologii.* Sukhumi, 1968. Pp. 229–239.   (b)

Startsev, V. G. *Nevrogennaia zheludochnaia akhiliia u obez'ian.* Leningrad: Nauka, 1972.

Startsev, V. G., & Kuraev, G. A. *Zhurnal Nevropatologii i Psikhiatrii,* 1967, **67(6),** 880–886. (English translation in *Soviet Psychology,* 1970, **9(1),** 92–102.)

Startsev, V. G., & Ianson, V. N. In *Voprosy fiziologii i eksperimental'noi patologii.* Sukhumi, 1968. Pp. 21–25.

Startsev, V. G., Repin, Iu. M., & Shestopalova, S. K. Novaia model' nevrogennoi ishemicheskoi bolezni serdtsa v eksperimente na obez'ianakh. *Biulliten' Eksperimental'noe Biologii i Meditsiny,* 1972, **73(1),** 35–38.

Stetten, D., & Mortimer, G. E. Carbohydrate Metabolism. In R. H. Williams (Ed.), *Diabetes.* New York: Hoeber, 1960. Pp. 89–101.

Sysoeva, A. F. In *Voprosy fiziologii, eksperimental'noi patologii i radiobiologii.* Sukhumi, 1965. Pp. 34–38.

Tareev, E. M. *Vnutrennie bolezni.* Moscow, 1952.

Tiufanov, A. V. Opyt massovogo patologo-anatomicheskogo issledovaniia obez'ian, zabitykh dlia prigotovleniia vaktsiny protiv poliomielita 1-ia Nauchnaia sessiia Instituta po Izucheniiu Poliomielita. Moscow: Tezisy Dokladov, 1957. P. 36.

Trusevich, B. I., & Shapiro, Ia. E. *Vrachebnaia Gazeta,* 1930, **16,** 1215–1218.

Ukhtomskii, A. A. *Sobranie sochinenii.* Leningrad, 1949. Pp. 5–328.

Vadova, A. V., & Gel'shtein, V. I. In I. A. Utkin (Ed.), *Problems of medicine and biology in experiments on monkeys.* New York: Pergamon, 1960. Pp. 137–158.

Vasilenko, V. Kh. *Vnutrennie bolezni.* Moscow, 1951.

Vetiukov, I. A. *Trudy Fiziologicheskogo Nauchno-Issledovatel'skogo Instituta,* 1936, **17,** 56.

Voitonis, N. Iu., & Tikh, N. A. *Trudy Sukhumskoi Biologicheskoi Stantsii AMN SSSR,* 1949, **1,** 164–225.

Voronin, L. G. *Trudy Sukhumskoi Biologicheskoi Stantsii AMN SSSR,* 1949, **1,** 67–69.

Voronin, L. G. *Tezisy dokladov na rasshirennom zasedanii Biuro Otdeleniia Mediko-Biologicheskikh Nauk AMN SSSR, Posviashchennomu 25-Letiiu Sukhumskoi Mediko-Biologicheskoi Stantsii AMN SSSR,* Moscow, 1953, 4–5.

Voronin, L. G., Kanfor, L. S., Lakin, G. F., & Tikh, N. A. *Opyt soderzhaniia i razvedeniia obez'ian v Sukhumi.* Moscow, 1948.

White, P. Juvenile diabetes. In R. H. Williams (Ed.), *Diabetes.* New York: Hoeber, 1960. Pp. 381–388.

Zakhar'in, G. A. *Klinicheskie lektsii.* Moscow, 1910.

Zavriev, Ia. Kh. Materialy k fiziologii i patologii zheludochnykh zhelez sobaki. Dissertatsiia, St. Petersburg, 1900.

Zel'geim, A. P. *Trudy VIEM,* 1934, 1(3), 93–99.

Zhodzishskii, B. Ia. *Sovietskaia Meditsina,* 1938, **4,** 20–21.

Ziabbarov, A. A. *Trudy VII vsesoiuznogo s''ezda rentgenologov i radiologov.* Moscow, 1961. Pp. 75–77.

Zimnitskii, S. S. *O rasstroistve sekretornoi deiatel'nosti zhelundochnykh zhelez s tochki zreniia funktsional'noi diagnostiki.* Moscow, 1926.

Zuckerman, S. A rhesus monkey (*Macaca mulatta*) with carcinoma of the mouth. *Proceedings of Zoological Society,* London, 1930, **1,** 59.

Subject Index

Negative stimulus, *see* Differential stimulus
Nembutal and ovulation, 147
Neoplasm, *see* Tumorogenesis
Neurogenic disorder, 3–4, 11, 15, *see also*
    Experimental neurosis
  cardiovascular, *see* Cardiac arrest; Cardiac
      arrhythmia; Coronary insufficiency;
      Hypertension; Hypotension; Myo-
      cardial infarction
  of conditioned behavior, *see* Alimentary
      CR, pathology of; Disinhibition;
      Equalization pattern; Excitatory
      pattern; Inhibitory pattern; Learning
      disability; Paradoxical drug effects;
      Paradoxical pattern; Ultraparadoxical
      pattern
  gastrointestinal, *see* Diarrhea; Gastric
      achylia; Gastric adenomatosis; Gastric
      anacidity; Hypopepsia
  infections, *see* Dysentary
  metabolic, *see* Diabetes mellitus; Hyper-
      glycemia; Hypoglycemia
  motor, *see* Convulsions; Hyperkinesis;
      Hysterical motor disorders; Paralysis;
      Tremors
  sensory, *see* Analgesia, hysterical; Blind-
      ness, hysterical
  sexual, *see* Menstrual cycle; Sexual cycle,
      disorders of
  of spontaneous behavior, 16–22, 32,
      36–38, 48
  trophic, 92, 131, *see also* Gastric
      adenomatosis; Gastric ulcer; Tumoro-
      genesis
Neurosis, *see also* Experimental neurosis;
    Neurogenic disorder
  general, 15
Nitroglycerine, 23
Nomenclature, *see* Terminology

O

Overstress of neural processes, 6
Ovulation, *see also* Menstrual cycle; Sexual
    cycle
  chlorpromazine and, 147
  follicle-stimulating hormone and, 147
  hypothalamic lesions and, 147
  in lower animals, 146–147
  luteinizing hormone and, 147
  morphine and, 147

Ovulation (*contd.*)
  nembutal and, 147
  reserpine and, 147

P

Paradoxical drug effects
  adrenalin, 21
  amphetamine, 21
  atropine, 23
  ephedrine, 21
  nitroglycerine, 23
  pilocarpine, 23
Paradoxical pattern, 7, 18
Paralysis, 139–140, 175, *see also* Hysterical
    motor disorders
Paresis, *see* Paralysis
Pavlovian pouch, 82
Pepsinogenesis, *see* Hypopepsia
Pernicious anemia, 96
Personality factors, *see* Type of nervous
    system
Phenobarbital, 98
Phobia, 8
Pilocarpine, 23
Pituitrine, 25
Polyposis, *see* Gastric adenomatosis
Positive stimulus, *see* Conditioned stimulus
Poststressor phase, 3–4
Pregnanediol and sexual cycle, 147
Prestressor phase, 4
Professional spasms, 127
Prostigmine and menstrual cycle, 147
Psychosomtic disease, *see also* Neurogenic
    disorder; Symptom specificity
  emotions and, viii
  organ weakness theory of, ix
  stimulus–response theory of, ix, 7
  western concepts, vii–x, 1

R

Rat, 16
Reactive changes, 4, 21, *see also* Defensive
    response system
  in autonomic functions, 32
  in blood glucose, 163
  in cardiovascular function, 178–179
  in conditioned behavior, 20
  death, 31
  drug suppression of, 106–107
  in gastric function, 60, 106